SISTERS IN
RESISTANCE

ALSO BY TILAR J. MAZZEO

Eliza Hamilton: The Extraordinary Life and Times
of the Wife of Alexander Hamilton

Irena's Children: The Extraordinary Story of the Woman
Who Saved 2,500 Children from the Warsaw Ghetto

The Hotel on Place Vendôme: Life, Death, and
Betrayal at the Hotel Ritz in Paris

The Secret of Chanel No. 5: The Intimate History
of the World's Most Famous Perfume

The Widow Clicquot: The Story of a Champagne Empire
and the Woman Who Ruled It

SISTERS IN RESISTANCE

How a German Spy, a Banker's Wife,
and Mussolini's Daughter
Outwitted the Nazis

Tilar J. Mazzeo

GRAND CENTRAL
PUBLISHING

NEW YORK   BOSTON

Grand Central Publishing
Hachette Book Group
1290 Avenue of the Americas, New York, NY 10104
grandcentralpublishing.com
twitter.com/grandcentralpub

First Edition: June 2022

Grand Central Publishing is a division of Hachette Book Group, Inc. The Grand Central Publishing name and logo is a trademark of Hachette Book Group, Inc.

The publisher is not responsible for websites (or their content) that are not owned by the publisher.

The Hachette Speakers Bureau provides a wide range of authors for speaking events. To find out more, go to www.hachettespeakersbureau.com or call (866) 376-6591.

Print book interior design by Jeff Stiefel

Library of Congress Cataloging-in-Publication Data
Names: Mazzeo, Tilar J., author.
Title: Sisters in resistance : how a German spy, a banker's wife, and Mussolini's daughter outwitted the Nazis / Tilar J. Mazzeo.
Other titles: How a German spy, a banker's wife, and Mussolini's daughter outwitted the Nazis
Description: First edition. | New York : GCP, 2022. | Includes bibliographical references and index.
Identifiers: LCCN 2021053690 | ISBN 9781538735268 (hardcover) | ISBN 9781538735275 (ebook)
Subjects: LCSH: Ciano, Edda Mussolini, Contessa. | Purwin, Hilde, 1919-2010. | Ciano, Galeazzo, conte, 1903-1944. The Ciano diaries. 1946. | World War, 1939-1945—Italy. | Italy—History—German occupation, 1943-1945. | Espionage, German—Italy—History—20th century. | World War, 1939-1945—Secret service—Germany. | Nationalsozialistische Deutsche Arbeiter-Partei. Schutzstaffel. Reichssicherheitshauptamt. Amt VI. | Ciano, Galeazzo, conte, 1903-1944—Death and burial. | Italy—Politics and government—1922-1945.
Classification: LCC DG575.C52 M39 2022 | DDC 945.091—dc23/eng/20211112
LC record available at https://lccn.loc.gov/2021053690

ISBNs: 9781538735268 (hardcover), 9781538735275 (ebook)

Printed in the United States of America

LSC-C

Printing 1, 2022

CONTENTS

Contents

Cast of Characters

Edda Mussolini Ciano—Favorite child of Italy's blustering dictator, **Benito Mussolini**, she was forced into a desperate attempt to blackmail her father and Hitler to try to save the life of her husband, **Galeazzo Ciano**. While on the run from the Gestapo, she used the pseudonym **Emilia Santos**. She was mother to three young children during the war: **Fabrizio**, **Raimonda**, and **Marzio**. Her wartime lover was **Emilio Pucci**.

Galeazzo Ciano—Mussolini's foreign minister and son-in-law, he was repulsed by the state secrets of Nazi Germany and fascist Italy and tried to organize a coup to remove Mussolini from power and to broker a separate peace with the Allies. His devout mother, **Carolina Pini Ciano**, disapproved of his wife. His brother-in-law **Massimo Magistrati** held a diplomatic post in Switzerland.

Benito Mussolini—Italy's fascist dictator, he inspired the young Hitler but found by the middle of the Second World War that now the

vii

Führer gave the orders. Confronted with the choice between pardoning his son-in-law and pleasing Hitler, Mussolini wavered. His wife was **Rachele Mussolini**. His mistress was **Clara Petacci**. He sent his son **Vittorio Mussolini** to hunt down and return Edda, by whatever means necessary.

THE OTHER ITALIANS

Emilio Pucci—An expert skier and a wealthy aristocrat, he flew in the Italian air force and attended Reed College in Oregon. One of **Edda Mussolini Ciano**'s athletic younger lovers, he reconnected with her during the Second World War and, when circumstances required, gallantly risked his life to protect Edda and the diaries of **Galeazzo Ciano**. After the war, he became famous as a fashion designer.

Vittorio Emmanuel III—King of Italy, he was sidelined during the dictatorship of **Benito Mussolini** but, when given the opportunity to choose, selected ardent fascist **Pietro Badoglio** as his second wartime prime minister, precipitating the Ciano family's flight from Rome.

Zenone Benini—A school friend of **Galeazzo Ciano** from their youth and a beneficiary of Ciano's rise to power, he witnessed firsthand Galeazzo's incarceration in Verona and his deepening love affair there with German spy **Hilde Beetz**. Zenone assisted American intelligence in contacting **Edda Mussolini Ciano**.

Susanna Agnelli—Heiress, socialite, and staunch friend to **Galeazzo Ciano** and **Edda Mussolini Ciano**, she was engaged to marry **Prince Raimondo Lanza** but dreamed of becoming a physician. With her half-American mother, **Virginia Agnelli**, she and her sisters Maria Sole and Clara played a pivotal role in Switzerland in the race to aid **Edda Mussolini Ciano** and save the diaries.

Tonino Pessina—Along with his wife, **Nora Pessina**, and their friend **Gerardo Gerardi**, Tonino tried to help old friends Edda and Galeazzo at great personal cost.

Delia di Bagno—Loyal friend of **Edda Mussolini Ciano**; Edda and Delia were reputed to share their husbands with each other. Delia and her mother, the **Countess of Laurenzana**, bravely offered to help Edda and Galeazzo. Some sources suggested that they drew the celebrated Polish-British spy **Christine Granville** (Krystyna Skarbek) into their circle of confidence.

Dr. Elvezio Melocchi—Along with his brother **Dr. Walter Melocchi**, he ran the rest clinic at Ramiola where **Edda Mussolini Ciano** and **Emilio Pucci** resided. Active in the Italian resistance as partisans, the two doctors agreed to deliver Galeazzo's papers only to someone who knew the secret code word.

Father Guido Pancino—A Catholic priest and the Mussolini family confessor, Father Pancino was also working as a spy for the Germans, in the same division as **Hilde Beetz**. The priest was sent to Switzerland to try to trick **Edda Mussolini Ciano**. There he discovered that **Hilde Beetz** was acting as a double agent.

Mario Pellegrinotti—A sympathetic jailer in the Scalzi Prison at Verona, he witnessed firsthand the deepening love affair of **Galeazzo Ciano** and **Hilde Beetz**.

Cast of Characters

THE GERMANS

Hildegard Burkhardt Beetz—Also known simply as **Hilde Beetz** or by her code name, Felicitas, she was a brilliant, beautiful, and ambitious young Nazi spy, assigned as her first mission to seduce Mussolini's son-in-law **Galeazzo Ciano**.

Joachim von Ribbentrop—Hitler's foreign minister and Galeazzo Ciano's German counterpart, he was the man that even the other Nazis hated and was a notorious war criminal. Vain, cruel, pompous, he hated **Galeazzo Ciano** and was determined to destroy him. Inside the Nazi machinery, there were other senior German officials looking for the opportunity to destroy him, among them **Heinrich Himmler** and **Ernst Kaltenbrünner**.

Ernst Kaltenbrünner—Head of Nazi Germany's main security office (the RSHA) and among the architects of the Holocaust, he was a senior member of Hitler's inner circle, despised **Joachim von Ribbentrop**, and was **Hilde Beetz**'s "big boss" in intelligence operations.

Wilhelm Harster—A Nazi general, war criminal, and director of German intelligence operations (the SD) in **Hilde Beetz**'s sector during the trial of **Galeazzo Ciano** and following, General Harster was Hilde's immediate supervisor in Verona. His trusted liaison officer was **Walter Segna**.

Eugen Dollmann—An SS man loyal to **Heinrich Himmler**, he drove a flashy Mercedes, had a vicious attack dog named Kuno, and was a favorite of aristocratic Italian socialites, who didn't hesitate to ask him for special favors. Among his lady friends were **Virginia Agnelli** and **Edda Mussolini Ciano**, both of whom turned to him for help when they found their lives and the lives of their families in danger. His superior in Rome, **Herbert Kappler**, helped to arrange the Ciano family's flight to Germany.

Wilhelm Höttl—**Herbert Kappler**'s counterpart in Munich, he worked with German foreign intelligence and helped to arrange the German side of the Ciano family's flight and their surprise house arrest in Bavaria, where he dispatched a young secretary and translator named **Hilde Beetz** on her first spy mission, charged with gaining the confidence of **Galeazzo Ciano**. Höttl would not be the first or the last of Hilde's supervisors to become infatuated with the beautiful young agent.

THE AMERICANS AND OTHERS

Frances de Chollet—A middle-aged American socialite and mother, married to banker and aristocrat **Louis de Chollet**, living in Switzerland, she was the hostess of the "house of spies," where Allied intelligence and military command mixed with well-placed refugees and foreign contacts under the guise of raucous house parties. Frances was soon drawn into the world of spycraft as an amateur agent by fellow American **Allen Dulles**, charged with helping to persuade **Edda Mussolini Ciano** to give her husband's incendiary diaries to the Allies.

Allen Dulles—A pioneer of American spycraft, he was posted to Bern to lead the Swiss branch of the Office of Strategic Services (OSS), the precursor to the Central Intelligence Agency (CIA). Career spies **Cordelia Dodson** and **Tracy Barnes** were operatives affiliated with his office and assigned to the **Edda Mussolini Ciano** mission. Short of professional agents during the Second World War, he also turned to private American citizens in Switzerland, asking men and women such as

Frances de Chollet to serve their country and the anti-fascist cause with sometimes extraordinary missions.

Werner Balsiger—A senior official with the Swiss police, he was not entirely neutral. Frequently a guest at the house of spies, he assisted the Allies with sensitive matters, and **Frances de Chollet** considered him and his wife trusted friends.

Paul Ghali—A correspondent for the *Chicago Daily News*, he was among those who worked informally with **Allen Dulles** as part of the Allied intelligence circuit in Switzerland. Pulled into the hunt for the Ciano Diaries in order to assure Edda that there was a willing publisher and financial opportunity, he worked directly with **Frances de Chollet**.

The Inferno

In the middle of the road of our life
I found myself in a dark wood,
Where the straight path forward had been lost.
It is hard to talk of what it was like.
The forest was so wild and harsh and thick
That even the thought of it now frightens me!
It is so bitter, too, that a little more would be the bitterness of death;
But to be faithful to the good that I found there,
I will speak of those things too.

—Dante, *The Inferno*, I

This is a book about the moral thicket, about a group of people—and a group of nations—lost in darkness.

I have spent a career now writing the stories of women and resistance and war, and sometimes I have written books about inspirational people, people like the Polish heroine Irena Sendler or the French-American wartime partisan Blanche Rubenstein Auzello, who both saw the path of righteousness with a blinding clarity and simply acted. This is not that story, and, apart from the notable exception of a banker's wife—a socialite living in a failing marriage who found at midlife something so important that nothing that came after mattered—these are not those people.

But this is a story of courage. It is the story of how people who, finding themselves on the wrong path in the middle of their life's journey, discover the courage to change and to wrestle with the darkness and with the reckoning that follows. A Nazi spy. Mussolini's daughter. A fascist diplomat. At the story's heart is Mussolini's son-in-law, a flawed man, a playboy and Italy's foreign minister, who found the strength to repudiate fascism and stare down his executioners. It is also the story about his candid wartime diaries and the men and, especially, the women who risked their lives and their families to preserve the truth about the crimes recorded in those papers.

His diaries—known to history as the Ciano Diaries—were written during his time as Benito Mussolini's second-in-command and part of Adolf Hitler's inner circle. As "the most important single political document concerning recent Italian foreign affairs in existence," they record a journey so wild and tangled that even he became horrified with it. Galeazzo Ciano, for all his sins, acted, however belatedly, on that self-knowledge when it came to him mid-war. So did the women who saved some part of his papers from Nazi destruction. The manuscripts they preserved served after the Second World War as crucial evidence at Nuremberg and remain among the most significant historical records of the Third Reich and the intentions of its leaders.

These were men and women who, for the most part, defy neat, polarizing categories. There is a great temptation when writing of the period from 1939 to 1945 to speak of good versus evil, of categories of white and black, clarity and moral darkness. The trouble is that most history, including the history of the human heart, takes place in the shades of gray and among the shadows. You must tread carefully here. How do you tell the story of the courage of a Nazi spy or a dictator's daughter without making her a heroine, without dishonoring either the six million whom fascism targeted or the forty million civilians who perished? What does it mean, in writing of fascism and Nazism, to be, as Dante imagined of his descent into hell, faithful to the good things, as well as to the horrors? To the moments when those guilty of crimes and grave sins choose a different path forward?

This is not a book that asks for forgiveness for them. Forgiveness belongs only to their victims. But this book does ask us to consider the honest and essential human drama of how people—and, Galeazzo Ciano argued, nations—can recognize and repudiate their errors and attempt some reparation. The race to save the Ciano Diaries is, by any measure, the story of an astonishing rescue mission, worthy of any spy thriller, but it is also the story of how these men and women, in trying to save a set of papers documenting crimes that called out for justice, rescued themselves first and foremost.

SISTERS IN RESISTANCE

The German Spy and Mussolini's Daughter

August 31, 1939–February 5, 1943

Where is Ciano? Dinner had been cleared away. Galeazzo Ciano had been expected. The houseguests nursed after-dinner drinks. On this last night of August 1939, the air was hot and still even this late in the evening. Just like always in Rome in the late summer.

But the city beyond the walls of the villa was already unrecognizable. Coffee had been rationed since spring. Workingmen paused now for a *caffè corretto*—a bitter chicory brew "corrected" with grappa. Irate housewives muttered words tantamount to insurrection as they waited in long lines outside shops, only to find there was no beef or butter. Private automobiles were forbidden, and a creaking bicycle passing through an empty street at night brought curious neighbors to peer out of darkened windows. Something anxious hung in the air. The businessmen in the salon that night knew that their office secretaries quietly kept gas masks tucked away in desk drawers, alongside their powder compacts and lipstick cases. People said to each other privately now that the real shortages were still coming.

Across Rome, all but the most fortunate felt the bite of austerity. In the grand homes of the wealthy and well positioned such as this one, with access to the halls of power, though, only the mood had changed substantially. The guests were gloomy and fretful, and they were focused on just one thing: Ciano.

Everyone in Italy knew Ciano.

Count Gian Galeazzo Ciano—his black hair slicked back and shining with pomade, his clothes elegant; foppish, vain, and ultimately foolish—was the second most powerful man in fascist Italy. He was the son-in-law of strongman Benito Mussolini, as well as Mussolini's political heir apparent, and as the nation edged closer to the precipice of war that night, Galeazzo Ciano was also still the man in charge of the faltering international relations: Italy's foreign minister.

A single question held Italy breathless: Would there be war in the morning? Ciano would tell them.

* * *

Only Benito Mussolini held more power, and war was not what Mussolini wanted, though he talked a good game. Mussolini had thrown his support behind Hitler's Third Reich, and now, unless the Allies blinked, Italy risked being drawn into a German-led conflict that Mussolini knew Italians didn't want and its military couldn't manage. Still, Mussolini was optimistic. The Allies would bluster and moan. They would ultimately *do* nothing. They had done nothing when Hitler took control of Austria, then Czechoslovakia. They would not fight now for Poland.

* * *

Galeazzo Ciano was not so certain. In fact, Galeazzo had many doubts both about a war and about the Third Reich.

Since the beginning of the year, Galeazzo had been keeping a diary. The uncensored and indiscreet views he recorded in those pages did not paint flattering pictures of his father-in-law or the Germans. He despised in particular his German counterpart, Hitler's foreign minister, Joachim von Ribbentrop, a thin, cruel man with unsettlingly pale eyes, whose lust for power and political bootlicking earned him the contempt of nearly all who met him. The American diplomat Sumner Welles rather undiplomatically remarked of Ribbentrop that "The pomposity and absurdity of his manner could not be exaggerated." One German counterpart remarked that "One could not talk to Ribbentrop, he only listened to himself"; another described him as "a husk with no kernel." Here was the kind of man who plotted revenge simply because another hapless lieutenant's name was mentioned before his own in some bureaucratic document or another. Already many in Hitler's inner circle were eager to see Ribbentrop stumble. His fall from power would be welcome. In the pages of his diary, Galeazzo summed Ribbentrop up in two simple words: "revolting scoundrel."

Ribbentrop, in return, hated Galeazzo Ciano. He hated the count's casual aristocratic manner and his unabashed love of the English. He hated that Galeazzo did not feign deference and how he impertinently questioned the wisdom of the Führer. When the time for vengeance came—and he did love vengeance—Joachim von Ribbentrop would take great pleasure in destroying the Italian foreign minister.

If Ribbentrop was, in the view of the Italian foreign minister, a fool and a sycophant, Galeazzo Ciano had no illusions left about Hitler by the summer of 1939 either. Only weeks earlier, he had met with the Führer and returned, he confided dangerously to his diary, "completely disgusted with the Germans, with their leader...they are dragging us into an adventure which we have not wanted...I don't know whether to wish Italy a victory or Germany a defeat...I do not hesitate to arouse in [Mussolini] every possible anti-German reaction...they are traitors and we must not have any scruples in ditching them. But Mussolini still has many scruples."

* * *

Mussolini equivocated. One moment, he was full of talk of war and honor and determined to prove to Hitler that he was as eager for imperial expansion as the Germans. The Italians were the heirs to the Roman Empire. He dreamed of a return to sweeping greatness. The next moment, however, reality pressed on Mussolini. Italy was not prepared for this kind of war, and he railed against the pressure the Nazis were placing on him. All that day, Galeazzo had been working feverishly behind the scenes to avert disaster and to prevent the conflict in Europe from exploding. A last-minute British agreement to a peace conference with the Germans took all evening to hammer out. It would solve nothing, but it would buy them some room to navigate. By the time Mussolini had been brought on board, Galeazzo was hours late for his dinner engagement.

When he strode at last through the doors of the salon, eager faces turned toward him, and Galeazzo Ciano smiled brightly. He was a show-man. This was his stage. They could sleep well, he assured the guests laughing, confident: "set your minds at rest…France and England have accepted the Duce's proposals." The British had blinked after all. Of course. *Appeasement* was once again the word of the hour. There would be no war tonight. The guests chuckled and refilled their glasses before slowly wandering off to their bedrooms.

For a brief moment that night, Galeazzo was as relieved as anyone. It didn't last. By midnight, the peace was unraveling again. Galeazzo was back in a ministry car, the smartly uniformed driver swerving through Rome's narrow streets toward an office overlooking the storied Piazza Colonna. Someone passed Galeazzo a sheet of paper. There were quick steps in the corridor. Word was filtering in now over the diplomatic wires. Hitler was having none of a peace conference. The headlines for the morning papers in Berlin were already at the presses, announcing the German invasion of Poland. By dawn came word that Poland was falling. Galeazzo knew what it meant. Mussolini would not join the Allies. His friendship with Hitler would prevent Italy from taking up arms against Germany. But perhaps Mussolini could be persuaded to remain on the sidelines. In the tragedy that was coming, the only hope was somehow to keep Italy neutral.

* * *

For nearly a year longer—until June 1940—Galeazzo Ciano and his allies in Rome would manage that feat. Hitler knew perfectly well who he blamed for this stalling in Rome. He would later say of Galeazzo Ciano, "I don't understand how Mussolini can make war with a Foreign Minister who doesn't want it and who keeps diaries in which he says nasty and vituperative things about Nazism and its leaders." Already those diaries were seriously aggravating Hitler.

In the end, Mussolini could not be tempered. He was at once too weak and too proud. Belligerence was too deeply ingrained in his character. At ten, Benito Mussolini had been expelled from school for thuggishly stabbing a classmate. By twenty, he had stabbed a girlfriend. By thirty, he was the founder of the Italian Fascist party, which rose to power by the simple stratagem of systematically murdering thousands of political opponents so there was no one left to oppose him. By forty, Benito Mussolini had wrested power from the king of Italy through the force of a cult of personality, an act that inspired a younger and admiring Adolf Hitler to attempt a similar Beer Hall Putsch in Germany. Within a year or two, by 1925, he cast aside any pretense and ruled as a fascist dictator, riding a wave of populist support, buoyed by invective and a swaggering, cocksure rhetoric of nationalism and nostalgia that exhilarated his followers and terrified his critics.

Machismo was at the heart of Mussolini's claim to power. In the world that Mussolini had created, "real men" did not back down from a fight and "real Italians," men who were heirs to the Roman empire that had conquered the world, conceded to no one. This created a political dilemma that was clear to him: "The Italians having heard my warlike propaganda for eighteen years…cannot understand how I can become a herald of peace, now that Europe is in flames….except the military unpreparedness of the country [for which] I am made responsible." Mussolini did not want war. But he would not lose face either.

* * *

Galeazzo Ciano fought in every way he knew to keep Italy from entering World War II on the side of the Germans. From the rearview mirror of the twenty-first century, that much is maybe even valiant. For all that, though, it would be a stretch too far to claim Galeazzo Ciano as any kind of hero. He prosecuted other wars, against those far less equipped than France or Britain, with few scruples himself; he was widely and probably accurately considered, like his father-in-law, to have played a role in the extrajudicial execution of political opponents; he enriched himself in office, while much of Italy went hungry; his politics, even when anti-German or anti-Nazi, were not yet anti-fascist. He was, by most contemporary accounts, frivolous, indiscreet in his gossiping, and an incorrigible womanizer. Joseph Kennedy, then the US ambassador in Rome, observed of him in 1938, "I have never met such a pompous and vain imbecile. He spent most of his time talking about women and spoke seriously to no one, for fear of losing sight of the two or three girls he was running after. I left him with the conviction that we would have obtained more from him by sending him a dozen pretty girls rather than a group of diplomats." The Americans were not the only ones to draw this conclusion. Galeazzo Ciano's weakness for attractive women had also caught the attention of the Germans.

* * *

Still more would it strain credulity to claim Galeazzo Ciano's wife, Edda, as a heroine in this story, although this is certainly a book about her and about the astonishing courage, intelligence, and resolve she demonstrated in what was to come.

Edda was also someone known in 1939 to every Italian. She had been known to every Italian for at least those eighteen years of Mussolini's reign, first as the favorite eldest child of Italy's autocratic ruler and a young hellion, and then, after the celebrity Ciano marriage in 1930, as the glamorous and flamboyant Countess Ciano. Twenty-eight on the eve of war—September 1, 1939, would be, as chance had it, her twenty-ninth birthday—Edda's reputation was not a sterling one, and diplomats around the world were very much keeping an eye on her as well.

The British ambassador in Rome, Sir Percy Loraine, reported to Prime Minister Neville Chamberlain that spring that Edda "has become a nymphomaniac and in an alcoholic haze leads a life of rather sordid sexual promiscuity." She drank too much gin and played poker for high stakes poorly. While Galeazzo spoke with a high-pitched, nasal twang and talked endlessly about his passion for antique ceramics—hardly the Mussolini idea of machismo—Edda scandalously wore men's trousers, smoked, wore makeup, and drove a sports car while her husband rode along as passenger. While Galeazzo took to bed in a love-them-then-leave-them fashion so many of her aristocratic girlfriends that people in Rome simply talked of "Ciano's widows," Edda's bedroom tastes ran to sporty and fit younger men like the aristocratic Marchese Emilio Pucci, a twenty-four-year-old Olympic skier and keen race-car driver (as well as, later, renowned fashion designer). No one is quite certain when their on-again, off-again liaison started. It probably began sometime in 1934 on the ski slopes in Cortina. By 1939, Emilio Pucci was back in Rome and once again seeing Edda, though no one supposed that Emilio was her only lover.

Why did foreign diplomats care so much about the dissipated life of the Italian foreign minister's wife and Mussolini's daughter? Quite simply: her influence with her father. Mussolini doted on his eldest child, and, unlike her husband, Edda was enthusiastically pro-war and pro-German. Galeazzo would later write in the diary that, at the crucial moment in the spring of 1940, on the eve of the invasion of Belgium and Holland:

> I saw [Mussolini] many times and, alas, found that his idea of going to war was growing stronger and stronger. Edda, too, has been at the Palazzo Venezia and, ardent as she is, told her father that the country wants war, and that to continue our attitude of neutrality would be dishonorable for Italy. Such are the speeches that Mussolini wants to hear, the only ones that he takes seriously....Edda comes to see me and talks about immediate intervention, about the need to fight, about honor and dishonor. I listen with impersonal courtesy. It's a shame that she, so intelligent, also refuses to reason.

Italy entered the war at last on June 10, 1940, and threw in its lot with Hitler's Germany. Galeazzo Ciano saw that it could only end in disaster. Edda conceded that it was a gamble. But Edda, like her father, thrilled to the show of boldness. Danger invigorated Edda. Besides, in the late spring of 1940 it very much seemed to both Edda and her father that Italy was putting its chips on a sure winner: Hitler.

It was the first of Edda's brash wartime gambles. Only after it was too late would she come to understand that the stakes were higher than she had imagined and that trusting Hitler was a fool's errand.

* * *

That Germany would lose the Second World War was not obvious. For the next two and a half years, in fact, it looked very much like Edda Ciano and Benito Mussolini had been right, at least on balance. The German and the Italian empires expanded steadily. By the end of 1942, Mussolini controlled large territories on the eastern Adriatic, in northern Africa, and on the Mediterranean, including areas taken from neighboring France when it fell to the Axis in 1940. Hitler's Third Reich had reached its greatest extent of the war by 1942 and ranged from Eastern Europe to Norway and Paris. Continental Europe, with the nominal exception of Free France, was effectively divided among three dictators: Hitler, Mussolini, and, on the Iberian Peninsula, Franco.

But Galeazzo Ciano saw the tide turning. He had seen in 1939 that joining Hitler could only bring disgrace and defeat for the kingdom of Italy. The year 1942 had not been easy for the Axis powers. The United States had entered the war, and there had been setbacks and frustrations for Hitler. Galeazzo remained convinced that Mussolini was leading the nation to disaster, but he mostly confided his worries now to his diaries. He already knew better than to say what he thought too openly or too often. He had witnessed the fate of another of the war's prominent skeptics, Pietro Badoglio.

Galeazzo and Pietro Badoglio had been rivals for more than a decade, tussling for power and influence, and neither was above backstabbing the other. They didn't hate each other with the same passionate intensity that Galeazzo reserved for the German foreign minister, Joachim von Ribbentrop, but there was plenty of antagonism. Galeazzo had used the power of the secret police to amass a wealth of embarrassing and compromising information about Pietro Badoglio. Badoglio knew it. One day, that was a score he too would settle.

Still, Galeazzo Ciano and Pietro Badoglio agreed on one thing:

Mussolini was giving foolish military orders and fighting a war that was unwinnable and unworthy. Badoglio had unwisely shared that view with Mussolini one time too many and was passing the war under house arrest at his lavish villa outside Rome, stripped of his military command and with a pampered pet poodle for company. Galeazzo recorded his thoughts privately and was careful to lock up the papers each night before leaving his office. The best thing: simply to keep quiet.

In his private recollections, however, Galeazzo was unsparing. Still foreign minister, he had a front-row seat to Italy's unfolding tragedy and maintained a clear-eyed view of both his German counterparts and his father-in-law's foibles. He was privy to state secrets. His private depictions captured the Nazis in all their brutish malevolence.

Hermann Göring appears in the pages of Galeazzo Ciano's diaries as a pathetic child, desperate for praise and baubles, but the only Nazi with any touch of vulnerability. "[He] wore a great sable coat," Galeazzo wrote of Göring in February 1942, "something between what automobile drivers wore in 1906 and what a high-grade prostitute wears to the opera. If any of us tried a thing like that we would be stoned in the streets. He, on the contrary, is not only accepted in Germany but perhaps even loved for it. That is because he has a dash of humanity." Hitler, depicted as not just a bully but a tedious blowhard, is chided for giving endless, self-congratulatory speeches, which bored everyone. "Hitler talks, talks, talks, talks," Galeazzo confided that April, wryly noting: "Mussolini suffers— he, who is in the habit of talking himself, and who, instead, practically has to keep quiet....the Germans. Poor people. They have to take it every day." Ciano's archrival, Joachim von Ribbentrop—sniveling, back-stabbing, glad-handing—appears as a man who makes a fool of Hitler. But it is Mussolini who comes across in the most unflattering light of all: a puppet dictator, afraid to stand up to the younger man who once held him up as a hero and who now treated Mussolini as a pawn in a large game of world politics—and like a pawn, expendable.

Above all else, in the diaries Galeazzo chronicled, blow by blow, the political squabbles in the Third Reich's inner circle as Himmler, Goebbels, Göring, and Ribbentrop vied among themselves for power and influence with Hitler, as well as the Germans' relentless pursuit of war simply for the sake of domination and plunder. In the hands of any one of those Nazis, Ciano's diary had all the power of a weapon. It had the power as well to strike a mortal blow against Mussolini in the eyes of the Führer.

Galeazzo Ciano, scribbling away, was oblivious to the danger. He wasn't discreet either. He was an inveterate gossip, incapable of keeping a secret, especially from a pretty woman. He carelessly chatted about his diaries to everyone from foreign diplomats to his father-in-law. And even as tensions between Italy and Germany grew explosive, he kept writing.

* * *

On New Year's Eve in 1942, Hitler acknowledged to the German armed forces that it had been a challenging year and that challenges remained ahead of them. "Hitler looks tired," Galeazzo noted. "The winter months in Russia have borne heavily upon him. I see for the first time that he has many gray hairs." Hitler was tired, but he was also "strong, determined, and talkative." "The year 1943 will perhaps be hard but certainly not harder than the one just behind us," Hitler admitted to the troops, as he confidently predicted a decisive Axis victory on the near horizon.

One step in that renewed surge toward victory was a shake-up in the German security service at the end of 1942. The organizational structure of the Nazi regime was notoriously complex, but, put simply, the *Reichssicherheitshauptamt* or RSHA was the German main security office. It had been headed by Heinrich Himmler on a temporary basis since the assassination of Reinhard Heydrich in June. The head of the RSHA oversaw the operations of two sub-agencies, the *Sicherheitsdienst*

(SD) and the Gestapo. The role of the SD was to ferret out enemies of the Third Reich. The role of the Gestapo, Nazi Germany's "enforcer," was to arrest and interrogate those enemies, and its tactics generally included torture.

At the end of 1942, Himmler was being promoted to minister of the interior and head of the German state police forces, and he delegated leadership of the RSHA to an Austrian lawyer-turned-SS-man named Ernst Kaltenbrünner. In January 1943, Kaltenbrünner, in turn, promoted a young would-be spy who, in the eventual assessment of US intelligence, would turn out to be "one of the outstanding RSHA operators of the war." This young agent, elevated to the role of the executive head of foreign intelligence in Rome, a division known as Amt VI (Office Six), would soon be tasked specifically with dealing with the matter of Galeazzo Ciano for the Germans.

The name of this German spy was Hildegard Burkhardt. She was twenty-three in January 1943. She would come to be better known to history, following her marriage that spring to a high-ranking German officer named Gerhard Beetz, by her married name: Hilde Beetz. Hilde was exceptionally bright, and she had the advantage of more than usual beauty. According to government files, she had blue eyes and dark-blond hair, and stood five foot four. Unlike many German girls in the 1930s, Hilde had a fine education. At the gymnasium in her native Weimar, where only a handful of girls studied, she excelled especially in languages. She spoke fluent Italian and excellent English, as well, of course, as German. She was a member of the Nazi party.

Hilde had joined the intelligence services two years earlier, first as a mail clerk and then as a translator. She had moved quickly up to the role of executive secretary for a man named Helmut Löss, special assistant to the police attaché in Rome, whose office was part of a section focused on espionage at the Vatican, where a number of Catholic priests—including a man named Father Guido Pancino, who happened to be the confessor of Edda Ciano and her father—were positioned as part of the German network of SD informants. Hilde's office tapped the phone lines in and out of the papal city-state.

Helmut Löss had a reputation as an excellent agent runner, and he was the first to recognize that Hilde, with her innocent face and sharp intelligence, would make a brilliant spy. On his recommendation, the "big boss," Ernst Kaltenbrünner, made Hilde's transition into intelligence work official, assigning her responsibility for organizing all the incoming and outgoing top-secret filings in the Roman foreign intelligence office, just as the German worries about Galeazzo Ciano were getting serious.

The first hints that Galeazzo Ciano was becoming a problem came across Hilde's desk as the executive head of Amt VI in Rome almost immediately in her new assignment. People now said that the Italian foreign minister was refusing to give the fascist salute to German officers. There had been unsubstantiated rumors since the autumn of 1942 of an inside plot to depose Mussolini and whispers that Galeazzo Ciano was mixed up in it. The reports coming in now were more substantial: Agents were hearing that Galeazzo was working behind the scenes with a coalition inside the Italian Fascist party to overthrow his father-in-law and have him replaced with a new leader, a leader who would sue for peace with the Allies.

* * *

The telegram that blew everything wide open arrived in Hilde's office sometime in the last week of January or the first few days of February. It contained top-secret intelligence intercepted from the American communication channels, and it confirmed the German suspicions about Galeazzo Ciano. The intercepted message had been written by a jovial middle-aged career diplomat named Allen Dulles, who had arrived in Switzerland in early November 1942, based out of Bern. A staunch

Republican with a successful legal career and a failed congressional run behind him, Allen Dulles was ostensibly working as a special assistant to the American ambassador, though the Swiss newspapers soon reported that he was acting as President Roosevelt's personal agent in the country. None of that was true. Allen Dulles was, in fact, working undercover as the head of the newly created American Office of Strategic Services (OSS), the precursor of the modern Central Intelligence Agency, run out of a ground-floor rented apartment in Bern's picturesque medieval quarter.

The Germans would not discover the existence of the OSS until 1944, but they knew enough to be wary of this new arrival. Dulles exuded authority, and between his bearing and the rumors swirling in Bern, the Germans pegged him quickly as a government man whose movements and communications were worth watching. Surveillance paid swift dividends. In January 1943, the Germans broke Dulles's transatlantic code. Catastrophically, it would be months before Dulles would realize all his top-secret communications back to Washington were being read by the Nazis. By then, it would be too late for Galeazzo Ciano. Allen Dulles would wonder later, when he learned his code had been broken, to what extent he was to blame—good and bad—for what followed.

* * *

The intercepted telegram was a secret communication to the State Department containing Dulles's smoking-gun confirmation: A group of anti-German activists close to Mussolini did support a coup and could potentially deliver the Italian army and navy to the side of the Allies. Galeazzo Ciano, along with his exiled rival Pietro Badoglio, a man named Dino Grandi, and a number of prominent anti-war military leaders, were said to be among the party members plotting Mussolini's removal from power and Italy's exit from the conflict. Galeazzo, in fact, had covertly been in contact with the Americans as early as 1941, following Italy's entrance into the war, proposing "the Duce's overthrow and a separate Italian peace" to the Allies. Hitler ordered a copy of the decoded telegram sent to Mussolini in early February. When Mussolini read it, he understood immediately that Hitler expected action.

On February 5, 1943, within a day or two of receiving the intercepted American intelligence, Mussolini summoned his son-in-law to his office. There was no preamble. Mussolini was purging his cabinet. All of them were suspect. All of them would have to go. "What are you going to do now?" was all Mussolini asked. Galeazzo understood immediately that he was being fired.

Mussolini offered his son-in-law the choice of any number of other, trivial government positions, ideally located somewhere outside Italy, as a concession to family. "I [chose] to be Ambassador to the Holy See," Galeazzo stubbornly recorded in his diary. The Vatican *was* a foreign country after all. "To leave the Ministry for Foreign Affairs, where for seven years—and what years—I have given my best," he admitted, "is certainly a hard and sad blow."

Galeazzo Ciano was not a man of keen political instincts. Had his instinct been sharper, he'd have had the sense to take his father-in-law's advice and departed Italy that winter. If Galeazzo did not have the sense to flee, he did at least have the good sense to fret. One of his most loyal friends was a young woman named Susanna, though everyone called her Suni. She was the twenty-one-year-old daughter of Fiat industrialist Giovanni Agnelli—a household name in Italy—and came from one of the wealthiest families in Europe. While many of the Cianos' other friends melted away after Galeazzo's public demotion, Susanna stuck by him. She would remain loyal later too, even when it was perilous to care for Galeazzo and Edda. Susanna Agnelli recorded in her memoirs after the war that she remembered her visits that winter and into the spring to the Ciano family's palatial residence in Rome: "Galeazzo had fallen into disgrace and was no longer the Foreign Minister," she remembered. "He was worried, nervous, and plotting like everybody."

* * *

A few days after his dismissal from office, Galeazzo was contacted by Mussolini again. He wanted to know from his son-in-law the answer to a different question, one that should have been even more ominous: Did the count still have his diaries, and were those papers all in order?

"Yes," Galeazzo replied. "I have them all in order, and remember, when hard times come—because it is now certain that hard times will come—I can document all the treacheries perpetrated against us by the Germans, one after another."

The answer might have placated Mussolini, but it was ill contrived to reassure the person who was really asking: Hitler.

CHAPTER 1

The Grand Council

February 5, 1943–July 26, 1943

When he was removed from office, Galeazzo Ciano stopped writing.

He had been keeping a diary since at least 1937, and probably since at least 1936, the year he was appointed foreign minister. In inexpensive, flimsy eight-by-ten-inch calendar notebooks, he filled each day's allotted page with personal reflections on government meetings and diplomatic personalities before locking the diaries away in the small safe in his office for the evening.

His final regular entry was on Monday, February 8, 1943, three days after Mussolini fired him. There would be only one more entry, a coda of sorts, written for us, his imagined readers, penned two days before Christmas, still ten months in the future, when Galeazzo Ciano had no illusions left to shatter.

* * *

By summer 1943, it was clear that Galeazzo had been right about the war. Hitler's optimistic New Year's speeches had not stood up against the encroachment of reality. Germany was preoccupied with the Eastern Front. Mussolini was left to try to manage the Mediterranean, but Italy could not win that theater—not materially and not tactically. Mussolini, faced with the inevitable, needed reinforcements, but he could not persuade a monomaniacal Hitler to turn his attention back to the war on Italy's doorstep.

By July 10, 1943, word was circulating in Rome that the Allies had landed troops on Sicily. From there, the forces would slowly and arduously push their way northward, up the boot of Italy. By July 16, Italy's ambassadors, passing a secret message from Mussolini, warned the Japanese that "Italy was on the verge of collapse," hoping for some reaction. Mussolini urgently needed to persuade the Axis that his power was tenuous. He needed something to persuade Hitler that, without German reinforcements—and without the peace on the Eastern Front that such reinforcements would require—Italy would fall, and the Allies would take the Mediterranean.

So Mussolini decided to take a wild, last strategic gamble to force Hitler's hand. It would be, he hoped, the final wake-up call that the Führer needed. The plan would backfire catastrophically. And it would also be the moment when Galeazzo Ciano—whatever his moral qualms about his father-in-law and fascism—would have to decide whether to speak or to remain silent in the shadows.

* * *

Strictly speaking, Italy had remained throughout the fascist period a monarchy, ruled by King Victor Emmanuel III. However, the king was an ardent supporter of fascism and had appointed Benito Mussolini as his prime minister in 1922. By the 1930s, Mussolini ruled with an iron hand, with the king acting as a mere rubber stamp to his power. There was, by the time the war began, only one political party in Italy, the National

Fascist Party, and although the king was still asked, as a courtesy, to assent to Mussolini's decrees, in fact Victor Emmanuel had only one curb on his prime minister: the right (but not the obligation) to remove him from office, *if*—and only *if*—the Fascist party's so-called Grand Council voted to recommend it. And while the Fascist Grand Council, as an assembly of party loyalists, retained the right to select the party leader, only Mussolini could convene a meeting of the Grand Council. Quite simply: If the Grand Council did not meet, it could not vote. If Mussolini wished to rule forever, there was no one who could stop him.

Those political realities made Mussolini's call for a meeting of the Grand Council on July 24 to discuss the progress of the war all the more astonishing. The war was clearly not progressing well. He knew that the Grand Council would make it a referendum on his leadership. He knew there would be criticisms of his decisions. Perhaps there would even be calls to replace him with a different party chairman. Mussolini had been warned that a coup was brewing inside the party. He had seen the intercepted secret telegram written by Allen Dulles. Yet heedless of it all, Mussolini barreled ahead with the meeting. He didn't see any alternative. It was a last, reckless gamble.

In Mussolini's mind, the meeting was nothing more than political theater, with an audience of one: Hitler. He did not believe the Grand Council would dare to offer more than political posturing. Some of the ministers would complain and give long speeches. Then they too would settle on a strategy of appeasement. When all the roiling internal discontent was reported back to Germany, however, Mussolini calculated that a vote of no confidence would, at last, "scare [Hitler] with the impending collapse of fascism and…give an edge to the Japanese in their peace efforts," as one historian has summarized his strategy.

Mussolini was supremely confident of his grip on power. The Grand Council could talk all night about replacing him as party leader. As long as the king supported Mussolini's authority—and why would he not,

Victor Emmanuel had been cowed for decades and supported the Fascist party—his position was secure. He knew it, and he knew that the Grand Council knew it. The Grand Council knew, too, what had happened to Mussolini's other opponents.

* * *

The Grand Council meeting was called for the evening of July 24, 1943, a Saturday. Rome sweltered, and the air was heavy and muggy. Behind the scenes, the Ciano marriage was on the rocks. It had never been anything other than tumultuous. Edda and the three Ciano children had fled the capital for the seaside. Fabrizio, their eldest boy, was twelve, their daughter Raimonda was nine, and Marzio was a sturdy little boy of five that summer. The family had recently come into possession of an airy new oceanfront villa in the hamlet of Antignano, on the southern edge of Livorno, where the air was cooler. The villa had been expropriated under wartime anti-Semitic laws from a wealthy Jewish family, a fact that concerned neither Galeazzo nor Edda. Edda planned a series of beachfront dinner parties and, turning a blind eye to Galeazzo's Roman infidelities, comforted herself with tanned and athletic seaside alternatives.

Galeazzo did not need to be in Rome. His father-in-law assured him that his presence at his sinecure post was not strictly necessary. If he had wished to make his life easy, Galeazzo would have simply joined his family on holiday at the beach and kept his own counsel. But for a long time he had been uneasy. He had not supported the war or Hitler, even when serving as Italy's chief diplomat. He remained deeply opposed to the war and convinced that it would turn out to be a disaster for Italy. Now he felt certain that Mussolini was a danger. He was no longer certain that he could do nothing. There were twenty-eight members of the Fascist party's Grand Council, and Galeazzo Ciano was one of them. He had decided already: He would join the meeting at the Palazzo Venezia.

Once again, inexplicably in light of the circumstances, Galeazzo seems to have been blithely unaware of the pitfalls. His speaking was an act of courage. Galeazzo did what he did next from a sense of moral purpose. It would have been more courageous if it were clear that he understood fully what he was setting in motion.

Not all the Grand Council members were so sanguine or so confident. One of Mussolini's fiercest critics, the forty-eight-year-old Dino Grandi, the chief instigator of the planned coup, went into the meeting armed with live hand grenades in the event Il Duce tried to have him arrested. Dino Grandi had not always been a critic of Mussolini. He had been an enthusiastic Blackshirt in his youth and remained dedicated to fascism. But like Galeazzo, he had been purged from Mussolini's inner cabinet in February for daring to hint that Italy had made a mistake in joining the Nazi war effort.

Mussolini opened the meeting at just after five o'clock with a rambling speech. The tone was melodramatic. The scene in the palace was opulent and theatrical. The men sat ranged in a semicircle at boardroom tables, with Mussolini framed at the head of the room, flanked by portraits of Renaissance princes. Mussolini's remarks, to the minds of his critics, were just the same old excuses and platitudes. When Mussolini attempted to justify the German decision to abandon southern Italy to the Allies, there were groans of exasperation. There were then more flattering speeches, from more loyal council members, and Dino Grandi could clearly see that it was all heading in precisely one direction: nowhere.

Furious and impassioned, believing that he was fighting for Italy and for fascism, Dino Grandi rose to the floor. His words electrified the room. Not content to indict Mussolini, he demanded action. Grandi called on Vittorio Emmanuel III to resume control over the military and negotiate a peace treaty with the Allies. He called on the Grand Council to advise the king to remove Mussolini as the head of the party—and, in a one-party state, from power. The room gasped. Grandi was demanding—

there was no other word for it—a coup, and he was doing so face-to-face, mano a mano with Mussolini. The move took courage, even for a man armed with explosives under his jacket.

Dino Grandi's speech failed in one respect. He had wanted immediate action. Instead his call to arms set off hours of bitter and tedious debate in council. Mussolini listened to them all bicker patiently, confident that his goal had been accomplished: Here was enough dissatisfaction to shake Hitler out of his complacency. Surely the Führer would now see that he must rally around his friend and early mentor and send troops to Italy.

By midnight, Mussolini felt confident that enough had been said to spur Hitler to action. He had no intention of being removed from power. Banking on cooler heads in the morning, he called for an adjournment and moved to shut the meeting down. Papers rustled, and the council members eyed the doors. By dawn, all the hard words would be forgotten, and Mussolini—still Il Duce—would see to it that his loyal party members were rewarded.

Dino Grandi was having none of it. He was under no illusions about what awaited him in the cold light of morning. There could be no retreat now. And so he took the simple, radical, and entirely unprecedented step of demanding that the Grand Council vote on his motion before retiring. No one had ever asked for a vote against Mussolini. Dino Grandi had pulled the pin on the only grenade that mattered. The motion set off a fresh round of acrimonious debate. But it would have to end now with a show of hands. At two o'clock in the morning, voting started.

One by one, the members of the Fascist Grand Council placed their chips. For whether they wished for it or not, they all understood in that moment that the political wheel was spinning. Whether Mussolini survived or whether he fell, there would be consequences rippling out from consequences. Dino Grandi proudly, unrepentantly, voted no. He did not support Benito Mussolini as the leader of Italian fascism or its government.

Deaf and befuddled, the elderly General Emilio De Bono, once a formidable Fascist party founder, voted no as well, though it was very late and he was no longer quite sure what he was voting for.

Galeazzo Ciano stood. When he announced that he too chose not to support his father-in-law, the room fell silent.

For a man to vote against his party leader was one thing. But no Italian felt truly comfortable with a man betraying the patriarch of his family, even if that paterfamilias was Benito Mussolini. Galeazzo, in his own mind, was certain. He had been weighing this since 1940, when he first made note in his diaries of another passage from Dante, on the torment of those "hateful to God and to his enemies": It is the moment famously, if rather loosely, rendered into English as "The darkest places in hell are reserved for those who maintain their neutrality in times of moral crisis."

* * *

In the end, nineteen members of the twenty-eight-member Grand Council—a clear and decisive majority—cast their votes that morning to remove Mussolini from power. Mussolini, stunned, took the only avenue available. He promptly brushed aside the outcome, declared that black was white, and white was black, and recast the vote as "advisory." To some extent it was more spin than mistruth: The Grand Council's recommendation was not, in fact, binding on the king, who had long been loyal to his prime minister.

Even as he clung to power and swaggered into the predawn, Mussolini was undeniably damaged by the public rebuke. Behind the scenes, in moves worthy of a Renaissance drama and its princes, ministers were already jockeying for position. Back in his vast official residence at Villa Torlonia, one of Mussolini's first actions was to place a call to one of the few advisers he wholeheartedly trusted: his eldest child and favorite daughter.

Edda missed her father's call in the early hours of Sunday morning. The Allies bombed targets in central Livorno from the air that morning, and she and the children may have been huddled in the air-raid shelter when the call came, she conceded. Edda suspected something darker had been at work. She believed that the call had been blocked by those in the government already rushing to fill the power vacuum.

* * *

Unable to reach her father on the morning of Sunday, July 25, Edda, worried and anxious to hear the outcome at Grand Council, called Galeazzo. Her father, she predicted when she heard of the vote, would be furious. Galeazzo was not worried. "In a few hours Mussolini will have me arrested," he agreed, but "then the king will take away his power and I will be let out." Galeazzo privately hoped that he would be named as his father-in-law's successor as the king's new prime minister, and his first act would be to make official contact with the Allies. After all, he remained Mussolini's son-in-law and heir apparent. Galeazzo was about to encounter a rude awakening.

* * *

Mussolini was also about to have an unpleasant encounter with reality. He requested an appointment on Sunday afternoon to brief Victor Emmanuel III on the party meeting. The king, of course, would need to respond to the vote in Grand Council. Mussolini arrived rumpled, unshaven, and blithely confident of the king's support. Twenty minutes later, he left the meeting reeling.

"My dear Duce," the king told him bluntly as he entered, "it's no longer any good. Italy has gone to bits. Army morale is at rock bottom. The soldiers don't want to fight any more....The Grand Council's vote is terrific—nineteen votes for Grandi's motion.... You can certainly be under no illusion as to Italy's feelings with regard to yourself. At this moment you are the most hated man in Italy." Victor Emmanuel didn't see how he had any choice but to appoint a new prime minister. Mussolini was dismissed. Just like that, nearly two decades of autocratic rule ended.

Mussolini retreated down the steps of the Villa Savoia toward his waiting car. The king, Mussolini remembered later, "was livid...he shook my hand without looking me in the eyes." His mind was awhirl. Six policemen waited beyond the entrance. An officer of the carabinieri approached from somewhere, saluted, and asked Mussolini to enter a waiting ambulance. Only after the doors swung shut did Mussolini stop to wonder why they had sent a medical decoy and then comprehend that he was a prisoner of the king and whomever was destined to be the king's new government. Alarmed, Mussolini looked back at the doorway and saw the king watching.

No one imagined that Mussolini would accept defeat quietly. For the first month of his arrest, Mussolini was moved in secret from location to location, first to offshore islands and then, famously, to the mountaintop Hotel Campo Imperatore at Monte Portella, to await Hitler's daring liberation.

* * *

What Mussolini had not anticipated was that Victor Emmanuel had been looking for a chance to remove his autocratic prime minister for some time. The king had guessed what was coming at Grand Council and had met with Pietro Badoglio a week earlier and let him know that, if the vote were against Mussolini, he would be Il Duce's replacement. Badoglio had been against the war with Germany. But he was also a military hard-liner and dedicated party loyalist, and the king wanted, above all, a determined fascist.

For Galeazzo Ciano, the news of Pietro Badoglio's ascension to power was an unmitigated disaster. If there was one person whom Badoglio despised more than Mussolini, it was his son-in-law, who not only had amassed a vast and enviable fortune during his time as foreign minister but also held some private documents that incriminated Badoglio, who was himself reputedly crooked. The papers had been a sword over Badoglio's head when Galeazzo's father-in-law was running the government. Now Badoglio had a score to settle and—thanks to the vote of Galeazzo and the others in Grand Council—the means to do it. Pietro Badoglio relished the delicious irony. Galeazzo Ciano was, as yet, only dimly aware that he was in a great deal of trouble.

CHAPTER 2

Tramontana

July 24, 1943–August 14, 1943

The Grand Council meeting of the Fascist party cabinet took place on the Saturday night. The Ciano household was in turmoil on the Sunday. By the afternoon of July 25, word of Badoglio's ascension and Mussolini's arrest had trickled out. For the first time, Galeazzo was frightened. He knew that Pietro Badoglio was his enemy. He fully expected the knock on the door that said the police had arrived to search the house for the documents that compromised the new prime minister. Galeazzo doubted he would survive that visit.

If the police should come he fretted, perhaps for the first time, about his diaries. Some of the volumes contained indiscreet—and, considering Badoglio's new favor with the king, potentially deadly—references to "the pederasty of the crown prince." For years, rumors had circulated that Prince Umberto preferred the company of young military men to that of his determinedly anti-fascist wife, the Belgian-born Princess Marie José. Gossips said that, so strong was his disinclination for the embraces of his bride and perhaps, as well, for her politics, their four children had been conceived through artificial insemination.

Galeazzo hastily gathered up the notebooks. There were the diaries of his time as foreign minister but also his separate memoranda of his conversations with German officials and various other private notes and papers, including those with details about the predilections of Prince Umberto. These papers might embarrass any number of powerful men, in fact, and get him in a whole lot of trouble: The realization came as a shock to Galeazzo. He burned nearly a quarter of his manuscripts that day in the family's Roman apartment as a precaution, and he started thinking seriously for the first time about what he was going to do with the remainder. He was loath to burn any more papers. Yes, they were dangerous. But they might, Galeazzo considered, equally prove to be a powerful chip with which to bargain.

* * *

On Sunday, July 25, Edda was still in Livorno with the children, and Galeazzo was also growing uneasy about his family. News of the coup had not yet been made public. When it was released, he wasn't sure that the Mussolini family would be safe from the public, though he expected most of the opprobrium to be directed at his father-in-law. He called Edda that night, finding her in the middle of hosting a lively dinner party in the villa, unconcerned and unenlightened. "The call was very short," Edda remembered.

Ciano warned her: "There is a *tramontana* not especially for us. I'll be sending the car tomorrow morning. Telephone to my mother and make her leave with you." *Tramontana*—the Italian word for the bitterly cold winds from the north—was their personal code for "there's a bad wind blowing." "He probably already knew that my father had been removed from power by the King," Edda understood later. Galeazzo could not say so in that moment; he had to assume that their telephone conversations were being monitored. But Edda knew her husband—and she knew Pietro Badoglio. The call was enough to worry her.

When the dinner party had ended, Edda, rattled by Galeazzo's guarded message, hurried a lingering girlfriend out the door and placed a late-night call to Galeazzo's mother, Carolina Pini Ciano. Edda did not like her mother-in-law. The deeply religious Carolina returned the disdain for her son's unconventional wife.

As Edda's younger brother Romano put it, "Edda was an unusual woman. Of all [Mussolini's] children, she most resembled my father. She had his temperament (energetic to the point of restlessness), his analytical skill, and his raging sensitivity. She resembled him physically too, with that withering look she inherited from him." It was a look that Edda gave her mother-in-law often. "Stop looking at me with those Mussolini eyes" was one of Carolina Ciano's exasperated expressions. Even Carolina, however, could not fault Edda's courage. Edda had no official role in her father's government and made no policy decisions. She could not have been compelled to do anything, either in character or as the Duce's daughter. Despite having three small children, however, she had volunteered for the Italian Red Cross in 1941, serving in an active combat zone off the coast of Greece. Almost immediately after she joined, her hospital ship was bombed by the British, and Edda survived the shipwreck by swimming five hours in icy waters. She had been feted in the newspapers, and Galeazzo wasn't the only one with a riveting diary: Edda had kept a record of her wartime adventures, which maybe one day she would publish.

Edda, in fact, had ended her Red Cross service only that year, in 1943, and she was taking the summer at the seaside to spend time with the children. The idea of having to manage her mother-in-law now was exasperating, but Edda dutifully placed the call to let her know to be ready. Typically, Edda found Carolina Ciano stubborn and dramatic. "There was some difficulty in making her realize that the expedition of the morning would not exactly be a pleasure trip and she had better not embarrass herself and the others with huge suitcases, personal maids and other luxuries necessary in normal times," Edda noted wryly. Then Edda decided she'd best tell the children about their grandfather's fall from power and what it meant for their family. Reading Edda's account of that conversation, one's heart goes out to the young Ciano children.

"What do you suppose is going to happen to us? Shall we all be killed?" the children asked their mother, when they understood their grandfather was no longer prime minister.

Edda did not sugarcoat her answer. "Not yet anyhow," she told them coolly, "but we must be ready for anything. In the best hypothesis, your father will lose his job, his fortune will be taken and we will all become private citizens. But it's much more probable that we'll go through the usual routine: prison, death, or, if we are lucky, exile." "[The] children understood," Edda assured herself: "They are clever....Hope is very hard to die. But I had no illusions. Tragedy had entered my house...we were doomed." She said later that she "went to bed, and for one more night, in blissful ignorance, I was still a dictator's daughter."

* * *

From their remote seaside estate, Edda could not hear the noise that arose in the streets across Italy that evening. If she had, she might not have slept at all. At 9:45 P.M., the national radio broke away to an announcement from the king, informing Italians that Benito Mussolini had been deposed and arrested. Twenty years of dictatorship had ended. Italy went wild. People flooded from their homes and into the streets that night, the radio broadcast coming in stereo from every open doorway. They kissed each other. They sang. Men swept women into their arms for impromptu dances. Everywhere there was laughter. For the people of Italy, this was no less their liberation than the day, still nearly a year in the future, when the Allies arrived to free Nazi-occupied Paris.

Edda was awakened by an early-morning telephone call. One of Carolina Ciano's sisters was calling in a panic, hoping to be evacuated when the car came for Edda and the children. "I'm afraid," she told Edda: "some men outside shouting they are going to break everything." Witnessing the street revelry in Rome and the angry denunciations, Galeazzo also understood for the first time that perhaps the *tramontana* was blowing in their direction after all.

* * *

What came next—the period from July 25, 1943, when Mussolini was deposed, to September 8, 1943, when he was freed by Hitler and returned to power as a puppet dictator—is known in Italian history simply as the Forty-Five Days. Ironically, Mussolini would get his last political wish: Germany would now have to focus its resources on the theater in the Mediterranean, though it was not the outcome he had predicted.

For one glorious night and into the next morning, Italians celebrated their liberation from Mussolini and what everyone said was the end of the war. It wasn't only the Italians who celebrated the hope of peace on the horizon. Across the Atlantic, the *New York Times* splashed the headline: "Mussolini Ousted with Fascist Cabinet; Badoglio, His Foe, Made Premier by King; Shift Believed First Step Toward Peace." In baseball stadiums across America, as news came in that Mussolini had "struck out," thunderous cheers brought games to a standstill and players rushed onto the fields in jubilation.

Outside Livorno on Monday morning, the car that Galeazzo had sent for Edda, his mother, and the children never arrived. There would be no more cars arriving for Mussolini's daughter. Instead, police knocked on the door of the villa and came to give orders. The family would need to return to Rome by train, like any other Italian family. It was nearly two o'clock in the afternoon of Monday, July 26, before they reached the station, and there, passing a newsstand, Edda saw the headline announcing the fall of her father's regime. The children spotted the freight cars along the tracks, now graffitied with the slogan DOWN WITH MUSSOLINI, and had to be cajoled to stop crying.

Edda, her mother-in-law, and the children arrived in the capital around midnight, four hours late, and by evening the mood had turned uglier still. Italians were coming to understand how little would change after all. It was a different leader, but the same old fascism. Pietro Badoglio, whose commitment to fascism was as unwavering as the king's, took to the radio in his first speech as prime minister and announced three words that stunned the nation: "*La guerra continua*"—the war continues. Galeazzo and Edda's friend Susanna Agnelli was in Rome that day, and she shrewdly noted: "The people thought that by getting rid of the Fascists the war would go. But they seemed to forget two things: that it was the Fascists who were voting against Mussolini and that the Germans, our allies, could be all over Italy in a few days."

The people knew who they blamed for this mess: Mussolini and his family. Edda was shocked to see crowds in Rome celebrating the arrest of her father as they waited for the bags to be unloaded at the station. Three armed police guards escorted them home—a necessary safety measure— but the guards had no deference left and scolded Edda the whole way for not having told her father that the Italians did not want war.

"We haven't the least chance of survival if we remain in Italy," Galeazzo said when he saw her. Edda knew he was right. They could not possibly stay in Italy with Badoglio in power and with the popular anger directed at the Mussolini family. Her father was in prison, in some undisclosed location, and no one in the Fascist party was prepared to lift a finger to try to free him. Her eldest brother, Vittorio Mussolini, was making hasty plans to flee to Germany. The next day, Tuesday, July 27, the Ciano family asked a friend with the Spanish embassy for visas and requested passports to leave Italy as well. They planned only to pass through Spain and to travel on to South America. Galeazzo was already ordering his bankers to move funds out of the country.

Edda and Galeazzo expected the passports to take a few days, perhaps as long as a week. While they waited, the situation in Rome deteriorated faster than they could have imagined and placed an additional strain on an already shaky marriage. The mood of the crowds in the streets turned from celebration to despair to fury. The military, on orders from the new Badoglio government, turned its firepower on the protestors. In the days that followed, nearly a hundred protestors were killed and more than sixteen hundred arrested across Italy. In the cultural clash of that moment—between those who despised fascism and those who believed that fascism had been betrayed by the removal of Mussolini—Galeazzo Ciano now emerged as someone everyone in Italy could agree to hate. He represented both the dictatorship and the betrayal.

The first of August came and went. Still the promised passports did not arrive. Without them they could not legally exit Italy. Edda began to be afraid of the reason. Friends, harboring the same fears, urged Galeazzo to get out now by whatever means necessary. He was the one in real danger, not Edda or the children. Not yet, anyhow. The door was closing. Pietro Badoglio had launched a smear campaign in the press and an investigation into Galeazzo, accusing him of enriching himself through corruption. Arrest and a trial were inevitable, and even if the trial was a fair one—hardly certain—the truth was that Galeazzo was almost certainly guilty. The couple was now under de facto house arrest in their city apartment at 9, Via Angelo Secchi, and bitterly fighting.

They fought about the risks, among other things. Edda saw the perils at home clearly: "The only way to avoid arrest, or perhaps even liquidation was to find refuge either abroad or on Vatican soil," she told Galeazzo. They attempted to secure refugee status at the Vatican. The Holy See, not wanting to cause problems for itself with the new fascist leader, refused to accept them. Edda wanted to leave Italy immediately, even if it meant going without passports. Galeazzo wanted to wait a little longer, confident there was no imminent danger and that the passports were coming.

By the summer of 1943, Susanna Agnelli was engaged to marry another of their mutual friends, the Sicilian prince Raimondo Lanza, himself an incorrigible playboy, and Susanna and Raimondo went to check on Galeazzo in person in the first week of August. By then, Edda and Galeazzo had been waiting more than a week for the passports. The Ciano marriage had never been an easy one, and the strain of the delay was showing. Locked in the house together and under police surveillance from outside, they were determinedly avoiding each other, entertaining friends and lovers in different rooms of the apartment. Galeazzo insisted that he and Edda were closer than ever, but Susanna, who was also a good friend of Edda's lover, Emilio Pucci, could at least guess at some of the drama that took place behind closed doors. For visitors to the Ciano apartment, Susanna remarked, "It was embarrassing and difficult."

Susanna and Raimondo were fond of Galeazzo, and Susanna hoped that he would find a way to get out of Italy. Dino Grandi slipped out of Italy that week, foreseeing the inevitable. Raimondo too was in a precarious position, "all mixed up in talking to the Allies, trying to get an armistice, getting rid of the Fascists, and turning against the German," as Susanna put it bluntly. They were debating whether Raimondo also needed a passport. When they arrived at the apartment, Galeazzo was on edge but glad to see friends. Few old friends came to see him now, he admitted to Susanna.

Susanna, an intellectual and bookish young woman who, unusually for a great heiress and socialite, aspired to be a physician, was legendary in their social circles for her brutal candor. Galeazzo challenged her now, joking: "Let's hear you who tell the truth, Suni. Do you think they are going to kill me?"

Susanna paused. Galeazzo was not a good judge of character. He surrounded himself with flatterers, and they were all telling him what he wanted to hear: that his life was not in danger. That his fortune could be saved. That there would be a solution. That he should wait for the passports.

"I smiled to make it less terrible," Susanna remembered.

"Yes, I do, Galeazzo," she told him.

"And who do you think would kill me, the Germans or the Allies?" he quipped.

"I'm afraid either one," she said slowly, regretting her words the moment she saw his face turn ashen.

Galeazzo turned. He was angry now and stung by her words. "Remember one thing, Suni," he said bitterly, "if they kill me, they will kill you, too."

"That may well be," Susanna quietly acknowledged. She and her family were already quietly making plans to flee to Switzerland.

Susanna took her friend's hand and squeezed. *Go to Spain*, she urged him. *Today.* Galeazzo had flown in the Italian air force. There were friends, pilots, ready to fly him to safety, passport or no passport. The Spanish ambassador in Rome had promised to help. She was pleading with him.

He didn't want to run away, he told Susanna. Privately, he confessed, he didn't want to flee without Edda and the children, and slipping away with a friend meant going without them. What if he left and never saw them again? What if they didn't make it out of Italy? He and Edda railed against each other, they fought and argued and raised their voices, but that did not mean that Galeazzo did not love his wife and his children. Their mutual infidelities might have caused storms and jealousy, but, in having them, their marriage was not any different from those of the vast majorities of their friends in Italian aristocratic circles, and Galeazzo was an especially doting father. He didn't feel that he could abandon his family as a man of honor. Things would turn out okay, she'd see, he assured Susanna as she turned to close the door behind her. Susanna smiled sadly.

On the street outside, Susanna exploded in frustration: "Why the hell doesn't he go away while he still can?" she burst out. Raimondo could only shrug helplessly. "I...wanted to help him," Susanna said later, "he had so many times helped people I had asked him to intercede for when one word from him could change their future from death to life. Now he was surrounded by people who...assured him that everybody loved him and that, certainly, his life was not in danger." Susanna, the sensible truth-teller, knew better. All their lives rested in the balance.

Another week passed: mid-August. The drumbeat pressing for an investigation into Galeazzo's financial corruption—and for his arrest—was growing stronger in the press. With Mussolini shunted to the sidelines, his prison location a secret, rage from all sides of the political spectrum was directed now at Galeazzo. Still the passports did not arrive. There was only one conclusion: The Badoglio government was stalling. Pietro Badoglio had a score to settle. He had waited a long time for this moment. There were not going to be any passports coming. The Ciano family's house arrest was tightened, and the prime minister began to consider moving them to more secure incarceration on a remote Mediterranean island, to prevent Galeazzo fleeing Italy while the politics of a show trial were navigated.

Galeazzo might escape Italy undetected on his own, with the help of friends in the air force or a sympathetic colleague in a foreign embassy. If they were to leave as a family, they would need the help of the Germans. Only a clandestine operation directed by Italy's Nazi allies could save Edda and Galeazzo from Pietro Badoglio's retribution. Edda trusted her personal relationship with Hitler, whom she considered an old family friend, and she made some quiet inquiries. When a friend inside the Third Reich learned of Edda's plan, he tried to stop the family from moving in that direction. Galeazzo had been frustrating the German war effort from inside Italy since 1939, to Hitler's considerable irritation. The Nazis also would take their retribution. "Warn Galeazzo that he should make sure not to fall into the hands of the Germans," he urged; "if they succeed in catching him, they will kill him."

By then, it was too late. The death of an old friend—the friend who had offered to fly Galeazzo to Spain—in a state-ordered execution brought home the reality: The Badoglio government had a hit list. Galeazzo was surely on it. Cornered, they threw caution to the wind. Edda asked the Germans to help them flee Italy.

CHAPTER 3

Flight to Exile

August 15, 1943–August 31, 1943

Lieutenant Colonel Eugen Dollmann was a well-known man-about-town in Mussolini's Rome. Fit and stylish, in his midforties, with blond hair, gray eyes, and a tight-fitting uniform, the head of the Roman SS swanned around the city in a Mercedes, accompanied by his vicious attack dog, Kuno, and he was known as one of the more ruthless and thuggish of Heinrich Himmler's enforcers. Attached to the German embassy in Rome, Dollmann spoke perfect Italian, and, although he could not be said to be handsome, with a bulbous nose, prominent ears, and gaunt cheekbones, he was nonetheless a favorite of the women in the aristocratic circles of Edda and her family. Rumor had it that he was particularly intimate with Susanna Agnelli's mother, the princess Virginia Bourbon del Monte Agnelli. Edda decided that Eugen Dollmann was the person to help them flee Italy. "What followed," Dollmann wrote blithely in his post-war memoirs, "was an exciting midsummer adventure in which Edda was cast as Marie Antoinette and I as her would-be rescuer."

Eugen Dollmann recalled the date as sometime around the middle of August. Edda remembered it as August 21 or thereabouts. Whatever the precise date, sometime in the second half of the month, Dollmann recalled, "I received a visit from a smartly dressed man whose civilian clothes did not disguise the officer beneath. He handed me a note." "Dear Dollmann," the note read, "The bearer of this, a family friend, is instructed to convey my regards and a request which I should be grateful if you would fulfil. Yours sincerely, Edda Ciano-Mussolini."

Eugen Dollmann later insisted that he also had tried to warn Edda. Perhaps he even did suggest that she think twice about going to Germany. Against Dollmann's self-serving post-war memories of the affair must be set Edda's willful and stubborn blindness. "You must be aware, Countess, that Count Ciano has not always been Germany's advocate," he claimed to have counseled her. Hitler liked Edda. But "I do not know what the Führer will decide about *him*," Eugen told her.

Edda brushed aside worry. She trusted Hitler and the men in his inner circle. She and the Führer were fond of each other, and there was a long-standing family friendship. Edda was certain that Hitler would never betray Mussolini's daughter. Dollmann shrugged and did as she asked. He made arrangements to meet with Edda in person sometime around August 23 to plan the logistics of a German-sponsored escape mission. The flight for the border would have to take place under the nose of Pietro Badoglio and in secret.

Edda's first concern was to smuggle out some of the Ciano family riches in advance of their departure. A parcel of her jewels was removed from the family apartment under the guise of a flower delivery. Galeazzo's valet left the country with the cache of valuables. One of Edda's girl-friends strolled out of their apartment in Rome wearing several of her fur coats, one on top of another, as elegantly as one could be said to stroll under such an incongruous burden at the end of August.

When Edda and Galeazzo counted up their assets, though, there was one that they knew, more than any other, might buy them financial independence and freedom. The diaries. How would they safeguard the manuscripts? They didn't ask Eugen Dollmann to help hide those. Whatever had been the history of their marriage and its indiscretions, when it came to her marriage and her children, Edda was fiercely loyal, and the diaries were a strictly family matter. They could not risk traveling with the notebooks, which were too large to hide easily and too precious to risk losing. They had to find a place to hide the manuscripts inside Italy. Somewhere they might be safe for years, but also somewhere a trusted friend could access. Edda and Galeazzo had already begun to think of the diaries as a kind of insurance policy, something they could barter with in a worst-case scenario.

* * *

The diaries included some very sensitive material. By 1943, a group of senior Reich commanders could see the German outlook in the war darkening, and these disgruntled Nazi insiders blamed Joachim von Ribbentrop's caustic and misguided "diplomacy" as the cause of the Third Reich's dangerous isolation. Heinrich Himmler and Ernst Kaltenbrünner were among those in the Nazi inner circle who particularly despised Ribbentrop and would dearly like to see his influence with Hitler diminished. Galeazzo hated Ribbentrop, and his diary was reputed to make the German foreign minister appear especially ridiculous. But the papers also recorded years of high-level secret conversations in which the Germans revealed their war strategy. In the hands of the Allies, the revelations could be damaging. As Edda would say later that summer: "The extraordinary importance of the notebooks was apparent to the Germans."

Galeazzo and Edda, determined to keep the manuscripts hidden in Italy, delivered a large cache of them in secret to his mother, Carolina

Ciano, for safekeeping. Then they delivered themselves directly into the hands of an enemy.

* * *

If they'd had longer to plan the operation, perhaps they would have reconsidered. But events unfolded quickly. Even the Germans sensed that the political climate in Italy was volatile. The Allies were slowly making progress northward, and in the third week of August all female operatives and staff in the German foreign office were evacuated hastily. Hilde Beetz, pulled from the foreign intelligence sector in Rome, was reassigned to the Munich office and demoted, set to working under an Austrian man named Wilhelm Höttl as his secretary and translator.

When Galeazzo's old friend and copilot Ettore Muti was assassinated on the instructions of Pietro Badoglio on Monday, August 23, 1943, they knew they had to flee. Neither of them doubted that, if they remained, Galeazzo would also be assassinated. Their fears were confirmed three days later when Raimondo Lanza made an emergency late-night visit to the Cianos at the apartment. He had a reliable source. The warrant for Ciano's arrest had been issued that evening. His arrest was imminent. Tomorrow. Raimondo came to warn his old friend: The time to go to ground was now.

Galeazzo and Edda discussed urgently what to do next. If they were going to flee Italy, it would have to be in the morning. They made late-night contact with Eugen Dollmann, and the Germans agreed to a hasty evacuation. Dollmann contacted his superior, Herbert Kappler, who headed up the SD in Rome. Herbert Kappler reached out in Germany to a colleague in the SD, Wilhelm Höttl, to close the circle. Someone in Germany would have to sign off on this kind of escape mission. A baby-faced, slender man standing five foot eight, Höttl was both unusually corrupt and notably clever. Though only in his midthirties, he had risen

41

quickly through the ranks and had jettisoned a pre-war calling as a professor of philosophy for a new career in espionage, under the direct patronage of Kaltenbrünner and Himmler. The Ciano family wanted to flee Italy? Wilhelm Höttl had the clearance to arrange it. He had a new secretary who spoke perfect Italian.

* * *

The mission was a go. The German security services would fly them to Spain. They would have to smuggle the Ciano family out of their apartment in Rome, under the nose of the Italian police, first thing in the morning. Getting Edda and the children out was relatively simple, as Eugen Dollmann recounted later: Edda was only loosely under house arrest and was still allowed to visit friends and walk the neighborhood. It was Galeazzo whom the Badoglio government wanted. Galeazzo was under constant guard by the carabinieri. Getting him out was the tricky bit. The family enlisted the help of Edda's pretty maid, who agreed to lure the police officer on duty to a nearby park.

Edda, stuffing as many of their last valuables as she could in her handbag, set off with the children for an early-morning walk, tailed on bicycle by an Italian minder. They fled wearing nothing but flimsy summer clothes, in order not to arouse suspicion, although one of the children refused to part with a toy duck that would escape with the family. "Behave normally. Pretend we are going for a walk," Edda admonished the children. The plan was precise. Edda walked the short distance west along Via Nicolò Tartaglia, then turned right onto the Piazza Santiago del Cile; an American car pulled up beside her, driven by a German Amt VI agent named Otto Lechner. She and the children jumped into the car when they heard the secret code word. Agent Otto sped off with a squeal of rubber, ditching a furiously pedaling police agent.

Galeazzo Ciano needed to leave the house only minutes later, and the timing was crucial. As soon as the police realized he was heading for the door or that Edda had fled, they would try to stop him, and surprise was his only advantage. When the minute struck, Galeazzo, playing his part with gusto, lowered his green-tinted aviator sunglasses and flung open the front door. As he stepped outside into the sunlight, blinking, a large black car with Nazi Herbert Kappler at the wheel slowed as it passed him. The door swung open, Galeazzo threw himself inside, and they tore off down the street, while on the doorstep the Italian secret police panicked.

The two separate cars headed for the German Academy, a short distance east. As they drew up, the gates opened and then closed again in a moment. Once both cars were safely hidden from view in the walled courtyard of the villa, the Ciano family, reunited, were met by operational lead Wilhelm Höttl, who had flown into Italy for the mission, and transferred quickly to a closed German army truck and then rushed to the small airfield at Ciampino, south of Rome. On their way to the airfield, the children nearly gave them away by giggling at the checkpoints. At Ciampino, a Junkers 52 transport plane, with engines running and loading doors open, was waiting. The army truck backed up to the loading doors so the family could board unseen. At the last minute, Wilhelm Höttl asked Otto Lechner, the Amt VI agent driving Edda and the children, if he would come along for the flight, to act as the onboard translator.

"The first thing we did," Edda remembered, "was to pin our Fascist insignia onto our lapels once again." Galeazzo made a quick inventory of their valuables: Edda's rings and bracelets, a gold cigarette case he had managed to slip into his pocket, some jewels that had been concealed in their daughter's little play handbag, a flask of brandy for Edda's nerves and to calm the children. They would be searched before the journey was over. He wanted a record of their possessions.

As they looked back down over Rome, it was without knowing

whether they would ever return to the country they had once ruled as the daughter and son-in-law of a dictator. The flight ahead of them was grueling. In order to avoid detection as the Junkers passed out of Italian airspace, they would have to fly at an altitude of eighteen thousand feet over the Alps, and the family, dressed in summer clothes, shivered miserably as the temperature plummeted.

Edda never recorded when precisely a more chilling realization dawned on her. She only remembered that it was early in their flight. They should have been heading west, toward the Atlantic. Instead, the plane banked to the northeast. The wrong direction.

The Germans had assured them that they would be taken directly to Spain, where they had been promised high-level asylum and a visa quickly onward to South America. It was a false promise. Hitler had already been persuaded that Ciano's diaries could not be permitted to reach the Allies, and the Germans had to assume that the family might be traveling with the manuscripts. Even if they were not, as long as the family was in German territory, where the Gestapo could reach them, Galeazzo attempting to do anything with the papers would be too dangerous. As Joseph Goebbels, Hitler's spin doctor and minister of propaganda, confided to his diaries: "The Führer rightly suspects that such memoirs can only be written in a manner derogatory to us.... There is therefore no thought of authorizing Ciano to leave the Reich: he will remain in our custody."

"I do not know what passed through his mind," Eugen Dollmann wrote afterward of the Ciano family's escape plan, "but [Galeazzo Ciano] can hardly have been thinking along the right lines. If he had been, he would never have embarked on a journey which would take him to the domain of Ribbentrop, who was his mortal enemy, or of Adolf Hitler, who despised him."

* * *

They were being taken to Munich.

The Junkers's pilot, a man named Erich Priebke, was one of Herbert Kappler's Gestapo men in Rome, and he offered honeyed words of reassurance to his passengers. They would land in Munich only for lunch and refueling. They would need to stop to pick up new passports and new identities for the family. Then, of course, the family was reassured, it would be onward to Spain, as promised. No need to worry.

Edda was too miserable during the five-hour flight to think. She took big slugs of brandy, trying to keep warm in her light summer dress, but the booze, combined with the airsickness pills she had taken, left her dizzy and disoriented as the plane lurched and shuddered in the turbulence.

Galeazzo refused to touch a drop. Every nerve was taut. They had made a catastrophic mistake. Rachele Mussolini later said of the decision, with crashing understatement, that it had been an "error of judgment." He had been such a fool. He needed to keep his wits about him.

* * *

When the plane jerked to a halt on the military runway in Germany, Wilhelm Höttl disembarked and strode forward. A car was waiting for them with the engine running. The Ciano family and their host were whisked away to the lakeside villa still nominally owned by Prince Sayn-Wittgenstein, some fifteen miles outside Munich in the Bavarian countryside, where they were to stay as distinguished "guests" of the Führer for what they were still promised would be a brief, if perilous, visit. Only when Wilhelm Höttl passed Galeazzo monthly ration cards for the family did the penny drop at last. "My God! I think they count on keeping us here for some time," Galeazzo whispered to Edda.

Erich Priebke, the SS pilot who flew them from Rome to Munich, would later talk of that flight as the moment he arrested the Count and Countess Ciano. Priebke had understood perfectly well since leaving

Rome that there was no intention of sending the family on to Spain that afternoon or any other afternoon. The house arrest at the rural castle was initially cordial, and in the beginning their hosts kept up the pretense of a social visit. Otto Lechner, the last-minute translator who made the flight with them from Italy, was assigned to stay with the family for the first several weeks, and there was a flurry of visits and messages, first from the Nazi security services chief, Ernst Kaltenbrünner, arriving with flowers, then a chivalrous note from Joachim von Ribbentrop, asking to call on his old friend Edda, and finally a personal request from Hitler to see her alone. No one spoke to Galeazzo. He was clearly persona non grata. "I was astonished," Edda confided. The Germans spoke "only to me and seemed to ignore my husband's existence."

* * *

It may have been in these first few days of princely captivity, as the peril of the situation began to dawn on him, that Galeazzo Ciano first made a bold proposition to Wilhelm Höttl. In the internal struggle for power within the Nazi ranks, Höttl's loyalties were to Kaltenbrünner and Himmler, which meant that Höttl and Galeazzo shared a common disdain for Ribbentrop, the German foreign minister. Galeazzo assured his minder that his diaries would discredit Ribbentrop. Otto Lechner observed that Ernst Kaltenbrünner made a surprising number of visits in the first few weeks the Ciano family were in Munich, perhaps a hint that the conversations began soon after their arrival. Galeazzo understood by now that he would need help from inside the Nazi party machinery if they were to get out of Germany. What if, Galeazzo proposed, they were to make a bargain: his diaries, with the power to bring down Ribbentrop, in exchange for his family's safe passage to South America? Wilhelm Höttl wanted to make sure he understood what Galeazzo was describing and wondered too what other secrets Galeazzo could be beguiled into sharing. Perhaps he could be seduced into revealing the location of the papers, which the Germans suspected he might have with him. Höttl brought in a crack young Italian translator who had just been transferred to his office from Rome, one of those attractive young women that were the count's weakness: Hilde Beetz.

CHAPTER 4

Gallo

August 29, 1943–October 15, 1943

Hilde Beetz's life had been thrown up in the air that summer. In Italy, she had been largely left to her own devices as the executive head of the foreign intelligence office. Evacuated in August, she was still settling in to a new, and less autonomous, position in Munich as Wilhelm Höttl's secretary and translator in the German-based intelligence office managing the Italian sector. She was an ambitious young woman, and it was undeniably a career step backward. Hilde was also settling into life as a newlywed. In June, in love, she married Captain Gerhard Beetz, a German military officer who happened to be an acquaintance of Galeazzo and Edda Ciano. Despite her time in Rome, Hilde had never seen the famous Count Ciano, and her first impressions of Galeazzo when she was introduced to him at the castle outside Munich were not flattering: "He was tall, well-built, physically attractive, sure of himself.…But he seemed to me a man too full of himself, too vain and frivolous." It was probably not an unfair assessment.

Hilde's first assignment was to serve as translator. She spoke Italian perfectly, and simultaneous translation was a rare talent. She quickly confirmed in reports back to headquarters that Wilhelm Höttl had correctly understood Galeazzo's proposed bargain. He would swap his manuscripts—guaranteed to damage Ribbentrop with his internal enemies—for the family's safe passage to Spain. The Spanish would provide them onward transit to South America, where Galeazzo had already transferred some assets. The family wanted only a quiet life and to flee Europe.

The proposed swap—the manuscripts for safe passage—set off eager internal discussion among Höttl and his superiors, especially Kaltenbrünner and Himmler. None of these men harbored any particular sympathy for Galeazzo Ciano. But they had no particular enmity toward him either. The opportunity to kneecap Ribbentrop, on the other hand, whom both hated, was simply too delicious to pass up. Perhaps they would find the diaries first and not need to follow through on the bargain. All things being equal, having the diaries to damage Ribbentrop *and* retaining control of the count would be the ideal outcome. But if the only way to secure the documents was to send the Ciano family off to South America, none of the key players in Munich especially cared. The Nazi security bosses signed off on an agreement to exchange the diaries for the family's freedom. The person conspicuously not in the loop was Hitler. No one imagined that Hitler would support an internal effort to damage Ribbentrop. Himmler and Kaltenbrünner were counting on the diaries to make their case for them.

Things seemed to be moving forward. By now, the Germans knew that the diaries were not at the castle. Agents were fanning out across Rome, trying to discover where Galeazzo might have hidden the papers. On Monday, August 30, perhaps as part of a plan to placate the family while the search for the diaries in Italy was under way, perhaps in earnest, the family had photographs taken, meant to be part of their false passports and new, post-flight identities. Galeazzo was to become an Italian-Argentine gentleman, and he now sported a fake glue-on mustache that sent the children into peals of laughter. Edda was to be an Englishwoman named Margaret Smith, born in Shanghai, China. They tried not to let on to the children how frightened they were, but by early September things were desperate. They had been promised that a plane would take them to Spain no later than September 5. When September 5 came and went, Edda began to think that perhaps Galeazzo had been right all along: The Germans could not be trusted. Galeazzo expected a double cross. After all, they had already been promised a flight directly to Spain from Rome. Look how that had ended.

* * *

The Germans were thinking the same thing about double-crossing Italians that week. The Axis had intercepted communications hinting that, in Italy, the king's new prime minister, Pietro Badoglio, was secretly negotiating an armistice, after all, with the Allies. When news of the peace treaty broke on September 8, the Ciano family's position at the castle became infinitely more complicated. Rome was now an open city. Hitler ordered a brutalizing occupation. The Italians had become enemies of the Reich. Galeazzo was a particular kind of enemy. He was widely blamed for instigating the coup against Mussolini and for Germany's loss of Italy as a strategic partner. Edda's brother Romano talked of the arrest of Mussolini that followed as the moment that "signaled the end of Fascism" in Italy, and Galeazzo was one of the men responsible.

Things took a disturbing turn at the castle after the announcement of the armistice. Wilhelm Höttl had been solicitous in his surveillance of the family as "host." His replacement in residence at the castle at the end of the second week of September was a man whose name was only recorded by Edda as "Otto." Perhaps this was the same Otto Lechner who had traveled with them from Rome as translator, though there were several other agents with the name of Otto who were ultimately involved with the Mussolini family. They quickly learned that Otto considered his role less as host than scourge and jailer. The SS commandant terrorized the Ciano children by murdering their pet cat in front of them and having them frog-marched off to bed each night at gunpoint. "I had never really hated anyone," Edda said later, "until I met Otto." The children's nanny, unsurprisingly, quit, and then, on September 10, a new arrival came to live with them at the castle.

* * *

Everyone knew Galeazzo's weakness for the ladies, and the new arrival was very doll-like and pretty, with an innocent face and an open temper. Her mission was to beguile Galeazzo into revealing the contents of the diaries, "including all details in its most specific form…most importantly every statement directed against Germany and, especially again, against Ribb." She was to get him to tell her, as well, where the diaries were hidden. The new arrival, of course, was Hilde. She had been promoted on an ad hoc basis from a secretary to an active intelligence agent. This was the career chance that she keenly wanted. She was clever and ambitious, and she was eager to be a spy. That her government was the Third Reich was not something that worried the twenty-three-year-old German.

Edda, no one's fool, was less than thrilled by the development. Her nickname for her husband was Gallo—the cock—and she saw where this was headed, even if Hilde was careful to appear emotionally remote and formal on arrival. Hilde appearing as a seductress would be counterproductive: Galeazzo loved the pursuit. She would let him be the pursuer. "Now we endured the impersonal correctness of a hostess—Frau Beetz, who stayed on with us till the end," Edda wrote crisply. Hilde's strategy worked. Galeazzo could not resist chasing after women.

It was Hilde Beetz's first assignment as an intelligence field agent, and, when she met Galeazzo a second time, on her introduction to the household, her impression was more favorable. Galeazzo by now was full of self-recrimination. He saw precisely how disastrous their decision to place themselves in German hands had been, and he blamed himself for it. "He had lost his self-confidence. He was downhearted, prostrate," Hilde noted. Part of her even felt sorry for him: "Instinctively, I felt solidarity with him," she remembered of those early days of her mission, "little by little he understood that he could trust me. He began to confide in me, to unburden himself. Our conversations became ever closer, more confidential. It came naturally to me to try to help him, to bolster his courage." Then again, charming Galeazzo out of his secrets was her mission.

* * *

Back in Rome, the capital was in turmoil by the second week of September. The Italians had changed sides in the war. Germany was furious. As German troops rolled into the capital to occupy the city, the king, queen, and new prime minister fled for their lives. Susanna Agnelli and Raimondo Lanza, still in Rome, were caught up in the national drama. The Germans were occupying the military barracks and shooting Italian soldiers. "I came home to find it was full of carabinieri who had jumped the wall from their barracks at the far end of the street into our garden," Susanna remembered. "They were asking for civilian clothes with which to escape capture." Within days, the Portico d'Ottavia—the Jewish quarter—was sealed off and liquidated. A handful of residents managed to flee by jumping from rooftop to rooftop over slippery clay tiles, which rained down in shards on the streets. Most residents were arrested and deported to Auschwitz.

Susanna's fiancé, Prince Raimondo, had been part of a network of Italians working in secret to negotiate the peace with the Allies, and he had been dangerously opposed to the Fascist party. Now he was desperately trying to get south to join the Allies before he was captured by the Gestapo as an enemy agent. Susanna found Raimondo a hiding place in a hospital cellar and then turned her attention to the plight of her half-American, English-speaking mother, the princess Virginia Agnelli, who, despite her long-standing friendship (and perhaps more) with SS man Eugen Dollmann, was also arrested and imprisoned as an Allied citizen. Then Susanna fled for the Swiss border, escaping with her sisters just days before the Germans liberated Benito Mussolini in a daring Alpine raid and put in motion plans to reinstall him as a puppet dictator.

In Switzerland, despite the vast Agnelli wealth and their royal connections, Susanna and her siblings found desperate wartime conditions in Lausanne. That winter, Susanna remembered, "We ate mostly corn flakes and milk that you could buy without food coupons" for lunch and drank "boiling soup to keep ourselves warm during the night" as a meager dinner. The only bright spot for Susanna: She still held on to her dream of becoming a physician, and she would be allowed to attend medical school in Switzerland. She would never marry Prince Raimondo.

* * *

The German plan to spring the Ciano family in exchange for the diaries that would bring down Ribbentrop was still moving ahead as late as the second week of September. Then Edda made a fatal, foolish error. She had been warned not to raise the subject with Hitler and to leave broaching it to his lieutenants. Edda barged ahead and insisted on asking for his personal permission. She trusted in her personal friendship with the Führer. Hitler, taken off guard and furious, summoned the security chiefs and immediately forbade any consideration of escape for Galeazzo Ciano. Mussolini was free and already under German protection. He would soon be returned to power in Italy, at the head of a fascist puppet state, and Hitler's view was that, when that return happened, his treasonous son-in-law should be sent as well to Italy, for Mussolini to deal with.

* * *

When they understood the deal was off, Galeazzo despaired. He talked openly of committing suicide. Edda, who had always been highly strung, was stricken by Hitler's refusal to help her family and the consequences of her mistake. She teetered on the edge of a nervous breakdown. They were still living under the reign of terror imposed daily by Otto. Hilde, whose cover as personal secretary and translator deceived no one, continued her careful charm offensive on Galeazzo. In hushed late-night conversations, Galeazzo and Edda worried to each other. They worried especially that the diaries' hiding place in Italy was not safe, especially now that the Germans controlled the capital. As long as the Nazis didn't have the diaries, there was a chance, something left to bargain with. If the diaries were discovered, neither doubted that Galeazzo would be executed—or assassinated.

In retrospect, leaving the papers with Galeazzo's mother had been too obvious, they realized. Galeazzo worried that it placed Carolina Ciano in danger with Germans actively hunting the diaries. Edda had a dim view of her mother-in-law and didn't credit her with much common sense. She would also feel better if the papers were somewhere more reliable. They could only see one solution. Edda would have to return to Rome. Galeazzo would not be allowed to go. They understood already that he was being detained in Germany. But there was no reason to deny her permission to return to Italy on a visit, especially as it was now occupied Reich territory. This time, she would hide the diaries carefully. She was already thinking of how to do it.

Both Edda and Galeazzo were distraught, then, when Edda's travel request was flatly refused. Her parents had been brought to Germany while operations were under way in Italy to prepare for Mussolini's return to power. Edda threw violent temper tantrums with her father, demanding that he insist that Hitler repatriate her. When that failed, she went on a hunger strike. Finally, the Germans, exhausted and convinced that she was mad, agreed to send her home.

By that point, there was another motivation for getting rid of Edda: her influence on Mussolini. Hitler and Ribbentrop wanted Mussolini as angry with Galeazzo Ciano as possible, and Edda staunchly and intelligently defended her husband. Some of Hitler's inner circle were privately sympathetic to her arguments. Even her father was increasingly swayed by them. Joseph Goebbels confided to his diary that, while in Germany, Edda "has succeeded completely in reversing the Duce's opinion of Ciano.... That means this poisonous mushroom is planted again in the midst of the new Fascist Republican Party." Mussolini, as the figurehead leader of the newly founded Salò Republic, would rule over the northern part of Italy under the direction of the Third Reich, based near Lake Garda. Sending Edda to Rome, nearly three hundred miles south and under German control, suddenly had certain attractions.

Perhaps more important, though, was the simple fact that, if Hilde Beetz was to have success in seducing Galeazzo to share his secrets, it would be more easily accomplished if his wife was in another country. Edda was permitted to leave Munich on September 27, 1943, on a military transport train. She traveled under a fake identity card in the name of Countess Emilia Santos, accompanied by three SS agents disguised as a Catholic priest and two nurses. Galeazzo was not permitted to leave. Neither—powerful collateral should Edda misbehave—were the young Ciano children, whom Hitler intended to hold as hostages. Galeazzo was a doting father. It was a terrible weakness.

* * *

Edda returned to a capital under direct German authority, and she put on a good show, playing the part of a dissipated party girl and meeting up with society girlfriends in order to deflect surveillance. She turned, in particular, to one old friend, Delia di Bagno. Rumor had it that the elegant and fashionable Delia had been Galeazzo's lover at the same time that Edda was carrying on with Delia's husband, the Marchese Galeazzo di Bagno. Edda's mother, the old-fashioned Rachele Mussolini, had been furious when rumors of this partner swapping had reached her. If the gossip was true, neither Delia nor Edda minded their husband's indiscretions. Galeazzo was in trouble, and Edda quickly confided to her friend what was at stake. Both Delia and her mother, Antonia, the Countess of Laurenzana, agreed to help Edda recover and more securely hide the diaries. Pulling some strings, Delia arranged the near impossible: a private automobile and petrol. The two women set off together, ditching their police minders, to retrieve the diaries from Carolina Ciano.

* * *

Carolina Ciano, however, had managed to lose her son's papers.

Edda's expectations of her mother-in-law were low, but this was unbelievable. Edda and Delia were beside themselves. Edda didn't care if anyone heard her swearing.

Carolina tried to explain. She had been concerned that her house would be searched. Not quite understanding the importance of the parcel entrusted to her, she had passed the diaries to Galeazzo's uncle Gino Ciano, who had divined that this might be something precious and had carefully buried most of them under a tree in the garden of a family house near Lucca. Unfortunately, Carolina explained, "someone seeing him do so and certainly believing them to be cash or jewels had dug them up and stolen them."

But it was a small village. Now that Carolina Ciano understood that the papers were being bargained for her son's life, she put out word locally that some important family documents were "lost" and offered a large reward for anyone who "found" them. A few days later, the missing parts of the notebooks appeared at the bottom of the garden. The remainder—including the all-important notebook recording Galeazzo's conversations with Ribbentrop—were recovered from Uncle Gino's second and happily more secure hiding place in Rome.

* * *

Galeazzo's "diaries" were not, in fact, all diaries. They were a mix of family and business papers. The "diaries" proper—Galeazzo's daily record of his time as foreign minister, written using flimsy Italian Red Cross planners as notebooks—ran to at least seven and perhaps eight handwritten volumes, one for each year from 1937 to 1943, and possibly a volume for 1936 as well, the year that Galeazzo took up the position.

Then there was a second set of papers, which they called the Colloqui or the Conversations. This set comprised at least five and possibly six volumes, bound in expensive green leather bindings; these records contained Galeazzo's memoranda of diplomatic conversations from 1938 to 1943. Some of those memoranda were copies of official papers. Others were personal records.

Finally, there was a third set of unbound papers, which Edda and Galeazzo called Germania—papers and supporting documents having to do with Italian-German relations. To this set of papers, they added a fourth loose-leaf collection of various personal and family letters and Edda's own action-packed wartime diary. Both Edda and Susanna Agnelli had served as nurses on hospital ships, and both had survived wartime shipwrecks. Edda's diaries, as the dictator's daughter, were a unique historical record.

These were the collective manuscripts that Galeazzo and Edda thought of as the "diaries." Together they were a hefty, unwieldy bundle. Moving the papers unnoticed was not easy. Most of the diaries had been left with Carolina Ciano. A smaller portion had been left with a friend at the Spanish embassy. Edda gathered the papers together and made a great show of packing up her extensive wardrobe in trunks and suitcases. Aided by Delia di Bagno, she used the occasion to transfer the diaries surreptitiously to a new location, apparently a trusted bank somewhere in Rome. Some sources say the two women placed them in a safe-deposit box under some concocted identity known only to Edda and Delia. Other sources—and probably the more reliable—say that the papers were bricked up behind some stonework at the top of an arched doorway in the building with the help of a family friend inside the institution. Her urgent mission accomplished and the diaries secured, Edda and Delia made their fond farewells, and then Edda headed north to Florence for a passionate reunion with her longtime paramour, the aristocratic Emilio Pucci, at his palatial estate in Florence.

Emilio Pucci, born in 1914 into one of Florence's most illustrious noble families and himself a titled marchese, was a glamorous and decorated wartime pilot, an ace skier, and a celebrated amateur race-car driver, but he was recuperating now at home from the aftereffects of a near-fatal tropical fever. Old friends and erstwhile lovers, Edda and Emilio had rekindled their passion in Capri in early 1943, just after the end of Edda's dramatic two-year tour with the Red Cross, and now, on the edge of nervous collapse and exhausted by her time as Hitler's captive and by the urgency of hiding the papers, she turned to Emilio for comfort. Edda told him of the danger to Galeazzo. And she told him about the diaries. She needed his help. "After listening to her story," Emilio said later, "I decided that it was my duty as an officer and an Italian to do all I could to help her…it was my duty as a gentleman to do my utmost."

For the moment, Edda needed a home base, and Emilio could see she needed a doctor. Jumpy, sleepless, and strung out, the Ciano family had lived in daily terror for their lives since July. Edda was cracking. There was no thought of her returning to Germany. First, she needed recuperation. Edda and Emilio checked into a fancy private health-care clinic in the small village of Ramiola, outside Parma, together but apparently in separate suites, in the middle of October 1943, placing Edda under the care of two brothers, Doctors Elvezio and Walter Melocchi, who, unknown to either Edda or Emilio, were "partisans"—members of the Italian anti-fascist resistance.

The clinic in Ramiola was an imposing if remote villa, with large windows and surrounded by shaded gardens, perched on a small hill overlooking fields and orchards. Edda—living under the assumed name of Countess Emilia Santos—collapsed gratefully. She would need new reserves, because the worst by far was still coming.

CHAPTER 5

Arrest

October 16, 1943–December 12, 1943

While Edda and Emilio settled into the Ramiola clinic, Galeazzo remained imprisoned at the castle in Bavaria with Hilde. Now that Edda had returned to Italy and had, he presumed, safely relocated the diaries, Galeazzo felt calmer, more buoyant. As long as the Germans didn't have the papers, he felt confident that he was not expendable. With Mussolini returned to power, Hitler surely would not harm Il Duce's daughter or her family. Hilde reported back to her superiors with satisfaction in intelligence briefings that Galeazzo had "made peace with the fact that he would remain in Germany for a long time. He never spoke of escape and abroad anymore." He expected Edda's return soon and, soothed by Hilde, began to talk of buying a family home and settling somewhere in Germany.

Having just settled into the idea that his stay in the Reich would be a long one and that he, Edda, and the children were not in daily peril, Galeazzo was surprised to receive a message on October 16, just a few weeks after Edda's departure, that he had been given permission to return to Italy. According to the notice, "the Duce wished to speak to him." The request was odd. Mussolini had been in Munich as recently as September. Edda's mother, Rachele, was still in Germany, wanting to be near her grandchildren and other members of the family, who had fled after the installation of Pietro Badoglio as prime minister. Galeazzo had talked with Mussolini then about the fiasco in July. Galeazzo had insisted to his father-in-law that "events after the Grand Council had gone completely against his and his fellow voters' intentions." That was a completely true statement, as far as it went: Galeazzo most assuredly had not wanted Pietro Badoglio in power. But Galeazzo *had* intended to see Mussolini removed from office as prime minister and had cooperated with the king and others to make that happen. Mussolini might have forgiven him, but Galeazzo was clear that his mother-in-law, Rachele, had not. She stared daggers at him. When she bothered to acknowledge his presence at all, that is. Years later, she would write her memoirs and notably had nothing good to say about her eldest daughter's husband.

When Galeazzo in response to this "invitation" suggested that he had made his peace with a quiet domestic life in Germany and no longer wished to return to Italy, the tone altered. Wilhelm Höttl arrived at the castle the following day, in the middle of a Sunday. Perhaps the count had not quite understood *Führerprinzip*. Nazism was based on one fundamental law, known in German as *Führerprinzip*—the Führer principle. Hermann Göring once offered a simple translation: "The Führer alone decides." Hitler had decided. Return to Italy was imminent and not actually optional. When Höttl then told Galeazzo and Hilde that the count would be accompanied south on Tuesday morning by two police officers, in case he had any "concerns" in transit, Galeazzo understood at once that Mussolini was not preparing him a warm filial welcome.

Galeazzo would be returned to Italy for his reckoning with Mussolini and the reconstituted Fascist party. The children would remain in Germany, as would their grandmother. Hitler already knew that Galeazzo would never attempt to flee for Spain or South America if it meant abandoning his children to the Nazis. On the Monday before his departure, he gathered his three children together in the grand salon. "Ciao, kids, we will not see each other for a while," his son Fabrizio remembered his father saying. Rachele, determined to let Galeazzo know just how much she hated him, poured the tea silently, scowling. "[A]lways behave with honor," he told Fabrizio gravely. "Don't forget ever that we are Italians," he said to his daughter, Raimonda. He just kissed his restless little boy, Marzio, whom he and Edda affectionately nicknamed Mowgli. Edda adored wild things. She had once kept a pet jaguar at the Villa Torlonia. They both loved in their youngest son his *Jungle Book* demeanor. Tea over, Galeazzo went out for a brief appointment in Munich. By the time he returned, the children and their grandmother were gone, and, except for Hilde and the SS, the castle was empty.

* * *

By now, Galeazzo and Hilde were inseparable. Hilde had been sent to prey upon Galeazzo's weakness for pretty women, and she had played the hand coolly. Galeazzo certainly found her charming. Hilde reported back to her superiors in the German security office in the autumn of 1943 that Galeazzo had fallen hard for her and was planning their future together. Whether Edda knew it or not yet, Galeazzo had come up with the idea that Hilde would join their household as his personal "secretary." "Should he be able, against his expectation, to live freely in Italy," Hilde wrote in her intelligence briefing to Wilhelm Höttl, "he would get his children to follow him immediately and would ask that I accompany them." Hilde and he would work together on preparing his diaries for post-war publication. Hilde was encouraging him to think about the diaries as a bestselling book and wanted to know all about their most thrilling aspects.

Galeazzo had a reputation for being an inveterate gossip, unable to keep a secret. True to form, he had already told Hilde where he and Edda had hidden the diaries before they left Italy. "[H]e had already told me in conversation, before the notice of his departure arrived," Hilde reported to her superiors, "that they are in three parts (originally, they were in 4, one part he had in Rome in his house and burned it on the 26th of July[)]....One part is held by a 'neutral' friend in Rome, two parts are buried in Tuscany." These were the papers held by the former Spanish ambassador and hidden by Carolina Ciano.

Edda, of course, had already moved those papers to a safe location, with the aid of Delia di Bagno, and in a sense Galeazzo was sharing with Hilde information that he hoped was already outdated. But the fact that he told her at all simply confirms what was inevitable: Galeazzo Ciano was infatuated and could not resist gossiping. Was Hilde Beetz in love with her target? She was a rookie spy, on her first real assignment, and Galeazzo was undeniably gallant and handsome. She had not been impressed with Galeazzo at their first meeting. Now she felt for the despondent count something that he perceived, at the very least, as a warm friendship and intense sexual attraction. Were those feelings real on Hilde's part or was the flirtation part of a ruse to gain his trust and accomplish her mission? There is no way to know for certain how things stood in the beginning. Perhaps both things were true simultaneously. Hilde later said that, before their sojourn in the Bavarian countryside ended, she had already "taken a strong liking for him and was working to save his life." At the same time, Hilde Beetz was ambitious and professional, she was newly married and apparently in love with her husband, and her career depended on her delivering up Count Ciano's diaries. Keeping him alive and infatuated was the best way to make that happen.

* * *

On Tuesday, October 19, as scheduled, a German transport plane took off from Munich, destined for Verona, the city at the heart of Romeo and Juliet's ill-fated love story. On board was Galeazzo Ciano, flanked by two grim-faced, gun-toting SS minders. He wore a gray flannel suit and a light raincoat. He had no luggage. No umbrella. He carried with him only a photograph of Edda and the children in his breast pocket and a Russian icon of the Catholic Madonna that had been a wedding present. Hilde Beetz was permitted to accompany him on the southbound flight, to keep him calm and compliant, though she would be expected to make the immediate round-trip journey.

The plane swept low on the approach. Galeazzo could see below them the Adige River winding through the city, a sprawl of red-tiled rooftops, and the stone husk of the Roman amphitheater. The transport plane came in fast, rattled, and then jerked to a halt. His minders nodded toward the exit. Verona in 1943 was under the nominal control of Mussolini, part of the so-called Italian Social Republic, often known simply as Salò, after the town on the banks of Lake Garda where it was centered. An Italian military police officer stepped forward as Galeazzo blinked in the sunlight, and a hand was on his arm in practically the same moment as his foot hit the tarmac: "Galeazzo Ciano, you are under arrest."

"I am aware of that," Galeazzo replied coolly.

He was determined not to let on that he was rattled. But he *was* rattled.

* * *

Hilde, soon back in Munich, was worried. She needed to figure out how to be reunited with Galeazzo and transferred to Verona. Maybe there was genuine sympathy for the count. But the reality was that unless Hilde could convince her bosses that, given just a bit more time with Galeazzo, she could deliver the diaries, she was back to being an office secretary. She was not going to miss her chance for a promotion by having her first mission disappear now.

Galeazzo had told her of the three sets of papers hidden in Italy.

Hilde saw the opportunity. On October 23, Hilde filed an intelligence brief with Wilhelm Höttl, her boss, making the case for continuing to be assigned to the mission. "I am determined even now to find out more about the documents," she pressed Höttl. "The Count would not be surprised by my arrival in Verona....He would certainly share his plans with me." Wilhelm Höttl, seeing a determined young Nazi agent keen to take her quarry, agreed to Hilde's proposed plan. By November 3, 1943, Hilde, along with Rachele Mussolini as a passenger, was on her way to Verona.

Internal Nazi party politics were a key driver in the decision to send Hilde Beetz back to Italy. The race was on for the count's diaries. Ribbentrop was worried about what Galeazzo Ciano might say if he were able to escape Italy now with the manuscripts and was pressing for a speedy execution as a decisive resolution. Wilhelm Höttl's boss, Ernst Kaltenbrünner, still wanted to kneecap Ribbentrop with Hitler, and Ribbentrop seemed awfully worried about something in those papers. That made Kaltenbrünner very curious about the reason.

* * *

The drafty stone building in which Galeazzo was being held prisoner had not always been a jailhouse. The seventeenth-century church of Santa Teresa degli Scalzi belonged to an order of Carmelite nuns. After that, for a time, it had served as military barracks, before being converted to a prison at the end of the nineteenth century. Located in the heart of old Verona, not far from the Castelvecchio or "old castle," Scalzi, as it was simply known, had a fearsome reputation in 1943 as a prison for fascism's political enemies. And that was how the new Fascist party of Italy saw Galeazzo Ciano. He had repudiated Mussolini's fascism at Grand Council, but fascism and Mussolini were not done with the count.

Galeazzo was not the only one of the party members at the Grand

Council who had been caught. All nineteen of those who had voted against Mussolini and betrayed fascism were being hunted. The ground floor of the church had been emptied out and reconfigured to house them as, one by one, they were captured. Some of the conspirators managed to flee to safety. Six of them were unlucky, among them Galeazzo Ciano and the elderly Emilio De Bono.

The impending trial of the Grand Council "traitors" in Verona was inherently political and partisan. Mussolini's new council of ministers set up a special court to try the men on charges of treason. Galeazzo was one of several indicted, but, as Mussolini's son-in-law, he was a particular lightning rod for party outrage. At the Fascist party conference in November, there were pounding feet and chants from the convention floor calling for "Death to Ciano," and it was hard to see how Mussolini could retain control over the party or prosecute any of the others if he pardoned Galeazzo. The outcome of Galeazzo's trial was not in doubt: This was not a jury trial but political revenge theater.

Hilde Beetz arrived on the steps of the Baroque prison on November 6, a Saturday, with orders that she have access to Galeazzo Ciano as a "translator." Everyone understood immediately that this was a euphemism: She was clearly a German spy, sent to keep an eye on the wily prisoner. The prison prefect, a man named Cosmic, readily agreed that Hilde would spend the afternoons and evenings each day with Galeazzo. When she was ushered into cell twenty-seven, Galeazzo was delighted. He wasn't a fool; he understood that Hilde worked for German intelligence. But he did not believe that Hilde was playing him. The chemistry between them he felt certain was genuine. He seems never to have considered that it was possible for Hilde both to find him sexually attractive and to act as a loyal Nazi, reporting everything that he said back to headquarters.

* * *

Galeazzo confided now that he was desperate to hear that Edda was safe and that the diaries had been hidden securely. He was not permitted to send messages out of his cell, and he didn't know if Edda was even aware that he was in Verona and had been arrested by her father's new government. Hilde, unsurprisingly, promptly offered to act as a confidential messenger between the two. She would hand-deliver to Edda any private communications about the diaries that Galeazzo wanted to send her. Galeazzo trusted her.

Hilde traveled north the next week to Ramiola, where Edda and Emilio Pucci remained in residence at the rest clinic, with Galeazzo's first message. Edda was surprised and somewhat startled to see their German "hostess." She had guessed since Munich that Hilde was a spy. There was no other reason for Hilde to have joined the family at the castle. She knew that she and Galeazzo had spent long weeks alone, and she knew that her husband could not keep a secret. She quickly concluded that Hilde Beetz must by now be "Gallo's" new mistress.

If Galeazzo was a trusting soul—and that had always been Susanna Agnelli's worry about her friend—his wife was not. Edda was Mussolini's daughter, and experience had been a good and hard teacher. She did not doubt that this very pretty young German spy would be happy to hear the locations of the diaries and convey the good news to Galeazzo, right after the Gestapo took possession of the documents. Edda was not going to give anyone the information about where the diaries were hidden. Not even Galeazzo. Edda knew her husband's weaknesses. She was pretty certain she was looking at her.

Edda demanded that she be allowed to see her husband in person. She was not going to pass messages. And she had no intention of negotiating with Hilde. Mussolini was nominally the leader of fascist Italy. Edda lived within his jurisdiction. Galeazzo had been arrested on his authority. Her quarrel was with her father. Mussolini, in truth, had little power as Hitler's puppet. Rachele was shocked to see, on her return to Italy, that the SS had taken over even their home. "I was stunned to find that, although back in his own home, he had retreated into a modest room, while the German officers assigned to serve and guard him ostentatiously occupied most of the house," Rachele remembered indignantly years later. But, hoping desperately for reconciliation with his daughter, Mussolini agreed that Edda be allowed to see Galeazzo, and her brother Vittorio, now returned to Italy, arranged for a private car to drive Edda from the clinic at Ramiola to Verona.

When Edda arrived at Scalzi and demanded to be taken to see Galeazzo, the prison prefect greeted her with an open hostility and calculated rudeness that startled her. Any deference due to Edda because of her father was more than outweighed in the prison director's mind by the fact that she was the wife of fascism's most infamous scoundrel. Edda brushed off the scorn, but privately it worried her. This, indeed, was a *tramontana*—a bad wind blowing. In the cell too, Edda was alarmed to see that their conversation was openly monitored. There would be no opportunity to discuss anything candidly, including her many questions about what had happened during those last days outside Munich. Soon the guard announced that the visit was over. Edda leaned to kiss her husband goodbye, and she only had time to whisper one short secret sentence, the thing above all she had come to tell him: "They are safe." She had saved the diaries. Galeazzo held her close for a long moment.

* * *

That whisper came with a price. Edda would not be allowed to see Galeazzo for weeks afterward, no matter how much she pleaded with or threatened her father. On the ground in Verona, Wilhelm Harster, the local SD commandant, was now Hilde's immediate supervisor. General Harster ordered that Hilde be given unrestricted access to Count Ciano, and she was with Galeazzo constantly from mid-November forward.

They played chess cozily late into the evenings; Galeazzo's favorite restaurant delivered gourmet meals to the cell. Anyone looking at the scene might have said it looked positively romantic.

Indeed, by now Galeazzo and Hilde were almost certainly lovers. Mario Pellegrinotti, a sympathetic prison warden who helped the couple, remembered clearly witnessing the "unequivocal behavior in which I casually surprised them once" sometime in late November or early December. They may have been lovers since as early as October outside Munich, when they were living together at the castle in Edda's absence and when Galeazzo first began talking of a future together and of bringing Hilde to live in the household with him and Edda. Hilde later insisted that she did not "make love" to Galeazzo and that she was not his "mistress." Perhaps in saying that she did not "make love" to him, Hilde only meant that she was not playacting the role of an Amt VI agent. Not entirely. Or perhaps she was simply noting what was almost certainly the truth: that, despite her being sent to spy on him and seduce him, it was Galeazzo who did all the pursuing. By the end of November, however, this much seems apparent: Hilde, despite all her clearheaded espionage intentions, *was* falling in love with Galeazzo Ciano.

Galeazzo's prison-house liaison with Hilde did not stop him from missing his wife or sending Edda genuine and tender love letters either. Theirs had been a tempestuous marriage, and sexual fidelity had never been either of their strong suits, but this was not the cultural expectation among Europe's aristocratic classes in the 1930s and 1940s. For Edda and Galeazzo, sexual fidelity was not the barometer of what it meant to be loyal to a marriage or a family. Galeazzo was truly grateful for Edda's fierce devotion to him and the children in times of trouble, now especially. "Life is sad," he wrote to her in a letter in November, "I read, read, read…I think of you a lot. With hope and sadness, according to the moment, but always with infinite longing. Kiss our three darlings, if they are with you, and take the most tender kiss of your Gallo."

Although Edda understood clearly where things stood by November, she too never faulted Galeazzo and Hilde. With Emilio at her side, how could she? "People have claimed that Frau Beetz behaved as she did because she was in love with Galeazzo," Edda explained after. "Certainly, but of what importance were feelings—or my reactions to this—when the life of my husband was at stake?...Frau Beetz was what she was, but she never betrayed me. She gave my husband the letters that I wrote to him, she delivered to me those he wrote to me."

For her part, Hilde explained it this way: "the Count and Countess trusted me from the very beginning and often complained [about] the way they were fetched from Rome to Germany and were treated in Allmannshausen where they officially were guests but really prisoners without any rights....Fortunately [Galeazzo] had mistrusted the Germans from the beginning—contrary to his wife—and had made his preparations at least to revenge himself." It would be revenge by publication of the diaries.

According to Hilde, on her return to Rome in the early autumn Edda had not just moved the originals to a more secure location. She had also placed copies of Galeazzo's diaries and perhaps a few crucial original documents with various friends, including several people in "neutral embassies." There were few neutral nations left by 1943, so it is not hard to guess their destination. The trusted recipients almost certainly included an unnamed diplomatic friend in the Spanish embassy, likely the same friend who had offered to help them flee in August, and former diplomatic colleagues at the Vatican, Galeazzo's last official appointment. Now, with Galeazzo imprisoned and his trial looming, Edda had sent instructions to their friends, Hilde reported, "authorizing them to publish those things, if later on they did not hear anything about him."

Was it true? It's hard to know for certain whether Edda had really made copies and left them in various locations. The papers ran to thousands of pages, and while electrophotography—photocopying—

had been invented, the technology was not common. Edda may, however, have had the diaries photographed and circulated in film canisters. On the other hand, it may have all been a bluff. Galeazzo and Edda may have only said that the diaries were in safe hands, in multiple locations, poised for publication, as a ruse, hoping to convince the Nazis that keeping him alive was the price of silence. They had circulated the story far and wide in Germany during their incarceration, and they had all the more reason to tell it now as the prospects grew increasingly dim in Verona.

There is one other tantalizing hint of another "friend" at a neutral embassy who, if the story is true, might have received copies of the count's diaries from Edda that autumn. Some reports have circulated—though they cannot be clearly confirmed, as is so often the case with classified wartime records—that Delia di Bagno and her mother, the Countess of Laurenzana, did more than just help Edda hide the diaries in October. They may have also helped connect Edda with a Polish aristocrat-turned-Allied-spy then living with the countess and operating under the assumed name of Christine Granville, who may have played an unrecorded bit part in the Ciano drama.

* * *

Christine Granville—better known as Krystyna Skarbek—was later one of the most celebrated British SOE (Special Operations Executive) agents of the war, and officially there is nothing to confirm that she was in Rome in the fall of 1943. Officially, there wouldn't be. Her personnel files either have not been located or remain classified. There are, however, some odd hints in the public records. Christine was studying Italian and expecting to be deployed on a secret mission in Italy sometime in 1943, possibly connected to a cell tied to the Polish resistance run by a former British diplomat, Lieutenant Colonel Ronald Hazell. Files show that her lover, a fellow spy, was deployed to Italy as early as January 1943, and perhaps they were sent together. Certainly, neither Britain nor Poland was neutral. But did Edda pass along copies of some of the diaries to friends in the diplomatic corps with the help of Christine Granville? We can't know for sure unless Granville's personnel files are uncovered somewhere, someday in the intelligence service archives. But if it ever proves to be the case, it would explain a curious thread in the story that unfolded in the year to follow: Galeazzo and Edda, at different times but each anticipating they might not survive, made eleventh-hour efforts to get a message to the British about the diaries.

* * *

By mid-December 1943, Galeazzo had been in prison for more than six weeks, and the political climate was only growing uglier and more vitriolic. The political show trial was moving ahead. Treason was a death sentence. It was clear by now to Galeazzo and Edda that, if they were going to save Galeazzo, they needed to leverage the diaries. This proposed deal more than usually interested Hilde, not only as an intelligence operative but also as the count's lover. By now, Hilde's feelings for Galeazzo were genuinely complicated. She wanted to have her cake and to eat it too: She wanted to save his life *and* deliver the diaries to her Nazi bosses in the bargain.

A preliminary idea soon emerged in conversations among the three of them. They would strike a fresh deal with the Germans, to complete the trade of the diaries for Galeazzo's life that had been sidetracked in Munich. This time, Edda would share nothing. But the Ciano children were still being held hostage by the Nazis in Germany. Before they did anything, they needed to get the children to safety so they could not be used against them in any covert negotiation.

"My father had a weakness" for Edda, one of her brothers noted pointedly later, "which he made no attempt to conceal," and Edda, knowing how much Mussolini hated refusing her anything, had been badgering her father to release Galeazzo from prison since November. Mussolini's reply to his favorite child had been blunt: She wanted to think about that demand carefully. The Gestapo would kill the children if he made a move to spare their father. Edda thought about how the vile Otto had terrorized the children at the castle casually, while they were under the personal protection of Hitler. She could not bear to think what would happen to the children if the SS were given license. She made up her mind now: She was going to get her children. She was going to smuggle them to Switzerland. Then she would turn her mind to saving Galeazzo's life and bargaining the diaries for their freedom.

* * *

She needed the children returned to her custody so she could plan a brazen escape. Who could resist a mother's plea? Her youngest child was not yet six. A mother asking for her children played to the Nazi image of ideal womanhood. She tearfully begged her brother Vittorio to intervene with her father and the Führer. Vittorio, moved by his sister's genuine distress, agreed, boldly demanding the return of the children to Edda and offering to escort them himself to their mother at Ramiola. Hitler could hardly refuse to have Mussolini's grandchildren returned to him without destroying any pretense of an Italian-German partnership, and so the request was ultimately granted. The Ciano children were reunited with their mother at the clinic just before mid-December.

By December, Fabrizio, Raimonda, and Marzio had not seen their mother for more than two months. Edda needed to prepare them now to be separated again from their parents for what might be considerably longer. She had thought about this carefully. There was only a very narrow window. She planned for the children to remain with her for just a few days. She would need to smuggle them out of the country immediately and in secret, before the Germans or the Italians thought to put monitors in place. Edda was not yet under intense police surveillance simply because no one expected that a mother would try to send her young children away within hours of their being returned to her. But that was precisely what Edda and Emilio were planning.

If her plan failed, she would not get a second chance. Edda knew there would be hell to pay, too, if her plan succeeded. They would try to keep the children's disappearance a secret for as long as they could, and that meant that Edda would not be able to travel with them to the border. The flight for the border was planned for December 9, less than forty-eight hours after the children were returned to their mother. Edda and Emilio had arranged for two old friends, Tonino Pessina and Gerardo Gerardi, to help get the children across the Swiss border. There are tantalizing hints—unconfirmed and as yet unconfirmable—that Christine Granville may also have been part of this operation. Christine was famous for her ability to cross borders—indeed, she was so good at crossing hostile borders that the British wondered if she might be a double agent.

Edda would need to remain at the Ramiola clinic and keep up the appearance that the children were with her. Emilio Pucci, pretending to be called away on military duty, would manage the transport. Emilio hustled the three youngsters to a waiting car on December 9, a Thursday. They headed north to Milan, arriving on December 10, where Gerardo Gerardi had an apartment. On December 11, they traveled again to the appointed border town, where Tonino Pessina was waiting to walk with the children across the mountain to Switzerland. They had bribed an Italian border guard to let them pass, paying him, Edda said, "with my diamond brooch given me by the King and Queen of Italy as a wedding present, a ruby bracelet, and a solitaire." All the time back in Ramiola, Edda carried on pretending that the children were with her in her rooms at the clinic, ordering extra meals and talking at doors to deflect attention.

* * *

The three young children would have to cross the mountain pass separating Italy from neutral Switzerland in the small hours of the morning. There was a full moon that night, and they trudged through snowfields, keeping to the edge of forest. It was cold, and the children understood that they were leaving their parents behind, perhaps until the war was over. Fabrizio, twelve, was old enough to understand that it might be far longer. Little Marzio struggled with the long walk through the half darkness. When they couldn't go on, the children slept for a few hours in an Alpine shepherd's hut, but they had to pass the border before morning, and they would have to make the last part of the journey alone.

When the children slipped at last through the barbed wire and netting before sunrise, they were met by the Swiss police from the village of Neggio, who had been warned that children were crossing alone. When a kindly Swiss guard offered them a piece of chocolate, Marzio was wide-eyed. Chocolate had been impossible to come by during the war with shortages and rations. He had only ever heard of such a marvel.

The Swiss police had been told that they were meeting the fleeing members of the Savoy royal family. They were in for an unpleasant shock when they learned that it was the Ciano children who had crossed the border. The Swiss would not have taken on the political complications that came with harboring the grandchildren of Mussolini had they been given the option, and diplomatic officials back in Bern were furious with the deception. But there was no option of sending children alone across a fascist border.

Edda had impressed upon the children that they would need to stay hidden even in Switzerland. They would be hunted by their grandfather and the Gestapo once their flight was discovered. Switzerland was safer than Italy, but Edda knew better than anyone the long reaches of the police and the intelligence services. The Swiss sternly gave the three children the same warning. "You must now forget your family name," they admonished. "You are a Spanish family named Santos." It was the assumed name Edda was already using at the border, a hint that somewhere along the way she had obtained for all of them false papers.

Emilio waited until morning on the Italian side of the border. When he heard nothing—a good sign—he drove back to Ramiola to let Edda know that the children were presumed to be safe in Switzerland. For as long as she could, she would carry on pretending in all her communications that the children were living quietly in Ramiola with her. As long as no one in her family visited her, the deception was unlikely to be discovered. On December 12, with the help of Hilde, Edda was smuggled into Galeazzo's cell in Verona for a brief and rare prison visit. She had another important message for her husband. "It's done, the children are safe," she whispered this time as they parted.

Now Edda planned to see about saving the life of her children's father.

CHAPTER 6

The Last Card

December 15, 1943–December 27, 1943

The relationship between Edda and Hilde was not precisely a friendship. But it was not unfriendly either. The two women definitely had their doubts about each other. Hilde, a cool, strategic thinker, worried that Edda was too hotheaded, too Italian. Edda's impulsivity and fearlessness had created all sorts of problems in Munich. Edda, for her part, didn't fully trust the younger woman's motives. Hilde was a Nazi intelligence agent, and it did not take a genius to figure out that her mission was to secure the diaries that the Germans so badly wanted. Whose team was she on, really? And which mattered to her more: Galeazzo or the manuscripts? Those questions niggled at Edda. But both women were running out of options by mid-December, when they turned to the only avenue either could see ahead: "the idea of my husband's escape in exchange for his notebooks."

Hilde—described by one commentator as "a semi-young German girl with the Dresden type of beauty"—saw this swap of the diaries for Galeazzo's life as a win-win solution to what was, for her, an otherwise intractable problem. Her mission as an agent was to get possession of the papers and pass them to her bosses, and her chain of command was Harster, Höttl, Kaltenbrünner, and, ultimately, Himmler. The shared objective of those four men was first to take down Ribbentrop, a project Galeazzo would have supported even had his life not hung in the balance, and second—this was where Galeazzo's aims and the aims of her Nazi bosses parted—to prevent the embarrassing publication of the count's diaries. Hilde still planned to execute her duty, and she acknowledged later that, at the time of her first meeting with Galeazzo, she was still a Nazi, holding the rank of an SS major.

Hilde needed—and wanted—to execute her mission successfully. But there was nothing in her assignment that required Galeazzo to remain in prison in Verona. The show trial was an internal Italian political melodrama, not a German state security matter, and her loyalty was to Berlin and not to Salò. Neither was there anything in her assignment that required Galeazzo's execution, which she saw already was where things were heading. Hitler himself doubted that Mussolini would have the mettle to execute the father of his grandchildren, though he certainly would have executed Galeazzo himself had the count been German.

Hilde had been sending back reports to her superiors throughout the fall and laying the groundwork for a plan to secure the diaries and free Galeazzo at the same time. They might have pulled off the swap back in Munich in September if Edda hadn't blundered into the situation and alerted Hitler. Edda had learned that lesson. Galeazzo intended to publish his diaries once the war was over, to restore the family's confiscated fortunes, and Hilde now advised Höttl that, since his incarceration, Galeazzo had taken the necessary steps to ensure that if he were executed they would be published immediately via the United Press International wire service. The diaries were in the hands of those diplomatic friends, poised to take action. This was a bold assertion and perhaps nothing more than a bluff of daring proportions, although on the whole the evidence suggests that Edda had passed at least part of the documents, either in the original or in copy, to diplomatic friends in the early autumn. Whether it was a bluff or the truth, Hilde's goal in making sure her superiors knew of the claim was to remove any incentive to have Galeazzo quietly assassinated before the location of the diaries could be discovered.

Why kill him anyhow? she reasoned to her bosses. He was willing to sell the papers instead to the Germans, Hilde noted in intelligence briefings. All Galeazzo wanted was safe passage for himself and his family and enough money to live on. "We practically have two options," Hilde advised her bosses: "to insist that he be executed [or] to conclude an agreement with him.... [i]f we buy the books for a generous price, and secure the needed guarantees [from him], we will be able to prevent this type of propaganda and get the useful knowledge ourselves." She assured her handlers that the diaries, while replete with "funny episodes [about Ribbentrop] that are not always indicative of an above average intelligence," were not critical of Hitler or Himmler. Mocking Hitler or Himmler would have been a deal breaker.

Where Galeazzo would go was a delicate question. Any escape would have to be a crossing at a land border. Flying to Spain and from there to South America was no longer an option. At first, Hilde thought perhaps Galeazzo could remain within the Third Reich once the diaries were exchanged, and in their initial planning an idea was floated to spirit him away to the remote estate of a friendly aristocrat in Hungary. But Hungary was still within the Reich, so that plan left Galeazzo potentially exposed to retribution from Ribbentrop, who would certainly be in a murderous mood when the content of the diaries reached him. Thus they decided that Galeazzo would also need to flee to Switzerland.

* * *

By December 1943, the broad outlines of a swap—the diaries in exchange for a prison break orchestrated by the German spy services—were coming together. Hilde was the broker and the chief architect. "It has been said," Edda wrote later, "that the person most active in this operation, set up by Kaltenbrünner and Himmler in order to cause Ribbentrop's downfall, was Frau Beetz. That is correct."

Hilde flew to Berlin in December, around the same time that the Ciano children were being reunited with their mother, to make a preliminary pitch for the swap directly to Wilhelm Höttl. Höttl approved of the plan. He asked Hilde to draft a formal memorandum that he could share with Ernst Kaltenbrünner, detailing especially "the possibilities of using Ciano's diaries to expose Ribbentrop's shortcomings." Hilde promptly delivered the memorandum, then returned to Verona on December 9 to await news of a decision, landing back in Italy just as Emilio and Edda were spiriting the Ciano children into Switzerland.

* * *

Hilde described the feelings that she held for Galeazzo as something "more intense than simple sympathy, something that arose from my heart," and she was constantly in and out of his cell, often staying for hours. Hilde was falling in love. It was a genuine complication.

Hilde confessed to Galeazzo that she was a German spy, and, although her bosses didn't know it, Galeazzo was by now drafting her intelligence briefings back to Berlin and Munich. They discussed for hours how to best make the case to Kaltenbrünner that the diaries were worth the trouble. As long as Galeazzo's enemy was the Italian Fascist party and not the Third Reich, Hilde did not have to choose between love and her country—a powerful motivation for the young agent to make this deal happen. Somehow, in this moment of moral crisis, Hilde still hoped to remain neutral.

* * *

Back at Scalzi, however, it wasn't just the friendly prison guard, Mario, who noticed certain "unequivocal" signs between Galeazzo and Hilde. Their conspiratorial intimacy was raising all sorts of red flags in the two weeks before Christmas. Afraid that she might be pulled from her assignment at the crucial moment if her personal feelings for Galeazzo were suspected and she was considered compromised, the couple embarked now on a campaign of deliberate misdirection. At his pre-trial hearing, Galeazzo put on a great show of irritation, demanding that the magistrate explain "who is that woman they have put at my side?...She stays continually with me. She prepares my coffee in the morning, she puts my cell in order, she stops to talk for a long time. She returns in the afternoon, she prepares my tea, she stops to play chess or checkers. In short, I don't manage to free myself from her. She is like my shadow." The magistrate, with a smug smile, was pleased to see Galeazzo was chafing under German surveillance, which he hoped the prison would ensure was ongoing.

Galeazzo's friend Zenone Benini was in on their secret, and he wasn't entirely sure what to make of Hilde. His assessment in December, though, was that Hilde was at least "slightly in love" with Galeazzo. Zenone Benini was among Galeazzo's oldest friends. Their relationship went back to their early days together at the same high school in Livorno, and they had worked together in close quarters. During his rise to political and social prominence, Galeazzo secured plum government assignments for Zenone, including a post as his undersecretary. Now Zenone was in prison in large part because of that friendship. Not a member of the Grand Council, he had not been involved in the July 25 vote against Mussolini, but he had been arrested anyhow and was being asked some hard questions about whether his loyalties were to friends like Galeazzo Ciano and Dino Grandi or to the Fascist party.

Smuggled into Galeazzo's cell by a friendly prison guard, presumably the amiable Mario, who let the old friends talk sometimes in the evenings, Zenone was surprised to meet there "a pretty, smiling young woman…with a light German accent, but her Italian was perfect."

"And who is that woman?" Zenone asked his friend.

"A spy," Galeazzo replied with a shrug, "but you can trust her."

"Aside from Frau Beetz, who was acting from selfish motives or perhaps because she was slightly in love with Galeazzo," Zenone wrote later, "the only person who attempted to soften Ciano's situation" was that friendly prison guard, Mario Pellegrinotti.

* * *

Meanwhile the political trial moved forward. They were all caught up in a complex political tangle of motives, Galeazzo especially. Some factions in Verona wanted the count out of the way. Both the German ambassador to Salò and the Italian-based SS pressed for the trial to continue. Ribbentrop, it now transpired, had been behind the count's forced return flight to Italy, and he looked forward eagerly to his rival's execution. The diaries could only cause problems for Ribbentrop, after all, and if they were to disappear along with Galeazzo—all the better. Hilde's superiors in the security service, especially Kaltenbrünner, on the other hand, took umbrage at the idea of Galeazzo's political execution by the Italians, and they hated Ribbentrop sidestepping judgment. That left the SD and its sister branch, the Gestapo, tentatively discussing at Hilde's urging a side deal to free Galeazzo secretly. Mussolini didn't seem to give a consistent answer from one day to the other. Negotiating a release would require delicate handling.

Mussolini issuing a pardon was the obvious solution. Edda made one last trip to Lake Garda to plead with her father in the middle of December. Mussolini casually assured Edda that Galeazzo would soon be free but insisted that, for the moment, he was powerless to stop a trial in process. Perhaps Mussolini truly could do nothing to help Galeazzo.

He was more or less a political prisoner of the Germans himself in his lakeside villa. More likely, Mussolini was weighing his political survival against the life of Galeazzo. What could he offer his daughter in the meantime? Galeazzo had written to Edda a moving letter. "I approach Christmas feeling very sad, without [the children], without you," he told her. Edda wanted her father's permission to see Galeazzo on Christmas Day. Mussolini promised.

* * *

Edda wrote to Galeazzo on December 23, telling him of Mussolini's promise for the holiday visit and announcing her visit. They would have at least a little celebration. "Truly I have moments in which I seem to be going mad," she wrote her husband. "I am sad and I love you so much and I am more than ever near you."

Galeazzo knew better than to trust his father-in-law. He had already accepted the inevitable. Galeazzo that same night, alone in his cell after Hilde had gone, wrote three letters: a letter to Vittorio Emmanuel III, the exiled king of Italy; a letter to the British prime minister, Winston Churchill; and a preface to his diaries, addressed to us, his future readers.

To the king, Galeazzo condemned his father-in-law as the sole author of Italy's tragedy. "One man, just one man," he wrote, was responsible for the war that had destroyed their country.

To Winston Churchill and the world beyond Italy, he placed the blame equally on Mussolini and the Germans. "I was never Mussolini's accomplice in that crime against our country and humanity, that of fighting side by side with the Germans," he wrote the British prime minister. He tried to explain that he had seen and known hellish darkness, and the diaries were the only atonement he could offer. "The crime which I am now about to expiate," Galeazzo wrote, "is that of having witnessed and been disgusted by the cold, cruel and cynical preparation for this war by Hitler and the Germans. I was the only foreigner to see at close quarters this loathsome clique of bandits preparing to plunge the world into a bloody war. Now, in accordance with gangster rule, they are planning to suppress a dangerous witness." Galeazzo already knew that he would be executed. But he wanted the prime minister to have the diaries.

Above all, Galeazzo wanted to explain to Churchill and the Allies the importance of those diaries that were his last obsession and his testimony:

> I put a diary of mine and various documents in a safe place, which will prove, more than I myself could, the crimes committed by those people with whom later that tragic and vile puppet Mussolini associated himself....Perhaps what I am offering you to-day is but little, but that and my life are all I can offer....This testimony of mine should be brought to light so that the world may know, may hate and may remember, and that those who will have to judge the future should not be ignorant of the fact that the misfortune of Italy was not the fault of her people, but due to the shameful behavior of one man.

To us, the future readers of those diaries, Galeazzo wrote: "Within a few days a sham tribunal will make public a sentence which has already been decided by Mussolini...I accept calmly what is to be my infamous destiny."

* * *

Galeazzo Ciano bore moral responsibility and had committed other crimes, passed over in his self-reckoning, but, as far as the letters went, they were the truth: Galeazzo had fought at every step against the Italians entering the war on the side of the Axis and had paid with his freedom—and he knew, would pay with his life—for having voted for a separate peace and for Mussolini's removal from power. He hoped his diaries would absolve him, but more important he hoped that they would absolve the Italian people for having gone to war with Hitler.

These letters would have been of great interest to the Nazis, who had every reason to wish to see them suppressed, as well as the diaries. Had the letters been intercepted, it would have been a death warrant for Galeazzo. In a sign of how certain Galeazzo was that he could trust Hilde, he gave all three letters to her the next day, with instructions to deliver them to Edda. And Hilde did, faithfully.

Edda, for her part, promptly posted the documents for the king and Churchill onward to Switzerland, asking her brother-in-law Massimo Magistrati, the Italian minister in Bern, to arrange their hand delivery. Galeazzo's letter to his future readers she added to the manuscripts. If Galeazzo had come to moral clarity about the war, and taken his faltering steps toward some kind of redemption, Edda's panic was completely personal. She just wanted to save the life of her husband. The Germans would get Galeazzo's letter if they set him free. If they betrayed her, she would make sure that the entire world read Galeazzo's last, bitter indictment.

* * *

Christmas morning was clear and bright in 1943 in Ramiola. That morning, Emilio and Edda set off in his military officer's car to Verona for her promised visit with Galeazzo. Edda was missing the children, but they were in good spirits. They stopped for a holiday lunch together in a little restaurant, and in the early afternoon Emilio dropped Edda off at the entrance to Scalzi Prison. She had put on a pretty dress for Galeazzo and carried with her a gift basket with a bottle of his favorite cologne, a bouquet of flowers, and a box of candy. At the gate, she was refused entrance. There was nothing they could do, an agent explained impassively. These were Mussolini's direct orders. Her father had personally instructed that she not be permitted to see Galeazzo. It was a crushing betrayal for Edda.

Hilde came out to stand in the cold and try to explain, because it was worse than Edda imagined, and Hilde was also reeling. Mussolini had decided that Ciano's trial would go ahead immediately. Galeazzo had been instructed to name his defense attorney that morning. His execution—because there was no doubt what the outcome of the trial would be—was expected before the new year. Her father didn't want Edda to upset herself by seeing her husband again. There could be no purpose. She would not ever see Galeazzo again. That was her father's Christmas message.

Edda, unsurprisingly, collapsed in hysterics of rage and grief in the prison courtyard. But no amount of weeping and wailing was going to change Mussolini's mind. He wasn't even in Verona. Emilio and Hilde bundled Edda back in the car, and there was nothing to do but take her back to the clinic for sedation. Hilde certainly was not going to tell Edda now what was worrying her desperately. The night before, Galeazzo had been abused in his cell, when drunken German soldiers arrived to show off their prisoner to local prostitutes. Hilde, afraid that Galeazzo would be tortured and lynched overnight, refused to leave the prison even for a moment. As Emilio pulled the car away, Hilde walked slowly back inside with Edda's gift basket. When Galeazzo saw his wife's gift and understood she had been turned away for what he knew would have been their last visit, he put his head in his hands and cried.

* * *

The only hope now was a German prison break. The operation to swap the diaries was still in the planning phase; Hilde would need more time to arrange it. Mussolini's decision to expedite the trial put all that in jeopardy. Hilde could only think of one person who could persuade Mussolini to spare the father of his grandchildren. She decided to write a letter directly to his mistress, Clara Petacci, asking her to stop an execution. Clara, moved by the plea, did what she could, writing, "My Ben, I have had a long, terrible night. Nightmares, anxieties, blood and ruins. Among the figures, known and unknown, appearing in a red cloud, was that of Ciano. Ben, save that man! Show the Italians you still control your own will. Fate, perhaps, will be kinder to us." Clara's dream would later seem like a premonition. Fate would not be kinder to either her or Mussolini.

* * *

On the long drive back to Ramiola, Edda wept, head against the window. By the time she and Emilio arrived back at the clinic, though, she had rallied. If her father would not budge and if Hilde could not help them— the plan to break Galeazzo from prison in a swap for the diaries now seemed stalled, and the clock was ticking—then, by God, Edda would mount the rescue operation herself. She decided to blackmail her father and Hitler. "I now realized," Edda said, "that there was nothing more to be done in Italy and that I had to flee my country to play my last card— blackmail—in neutral territory."

She would flee with the diaries to Switzerland, where her children remained in hiding, and, once there, with Emilio's help as a messenger, she would bargain for Galeazzo's life directly. Time was short. She would make everyone pay with the truth if they failed her. Edda and Emilio returned to the clinic late on Christmas. The next day was December 26. Galeazzo's trial was expected to begin immediately, with a verdict and sentencing on December 28. Execution, they assumed, would take place the following morning, December 29. If Edda was going to reach the

Swiss border in time to make her threats of retribution effective, she would have to leave now. She was ready.

They would have to be strategic in selecting which part of the diaries to take with her in her flight for the border. Edda would not be able to carry all of the diaries and papers. There were too many volumes. She had to be able to carry them hidden. She had to be able to cross a militarized border at a run with them. There were also some other immediate logistical challenges. Edda had some of the papers with her in Ramiola, but portions remained hidden in Rome, miles away. There would be no time to go to Rome that night and rifle through them.

Choosing the most important and damaging volumes from among those at the clinic, Emilio and Edda set off early in the morning for Como in Emilio's car, managing to lose a Gestapo minder on the road— Emilio had not been a race-car driver for nothing. They delivered the papers to Tonino Pessina, who promised to hide them somewhere near the border to be recovered in the hours before her crossing.

Those who whisper that Christina Granville played a role in arranging Edda's flight say that Christina, accompanied by Delia di Bagno, met Edda and Emilio at the Pessina residence that morning in Como. At least one report says that Edda gave Christina a copy of Galeazzo's preface to the diaries and allowed her to take photographs of the diaries, destined for the Allies, as Galeazzo had wanted. If true, those photographic negatives have never been discovered, although it might explain the astonishing lack of interest from British intelligence in recovering the Ciano files later. Until the wartime personnel files of Christina Granville are found, there is no way to know for certain.

Edda and Emilio were in Como only briefly. Almost immediately, they turned back south for the long drive home to Ramiola. No one could suspect that Edda was planning to make a break for the border. She had to show her face overnight at the clinic. Tonino Pessina, meanwhile, agreed to arrange things with a smuggler for the next evening. The plan was to return to Ramiola overnight, then drive to Verona early in the morning to see Hilde, so she could pass to Galeazzo the message that Edda was fleeing and planning to issue an ultimatum to her father and Hitler. They would turn then to the most dangerous part of the adventure: Emilio would drive her nonstop for the Swiss border, where the diaries would be waiting, and she would cross out of Italy on the night of December 27. Then she would blackmail Hitler.

* * *

The plan went smoothly the next morning. They hit the road in good time. They would have lunch with Hilde at noon in Verona. They planned then to drive on to Como and, at nightfall, the border.

They arrived to find Hilde determined to do whatever was necessary to stop them.

CHAPTER 7

Operation Conte

December 27, 1943–January 7, 1944

When Hilde met them for lunch, she explained: They would ruin everything if Edda disappeared now.

The deal to swap the diaries for a prison break was officially on. She had been pulling strings and pressing the case all the way up the chain of command straight to Kaltenbrünner and Himmler. She had high-level German approval. Edda and Emilio just needed to follow the original plan, she urged them. If Edda fled, then Germany would never agree to a swap and a prison break, and the result would be Galeazzo's certain execution. Operation Conte—"Operation Count" in English—had been green-lit from Berlin. Pressure would be brought to bear on the Italians to ensure that Galeazzo's trial would be postponed for a few days longer to give the secret team being flown in time for advance planning. The wheels were in motion. Edda just needed to stay put and trust Hilde.

Edda eyed Hilde warily. If Hilde were wrong—or, worse, if Hilde were playing them as a German agent—there would not be another chance to reach Switzerland in time to change the outcome. Hilde, reading Edda's hesitation, gave her a letter from Galeazzo confirming that he wanted her to try Hilde's plan for the diaries. Behind the scenes, Hilde was also pushing hard on the Germans, warning her supervisors that "If [Galeazzo] is shot, as is by now certain [unless freed], his diary and other German documents he possessed will be published immediately in America and England."

But there was another uncomfortable truth that Edda, at least, saw plainly. However much Hilde wished to save Galeazzo's life—and Edda did not doubt by now that Hilde was in love with her husband—in preventing Edda's flight to Switzerland with the diaries that afternoon, Hilde was also following direct Nazi orders. Hilde "told me," Edda recalled later, "that the Germans had decided to liberate Galeazzo in exchange for the notebooks, insisting at the same time that the initiative had come from her alone." Edda wasn't so certain. "I later learned," Edda said, "that General Harster, commander of the SS at Verona, had received a coded telegram from Kaltenbrünner, his immediate superior, sent in Himmler's name," instructing that Operation Conte be pursued as policy. Edda and Galeazzo had once again placed their lives in the hands of the Nazis. That made Edda very wary.

* * *

On the drive back to Ramiola with Emilio, Edda debated. She was still inclined to flee that night for Switzerland, while she had the chance. She had trusted the Germans once, to take her family to Spain, and their imprisonment outside Munich had been the result. She didn't trust them now, no matter what Hilde promised. Hilde was young. Edda had met Hitler and Himmler, knew their families, shared her name with Göring's young daughter. Edda wasn't confident that Hilde's instincts were based in experience.

Privately, Galeazzo shared his wife's concerns. He said to Hilde: "It is useless, nothing will come of it. However, the game is amusing. Let's go on with it." If Galeazzo and Edda had been free to speak freely, perhaps Edda would have fled that evening. But the worry went unspoken between them. Their only intermediary was Hilde, whose enthusiasm for the swap surely reflected her conflicting desires as Galeazzo's lover and as Himmler's agent. She wanted to save Galeazzo. In the months that they had spent together, real feelings had developed. But Hilde also wanted to deliver the diaries to her superiors and complete her mission.

In the end, Emilio Pucci was the one who persuaded Edda to wait. He understood, if Edda did not yet, that in crossing the border illegally she risked being shot or arrested. He convinced her that there was no harm in trying Hilde's plan first. It came with fewer risks for the woman he was trying to protect from the dangers pressing in around her. Emilio's concern just then wasn't Galeazzo or Hilde. It was Edda. He didn't doubt her courage. But people got shot all the time trying to flee to Switzerland. Besides, it was already later than they had expected. The plan to flee that night at least was aborted, and he assured her that they could still discuss it in the morning. Emilio and Edda returned to Ramiola. And at daybreak, Edda resigned herself. She would stay put and await new instructions from Hilde.

* * *

Hilde now swung into action on the German side. Galeazzo's trial had been delayed briefly, as promised. The next day, December 28, she went directly to General Wilhelm Harster, who confirmed that Operation Conte was definitely moving forward.

The men with whom Hilde was dealing—and whose work she was, it must be said, advancing—were not minor figures in the Nazi regime or nice people. General Harster before his appointment to Italy had directed the mass murder of Jews in Holland, and among the victims attributed to him are Anne Frank and her family. Kaltenbrünner and

Himmler, heads of the German security services and chief of the German police, respectively, were architects of the Holocaust already under way across Europe. Between them they had direct control of the Nazi spy services, the Gestapo, and the SS. Their interest was not in Galeazzo Ciano. They certainly did not place any value on his life as an individual. They wanted the count's diaries, and they wanted to take down the German foreign minister, Joachim von Ribbentrop, whose influence on Hitler they mistrusted. But Operation Conte served their interests, and so the mission was authorized. That was all that Hilde wanted.

For Edda, the pause in the next few days was excruciating. Emilio traveled to Florence over the New Year's holiday for a brief visit to his family, and for several days Edda remained alone in Ramiola.

The wheels were moving but slowly on the German side. On January 2, Hilde traveled to Innsbruck to meet in person with Ernst Kaltenbrünner and General Harster to formalize the agreement in an operational memo. Neither party trusted the other. Galeazzo didn't want to hand over the diaries until he was safe in Switzerland. The Nazis didn't trust that, safe in Switzerland, he would keep his promise. The swap would have to take place in increments, adding to the complexity of the escape plan.

In Innsbruck, Hilde managed to hammer out a deal. Galeazzo would pass over a portion of his papers, as a deposit. The trial was now rescheduled for January 8, 1944. The plan was to spring Galeazzo the day before, on January 7.

As soon as Hilde returned from Innsbruck, she traveled to Ramiola to update Edda, arriving at lunchtime on January 3. Galeazzo had warned Hilde that Edda would be suspicious of a trick, and so Hilde again brought to Edda two letters from Galeazzo. One letter was the official one, which Galeazzo knew would be read by German intelligence. Hilde would have to make a show of logging the correspondence in her reports to avoid suspicion. Hilde also carried a second, private letter, which she did not disclose to her bosses. It was a personal note from Galeazzo to his wife, which he trusted Hilde to pass to Edda unopened. Hilde, to her credit, did not read it.

In the letter to his wife, Galeazzo gave different instructions, telling Edda to be wary and to hold back some of the papers as a precaution.

* * *

Emilio returned to Ramiola from the holidays that evening, after Hilde had gone, and he found Edda packing furiously. She was making a break for the border that night. Something felt wrong to Edda about the plan. Galeazzo's private warning to her to be careful and watch out for a double cross confirmed her uneasy suspicions. She was sure that she should flee now with the diaries. Blackmail, she was more convinced than ever, was the only good option. It was the only kind of language Hitler or her father would understand.

For a second time, Emilio persuaded her not to trust her instincts. She was being paranoid. She was being anxious. He pressed her to trust Hilde and Galeazzo. They quarreled, arguing for several hours. Finally, exhausted, Edda gave up. She agreed to wait in Ramiola and to go along with what she suspected was an ill-fated operation. Once again, it was too late to make it to Switzerland that day anyhow. "I was…obeying [Galeazzo's] instructions," Edda wrote later, trying to make her peace with the decision, "when I accepted contacts with the Germans, and in particularly with Frau Beetz, Himmler's special agent, to try to arrange for an exchange of the notebooks and other documents for the life of my husband." She would do what Galeazzo asked. But she didn't like it.

No wonder Edda was doubtful. The plan that the Germans and Hilde especially had arranged involved a full-on spy romp that would make 007 blanch. Edda's instructions in the "official" letter from Galeazzo were to travel with Hilde and the Gestapo to Rome the next day and there retrieve the hidden papers relating to Galeazzo's time in the foreign office;

these papers, the so-called Conversations, were the most prejudicial to Ribbentrop and would serve as a down payment. The official letter implied that these would be all the papers (save only the actual diaries).

When the down payment was received and confirmed as genuine, German SS officers, disguised as Italian fascists in order to point the finger of blame back at the Italians, would break Galeazzo out of prison and escort him and Edda to Switzerland, with Hilde assigned as their monitor to ensure they followed through on their part of the bargain. Then, when they were over the Swiss border, Galeazzo would tell Hilde the location of the remaining papers—the diaries—and she would return to Italy to retrieve them for her superiors.

Galeazzo's private letter to Edda, however, was more discriminating. Specifically, he asked Edda to hand over only the Conversations, the papers in the green leather notebooks. She should *not* hand over a packet of papers stored in the same location and labeled GERMANIA. These were the unbound notes and manuscripts on German-Italian matters, and they would hold back those materials in case of a double cross. Galeazzo too suspected that the Germans might trick them, and he asked Edda to safeguard those papers carefully and to deliver them to the Allies if he was not freed. He did not speak of the diaries themselves, perhaps fearing that his communications with his wife would not be entirely confidential.

At just before midnight on January 3, Edda was in no condition to travel to Rome on a few hours' sleep. She was half hysterical with anxiety. She and Emilio had been fighting for hours. She felt beaten down and exhausted. They agreed that Emilio instead would make the trip to the capital with Hilde and the Gestapo. He set off from Ramiola at just after 3:30 A.M. on the morning of January 4, intending to rendezvous an hour later with Hilde and her two agents on the side of a road outside Parma. One of those Gestapo men was Walter Segna, the aide to Hilde's immediate supervisor in Italy, General Harster. From there, the four of them would drive nonstop to Rome, a journey that in the end would take them ten hours.

Edda had hidden the papers somewhere in a bank in Rome—perhaps a safe-deposit box, but more likely a nook in the masonry. One of the items secreted away was Galeazzo's will, which Emilio stealthily left behind. He took out two packets of papers, making a show of displaying one—the Conversations—to Walter Segna and the other agent. Emilio deftly tucked the other packet, Germania, under his bulky air force overcoat, hiding it as Galeazzo had instructed in his letter to Edda.

By late afternoon, the papers had been collected. By the time Emilio, Hilde, and the Gestapo men had eaten and were ready to depart for the return journey to Ramiola, darkness had fallen, and snow was falling heavily. On the road out of Rome, traveling at a creeping pace as the snowflakes dashed against the windshield, the car skidded off the slippery road into a ditch. Emilio, struggling to keep the secret portion of the papers hidden underneath his coat, got out with the two Gestapo men to push the car, and they finally managed in the small hours of January 5 to get it back on the roadway. But when they tried to start the engine, the car stuttered.

There would be no other foolhardy travelers along the road, and Emilio remained anxious not to have the hidden diaries discovered. Since he had the warmest gear, they agreed that he would walk back to have another car sent for them, leaving the packet of down-payment papers with Hilde and Walter Segna. For the next eighteen hours—from the early hours of the morning until the evening of January 5—Emilio struggled through knee-deep drifts of snow, trying to keep the papers dry and hidden, afraid that the ink would run if the snow soaked them, until Hilde and the Gestapo men, who had finally managed to get the car started, were able to find him. Hilde decided that they would need to head directly for Verona in order to save the operation, and the four finally reached this destination, after several more breakdowns, on January 6.

* * *

In Verona, Hilde personally passed the down-payment papers from Galeazzo Ciano to General Harster. For the young spy, it was a formidable success for which she would be handsomely rewarded.

The packet contained eight volumes, bound in green leather, dating from 1939 to 1943, sometimes typed and sometimes handwritten, with Galeazzo's notes on diplomatic conversations. Featured prominently, just as Galeazzo had promised, were devastating accounts of his conversations with Joachim von Ribbentrop, his counterpart in the German foreign office. General Harster, delighted, immediately ordered the diaries photographed and instructed two young SS lieutenants to spend the night translating the papers into German and preparing a synopsis for Berlin. Harster in the morning locked the copies and the synopsis into his personal safe and sent Walter Segna to Berlin by plane to hand-deliver the originals to Kaltenbrünner. On receipt, Kaltenbrünner, no less delighted with what he saw and eagerly looking forward to the receipt of the second half of the count's papers when the family safely reached Switzerland, telegraphed Harster his orders to proceed with freeing Galeazzo Ciano.

Hilde felt mostly relief. So far, Operation Conte was moving ahead, and Hilde, in love with Galeazzo and thrilled with her first big success as a spy, saw on the horizon the possibility of both saving the life of the man she loved and completing her mission to her country faithfully. Now they only had to spring Galeazzo from prison, get him and Edda across the border in secret, and collect the hidden remaining papers. After the war, she and Galeazzo would find a way to publish the diaries and to be together, as they planned in their late-night conversations. Hilde dared to believe that there just might, after all, be a happy ending.

* * *

Waiting in Ramiola for news and having expected Emilio's return on January 5, Edda was growing frantic at hearing nothing. Edda feared that the Germans had tricked her and was afraid that Emilio had been arrested. She paced her room for hours on January 6, trying to decide whether to wait or to flee, as Galeazzo's first set of papers was making its way to Berlin, but, as she had no car with which to flee, she mostly just cried and worried.

It was only late on January 6 or early on the morning of January 7 that Emilio, having suffered more car troubles, finally made it back to the clinic, where by now Edda was beside herself. Emilio had good news for her. He had managed to bring with him the hidden Germania papers, as Galeazzo had instructed. Things were on track despite the car trouble. Two SS agents—German files name them as Johanssen and Thito—had flown in to handle the prison break. Two Italian prison guards were in on the operation. With their assistance Galeazzo would be released sometime that day. Maybe he was free already. So far, all the Germans had was the down-payment papers, and soon they would see Galeazzo.

Edda just needed to keep her nerves steady, Emilio urged her. All she had to do was to meet the SS at eight o'clock that night at the ten-mile marker on the road from Verona to Brescia. There she would be reunited with Galeazzo. The SS agents and Hilde would drive them onward to the Swiss border. There was just one problem: Edda and Emilio had left the crucial packet with Galeazzo's diaries in the north, with Tonino Pessina, in anticipation of Edda's aborted solo flight at the end of December. They would have to make a hasty, secret trip to Milan to collect those papers before meeting Hilde and the agents at the rendezvous.

It was tight. They would have to set off immediately to make it to Milan and back in time for the 8:00 P.M. rendezvous outside Verona. It would mean a hard day of driving. Edda and Emilio left Ramiola around noon on January 7, carrying with them in a suitcase the Germania papers that Emilio had collected in Rome. These were papers that the Nazis didn't know existed: her last insurance policy. Edda planned to flee with them concealed on her person.

By the early afternoon, they had successfully retrieved from Tonino Pessina the additional seven notebooks that they had hidden there after Christmas—Galeazzo's diaries—which were the second part of the exchange with the Germans. These they put into a second suitcase. Edda's wartime Red Cross diary and some family papers went into a third bag, and then Edda and Emilio immediately set off back south for Verona, arriving around six in the evening. They could breathe a sigh of relief now. They were in plenty of time for the 8:00 P.M. meeting. It would only take another hour to reach the entrance to the highway along which lay the milestone. Then there would be Galeazzo and Switzerland and freedom.

* * *

The evening was bitterly cold, and there were only a few, intermittent vehicles on the highway. Throughout the German occupation, personal automobiles were forbidden on the penalty of death; they had transportation only because Emilio was an air force officer and Edda was the daughter of Benito Mussolini. Edda wrapped her fur coat tightly around her as they rolled on toward their destination, ten miles, nine miles. Soon she would see Galeazzo.

Then a thud, and Emilio jerked hard on the wheel. The sound of the tire flapping on the roadway was unmistakable: a flat tire. Emilio's look of panic said it all. The back tire was blown out. Emilio checked his watch. Just under an hour. There was no way to repair the tire in time to make the milepost.

Edda would have to hitchhike if she was to meet Galeazzo on time and save the operation. Emilio would stay with the car. If he could somehow get the tire fixed, he would pick up Edda for the last leg of the journey.

If not, Edda would have to try to get there on her own. She would have to carry with her the diaries—and would have to keep them hidden from the Germans until they were safely in Switzerland. If the Germans obtained the prize on the roadside, Edda was not foolish enough to imagine that either she or Galeazzo would ever make it to the border. She was gambling that the Germans would not think her mad enough to bring the manuscripts with her.

There was no way for Edda to walk with all the papers they had with them. They were in three suitcases and were meant to be Edda's personal luggage. Edda and Emilio on the side of the road prioritized the diaries, and Emilio, taking a bit of loose fabric, tied the most important papers around Edda's waist. The notebooks were large but flimsy, and, although the look was comic, underneath her big fur coat they hoped no one would notice. Then there was a rushed and anxious roadside farewell for the lovers.

Emilio would face some unpleasant questions when word of Edda and Galeazzo's escape leaked out, and Edda worried for him. Emilio worried that Edda might be walking into a trap with the Germans and would have preferred to have been there for the drop-off, to at least see that they really had Galeazzo. Of course, there was nothing to prevent the Germans shooting Edda and Galeazzo and simply taking the diaries—nothing except the fact that the Germans could not possibly imagine that Edda would be so brazen as to bring them with her.

She set off, stumbling through snow in the dark, and before long spotted headlights coming toward her. When she flagged down the car, she was horrified to realize that the men who had picked her up were two fascist government ministers, men who knew her father. If they recognized her, they would drive her straight to police headquarters. The Italian security services—who were being set up by the Germans in the mock prison break—were sure to have discovered her flight by now, and there would be a warrant out for her arrest. Edda pulled her fur coat tighter in the back seat of the sedan and tried to keep her head down and say as little as possible. When their route turned off and they dropped her on the roadside, having no idea that their passenger was Mussolini's missing daughter, she breathed a sigh of relief. She stood for a few minutes in the cold, hoping for another car in the distance, and then decided that she would have to keep moving, watching for lights over her shoulder. "I began to run down the road," Edda remembered, "stumbling over stones, turning my ankles, falling, but always clutching at the notebooks."

Finally, breathless, she heard another engine in the distance. A German transport convoy careened down the highway, and, afraid that they wouldn't stop to pick up a civilian, Edda stepped into the middle of the highway and held out her arms. The lead truck had no choice but to stop for this madwoman in the road, and, when they did, she rushed at the driver. Something in the look of urgency in her face convinced the convoy to take her a bit farther toward her destination. So it went, while precious minutes ticked by and the night grew darker. Her next ride came from a lecherous man on a bicycle, who let her ride double for the last few miles, all the while his hands wandering. Edda hardly cared any longer. She knew the deadline was long past. She had missed meeting Galeazzo. When she arrived at the stone milepost, she hoped against hope to see a car idling, to know that they had waited for her. There was no one.

She was two hours late, and she was now out past the wartime curfew. Arrest—especially with the papers on her person—would be disastrous. She could only hope that they would find a way to circle back for her. For nine hours, all throughout a bitingly cold night and into the winter dawn, Edda sat in the wet roadside ditch just beyond the milepost, watching. "Each time a car passed I raised my head, each time I had the same mad hope, each time the same bitter disappointment," Edda said later. At 5:00 A.M., with the end of the curfew on the morning of January 8, her fur coat matted but the diaries safe, she was able to hitch one last ride, back toward Verona, with two men. This time, when one of the men let his hand stroke her knee, Edda simply looked at him, with her hard, weary Mussolini eyes, and told him that she was too tired.

* * *

In Verona, Hilde was sick with worry. And she was furious.

The news had not reached Edda in time, but, in fact, the Germans *had* double-crossed her. There had been no car coming to meet Edda. The Nazis had double-crossed all of them. This time Hilde felt that she was included.

CHAPTER 8

Blackmailing Hitler

January 8, 1944–January 9, 1944

The double cross by General Harster had not been intentional. Once again, the problem was Hitler.

On January 6, 1944, the down-payment papers had been winging their way to Berlin with Walter Segna. Emilio had been en route back to the clinic at Ramiola with the hidden Germania packet under his overcoat. In Germany, Ernst Kaltenbrünner had given his official go-ahead for Operation Conte, and the SS men were on the ground in Italy and ready to deploy. Wilhelm Harster had been commanding the raid, and very soon Galeazzo Ciano would have been broken out of his Verona prison on January 7.

Then a phone had rung in the Verona headquarters. The call came sometime on January 6, as Emilio and Edda were driving toward Milan to collect the hidden diaries from Tonino Pessina. Harster went white when the line connected. Adolf Hitler was on the line. He had a personal message for his general: If Galeazzo Ciano disappeared from that prison, Harster would be the next one executed. As Walter Segna put it later: "Hitler had at the last moment vetoed Ciano's liberation."

The Führer had decided. General Harster was not going to debate such clear instructions. He knew how Hitler executed those who disobeyed his orders. It generally involved meat hooks and piano wire. The general promptly called off the rescue mission.

* * *

No one is quite certain how Hitler got wind of the plan to free Galeazzo Ciano. Some believe that Kaltenbrünner and Himmler decided to ask Hitler's permission at the last minute, repeating Edda's mistake in Munich. Some say Ribbentrop learned of the operation and informed the Führer. In Berlin, there are some hints Kaltenbrünner and Himmler may have tried to buy some time. Galeazzo's rescheduled trial was slated to begin on Saturday, January 8, and no one doubted that it would be a speedy verdict and a speedy execution. Someone in the German embassy reached out to the Fascist party in Italy on January 7, just after Operation Conte had been scuttled, asking if the trial could not be postponed a few days longer, though no one could understand the reason. Perplexed, party officials with Salò took the request to Mussolini, who was equally mystified. By now, though, Mussolini considered that the matter was settled. Turning to his personal secretary, he remarked: "No intervention now can halt the course of events! For me, Ciano is already dead. He will not be able now to maneuver around in Italy, to let himself be seen, to have a name. Whoever voted for Grandi's order of the day will be condemned for it."

* * *

Hilde learned that the deal was off—and that the Germans, naturally, were keeping the down-payment diaries—sometime on January 6 or possibly January 7. She confronted General Harster. He explained that there was nothing he could do: The orders came from the Führer. Hilde wrote to Kaltenbrünner to protest. She had brokered a deal in good faith, she said. Galeazzo would think she had tricked him. He had been dubious all along, and she had pushed for the deal wanting *both* to save him and to accomplish her mission. Kaltenbrünner couldn't care less what Galeazzo Ciano thought. She had finished her mission and should be happy. The papers most damaging to Ribbentrop were now in the hands of his internal enemies. Kaltenbrünner and Himmler were delighted. The fate of Galeazzo was not their interest. Kaltenbrünner's only reply to her plaintive message was to send Hilde a huge bouquet of roses with a personal note of congratulations.

She had completed her mission. So why did she feel so bad? "I was then a little naïve," Hilde said later.

* * *

Telling Edda that she had been duped for a second time by the Nazis was going to be unpleasant. Hilde was dreading it, especially since Edda would have to be persuaded to keep quiet. Edda would have to keep her head down now or there would be real trouble. Operation Conte had been a secret mission, and had it succeeded it would have been a stinging embarrassment for the Italian Fascist party. Talking about the failed mission could only harm Galeazzo in prison.

Edda, as yet, knew nothing of what awaited her. On the morning of January 8, she was desperately making her way back to Verona from the failed rendezvous and a cold night in a roadside ditch. She had waited all night for a car that was never coming. But she had been late and thought that, somewhere, Galeazzo was free, and she had simply missed the meet-up. There must have been a reason they could not wait for her. Maybe Galeazzo was already safe in Switzerland.

Bedraggled and wet, but hopeful that Hilde could reunite her with

Galeazzo in hiding, Edda made straight for German headquarters. When she gave her cover name, Emilia Santos, she got blank stares, and they refused at the front desk to let her see General Harster. When she lost her temper and announced that she was Edda Mussolini Ciano and commanded that she be taken to General Harster, she was immediately shown into an empty office, while the clerk considered. He called upstairs to Hilde. Hilde rushed down from her office and burst into the room where Edda was waiting. "She stared at me, incredulous and panic-stricken," Edda remembered. Edda was making a scene. It was dangerous. Worse, Edda's muddy fur coat bulged at the waist at funny, crooked angles. The diaries were still strapped to her waist. That they were here was obvious.

* * *

Hilde's brief was to get the diaries. Another tranche of the diaries was in front of her. With their discovery would come rewards and a major promotion. She had a husband deployed, and her success would buy him safety and security. This time, if she took the diaries from Edda here in headquarters, her reward would be more than a bouquet of flowers. All she had to do was say the word. Harster would order a search of Edda. Hitler would have his diaries. "Frau Beetz could have taken the notebooks then, if she had wished, because she knew that I had them on my person," Edda said of that moment.

Hilde also knew what would come after that. Edda would be arrested. The possession of the diaries would seal Galeazzo's fate. The Germans would have no incentive to stop his execution. Hilde had done her job and delivered up papers that could cripple Ribbentrop with his internal political enemies. She had pleased her bosses. She should have been glad. Instead Hilde felt terrible. She had been part of a trick on Galeazzo and Edda—the second trick that the Germans had played on them.

Hilde had come to realize in those last few weeks of December and the first week of January something else: She loved Galeazzo. Not half in love. Not sympathy and affection. Not sex and passion. Or not just sex and passion. They had been constant companions in a prison cell, facing together terror, death, and sorrow, thrown together over a holiday when Galeazzo ached for his children. Galeazzo had opened his heart. Hilde's heart had responded. Far fewer self-disclosures have been known to make strangers fall in love with each other, and Galeazzo and Hilde were not strangers.

* * *

General Harster, when he arrived, was grim-faced. Hilde looked at the general. She looked at Edda's bulging coat. Here was Hilde's dark thicket, and she chose what she could see was the only straight way forward. Her decision in that moment changed the entire course of her life, though Hilde could not yet know it. She said nothing.

* * *

Signaling to General Harster that she would manage the situation, Hilde waited until the corridor was quiet. Then she grabbed Edda by the arm and half dragged her to the street. "You are crazy to have come here," Hilde hissed in the courtyard, frightened. Edda demanded to know where Galeazzo was. Hilde tried to look her in the eye as she confessed that her superiors had called off the operation. Edda exploded.

Hilde urged Edda to be quiet. She would come and explain it all to her. But Edda must listen: She needed to check into a hotel and stay there. The terror in Hilde's eyes finally convinced Edda that the street was too dangerous a place for this conversation. After, in a nondescript Veronese hotel room, Hilde tried to explain to Edda that there had been no choice. Edda had no patience with excuses. "You have deceived us in the most despicable manner, and I would swear that you are ready to do it again. One can never trust you, not even when the life of a human being is in the bargain," Edda raged at Hilde. There was nothing Hilde could say. She knew it was true. There *had* been base treachery, though she had not meant to be a part of it, and she had not saved Galeazzo.

Hilde tried to explain that General Harster's own life had hung in the balance. Edda had to understand. The order had come directly from Hitler. Edda surely understood that Harster could not disobey the Führer. It was the same law with her father; the law at the heart of fascism. *Führerprinzip.* When Edda stopped crying, she took Hilde's hand, nodded, and thanked Hilde for trying.

Edda also had to know the rest. Hilde in a few words spoken in a hotel room in Verona that morning crossed a frontier from which there was no returning. To say nothing was one thing, a sin of omission. To help Edda—to aid her in the commission—was active treason and directly contrary to the interest of the German security services. American spymaster Allen Dulles would later see what Hilde Beetz said next as the moment she went from being a Nazi spy to being the Allies' self-appointed double agent.

The Germans, she confided to Edda, were still determined to find the remainder of the diaries. They did not suspect that Edda had the diaries on her, but they did suspect that she knew their location. Edda would be watched, and, ultimately, she would be arrested. They needed now to get Edda and the diaries out of the country. Edda had to run. Switzerland was the only hope if she were to save herself—and perhaps, in one last bold gamble, Galeazzo.

Hilde would help her make the escape and help her take the diaries with her. "I felt an obligation to repair the wrong," she explained later, and she didn't know how else to do it.

* * *

It would take a team of conspirators, in fact, to make Edda's escape now possible. Fleeing was a hundred times more perilous than it had been just forty-eight hours earlier. Edda and Hilde would need help in making the slip, and they knew they could count on Emilio Pucci. Emilio had waited that night with the car on the side of the road to Brescia, while Edda trudged on to the milepost; in the morning, he had finally been able to repair the flat tire. He arrived back in Verona around noon, not long after Edda. Hilde, expecting him, quickly intercepted his arrival.

He and Edda would be, from now on, she warned them both, under constant Gestapo surveillance. General Harster had a grudging admiration for Edda. She was a brave and charming woman. But he had been made personally responsible for making sure she did not go missing, and he was not willing to risk his neck swinging in a noose for Mussolini's impetuous daughter. If their plot succeeded, Harster would be in some considerable difficulty. If Hilde's role were revealed, the Nazis followed the ancient Aryan rule of *Sippenhaft*—kin punishment. She *and* her family in Germany would be executed as traitors.

When Emilio saw Edda in Verona that afternoon, he could hardly recognize her. How twenty-four hours could make such a difference, he could not imagine. The events of the last day had shaken and exhausted Edda. She looked old and ill and haggard. Emilio simply took her in his arms and said nothing.

For the time being, Hilde explained that they would have to turn themselves over to the Gestapo. Those were General Harster's orders. Surveillance was being mobilized. They would have to pretend to go along with the German instructions and appear to accept retirement in the clinic. Edda was bundled into a waiting car. Emilio was permitted to follow. A police convoy accompanied them back to Ramiola. Fourteen heavily armed SS agents and a contingent of Italian fascist police swarmed around vehicles on motorcycles, poised from sidecars to shoot in the event there was some undiscovered plot to free them. The clinic had been torn apart in a search, and Edda and Emilio would be under house arrest while the hunt for Galeazzo's remaining papers was under way in other locations. Little did the Gestapo know that the missing papers were at that very moment being escorted with Edda back to the clinic under guard, wrapped around her waist under her matted fur jacket. If the situation had not been so frightening, the irony might have been funny.

Before the convoy rolled out, Hilde had managed to pass to Edda one last private letter from Galeazzo, written from prison when he first understood that Operation Conte had been aborted. Only once she was back in her room in Ramiola that night, with the door locked, did Edda dare to open the letter. "Darling," Galeazzo had written in that long day when he knew the truth already and when Edda was still rushing toward a milepost on a highway shoulder, "meanwhile you are still living in the wonderful illusion that in a few hours we are going to be together again and free; for me agony has already started…bless the children and bring them up to respect and worship what is right and honorable in life."

It was too much for Edda. She had spent so long living in terror. They had been trying to flee to safety as a family since July. Now the hope that had kept her moving forward was gone. Galeazzo's trial, even now, was under way. There would be a verdict soon. She would need to be in Switzerland with the children before that verdict came if she were ever to see them again, because she did not doubt that Hilde was right: When the search for the diaries failed, she would be arrested.

Edda looked around her room at the clinic and decided to smash everything to pieces. She would bring the world crashing down with her. Mirrors, lamps, photograph frames, and whiskey glasses: She hurled them at the walls and windows, taking furious satisfaction in the sharp tinkle of glass as it fell and shattered. Emilio came rushing in and, alarmed, called the clinic doctors. The doctors tried to calm her, but she refused to be sedated. There was no sedating this anger. The doctors left to confer, and it was Emilio's blunt words that finally stopped her. They needed to get across the border. There was only one route left to them. She had children. And she still had most of the papers. They did not have time for drama, and they could not make the run for the border if Edda got herself arrested. Edda grew quiet. "I decided to go to Switzerland," Edda said after, "in order to stake everything on one last attempt with my father and with the Führer by sending them both letters that my friend Emilio Pucci would have delivered once I passed the frontier." She would blackmail Mussolini and Hitler. And if they did not spare her husband's life, she would make them suffer. She would be, she swore, an avenging fury.

A decision made, Emilio and Edda turned their minds immediately to the logistics. They would have to leave in the next few hours. First they would need to evade house arrest and the police stationed outside their bedroom windows. Then they would need to travel, undetected, hours north, and slip across a heavily guarded border in the winter. And they would need to select the most important of the papers for Edda to carry with her and find somewhere safe to hide the rest, because it was now even less possible to make for the border with three suitcases of documents.

Edda and Emilio selected the five most damaging of Galeazzo's seven wartime foreign-office diaries, and Emilio again wrapped them around Edda's midriff in a thick makeshift belt fashioned from the legs of her pajamas. The remaining two foreign-office diaries, along with the documents they called the Germania papers, Edda's personal records and her Red Cross diary, some jewelry, and some phonograph voice recordings, were carefully wrapped into a package, sealed with wax on the strings, and given to the clinic director. Dr. Elvezio Melocchi, they had learned, was a partisan in the Italian resistance, and the papers would help the

Allies. He agreed to hide the package inside a local electrical power plant, where the risk of electrocution would prevent anyone idly looking. If Edda and Emilio were caught and executed, the doctor promised to deliver the package to the Americans or the British.

There were now at least three sets of papers: those left with the clinic doctor, those notebooks already transferred to Berlin as down payment, and the diaries that Edda would carry with her in her flight. There may also have been other papers or copies of papers still lodged with friends in the diplomatic service. The package left behind at the clinic became known as the Ramiola papers and, later, simply as "the chocolates."

* * *

Edda would have to make her escape quickly if she were to have any hope of saving Galeazzo, whose trial was already under way, and by morning the net was tightening around her. On January 9, 1944, the following day, SS Lieutenant Robert Hutting rudely began his day with a seven o'clock Sunday morning phone call from his boss, General Harster. Kaltenbrünner had sent a warning telegram from Germany, reaffirming Hitler's orders and directing the SS in Italy to "Watch closely the daughter of Mr. Mayer [*i.e.* Mussolini]. She can move and go where she wants, but she is not to put a foot in Switzerland. An eventual attempt by her to leave must be impeded even by force. The diaries of the son-in-law of Mr. Mayer are still to be found. Search for them." Harster was putting Lieutenant Hutting in charge of making sure orders from Berlin were followed and that Edda Ciano went nowhere near the Swiss border.

Lieutenant Hutting immediately set off for Ramiola with another seven SS agents in tow, an entourage that this time included both Hilde Beetz and Walter Segna as operational supervisors, to ensure Edda remained at the clinic. By the time they arrived, they learned that Emilio

Pucci, still active in the Italian military, had been given permission to attend a previously scheduled medical appointment at the base in Ferrara and had departed early that morning in his air force uniform. That made Hutting nervous.

But Edda was the target of this operation, not the marchese. The Gestapo men on the overnight watch assured the SS lieutenant that Edda was still fast asleep in her room at the clinic. The doctors confirmed that she had asked for sleeping pills before going to bed, and, as staff observed to the Germans, they could see plainly that the note she had posted on her door in the early hours of the morning was still there: "I am very tired and I don't feel well. Please do not disturb for any reason." Placated by these reassurances, the SS returned to their posts with instructions to inform Hilde and Walter Segna as soon as Edda was available.

Hilde knew, of course, that Edda was already gone. Or at least she hoped that Edda and Emilio had made a break for it, because, if they had not, it was now too late for them. She would do everything she could to stall a search of Edda's quarters, to give them time if they had attempted a flight to the border. And this time, Edda and Emilio had not hesitated. Just after three o'clock in the morning, when the clinic was silent and they hoped their minders would be least attentive, Edda crept to the clinic basement and squeezed through a small window in the foundation. She trudged alone in the darkness through the fields and woods to a small country lane, where she waited for Emilio to arrive with his car just after seven o'clock in the morning. As Emilio pulled to the shoulder, engine still running, Edda dashed from her hiding spot in the thicket and leapt into the car. In a few moments, they were gone.

On the run, the couple had no way of knowing how long it would be before their escape was discovered, and they had a long and perilous journey in front of them. Every moment that put ground between them and the SS counted. All morning and long into the afternoon they followed small back roads north, trying to avoid detection or suspicion.

Hilde would do all she could at the clinic to delay Edda being "awakened" to give them as much of a head start as possible.

* * *

They were making for Como, where the Swiss border juts down deep into Italian territory south of Lugano. Tonino Pessina and his wife, Nora, had an apartment in Como and once again stepped into the breach to try to save Edda and her family. Tonino would arrange for a smuggler to take Edda across the border. But first they had to get to Como safely. There would be checkpoints. They knew that, when their flight was discovered, the police all across northern Italy would be searching for them.

The journey was less than 120 miles, but they crawled along the most obscure back roads, Emilio driving and Edda struggling to map out a route on the most remote byways possible. They could not risk the high-way. They traveled through countless small villages, skirting far around Milan, and always careful to keep Edda's face casually covered with a head scarf if they passed a transport truck or a roadside farmer. She would be instantly recognizable as Mussolini's daughter.

Darkness was falling when they crept into Como, and they allowed themselves a few hours with Tonino and Nora to rest, eat, and leave behind a cache of valuables—some say perhaps even a further cache of political papers—that Edda and Galeazzo might need to recover later. Then, taking advantage of the lull at the dinner hour and the early winter sunset, they set off again that night in a small convoy heading west, toward the village of Cantello-Ligurno, a mile or two out of Varese. From Cantello-Ligurno, they continued north, following the contours of the Swiss border, until they reached the small village of Viggiù, at the foot of the Poncione d'Arzo, a mountain peak separating Italy and Switzerland.

At 10:30 P.M., according to later German police reports, Tonino,

Edda, Emilio, and a man they called Uncle Piero checked into the Hotel Madonnina, while arrangements were made with a local smuggler to escort Edda across the border. She might have crossed that night, January 8, and it would have been far safer had she done so. But when the smuggler learned that it was Edda Ciano that he was to risk his neck for, the price of his services skyrocketed at the last moment, forcing Uncle Piero to spend the night working contacts in the black market to locate the sack of rice that the smuggler demanded as his bonus. The setback put them all in danger, and they spent all night listening to every sound, afraid their location would be discovered.

The delay of a whole day at the small border town was harrowing. They would have to evade arrest all of Sunday, January 9. The entourage had no choice but keep out of sight and wait for nightfall. They guessed that by now the Germans would be looking for them in towns along the Swiss frontier, and if their steps had been traced it would be all over.

In the hotel room that morning, Edda put the final touches on three letters. Emilio would hand-deliver them to Hilde as soon as Edda was safely across the border. All three letters were postdated. They were ransom demands, her last effort to rescue Galeazzo. One was for General Harster. One was for Hitler. And one was for her father. They would go down in history as the most fearless and reckless letters anyone would ever write to either Hitler or Mussolini and as the central elements in one of World War II's most determined rescue missions.

* * *

All day at the hotel, the conspirators tried to remain inconspicuous and to keep quiet. The tension of waiting was nerve racking. Twilight came at 5:00 P.M. As dusk settled, they finally moved. Emilio drove Edda east to the border alone. They didn't dare to risk headlights. He stopped the car a few hundred yards away from the heavily policed crossing, and standing on the side of the road he embraced Edda one last time. Then he looked at her seriously and placed into her hands his loaded military pistol.

If they stopped her, she must use it and try to defend herself. She had to get across the border. If she were stopped and could not escape, they would brutalize her. Did she understand? Edda nodded. "As I said good-bye to her," Emilio remembered, "she was extremely calm and firm. I gave her a revolver to shoot if the German or Italian guards tried to stop her, and to shoot herself if they got her. Then she went."

In the darkness the smuggler was waiting for Edda in a small roadside wood. There was a bright moon—not good, but they did not have the luxury of waiting days for nighttime cover and passing lunar phases—and they would have to watch carefully and cross in between armed patrols. Crouched to the ground, Edda and the smuggler waited, taking care not to break a twig or make a sound. Edda would have to run, bent over as low as she could manage, across an open field in the last approach to the border, and the smuggler would tell her when to go. If she were spotted, she should expect gunfire. She should try to zigzag and not let razor wire stop her. Once she stepped into that no-man's-land, it was Switzerland or nothing.

As a German patrol passed out of range, the smuggler hissed to Edda, "Go, now!" She knew she was supposed to bend and keep down as she made her way through the grassland. But she didn't. She couldn't. She was tired of being frightened and broken, and perhaps fear too made her delirious. "I don't know why, but at that point I didn't care what might happen to me," she remembered. Standing tall, Edda Ciano walked slowly, majestically across the field of no-man's-land and strolled into Switzerland.

* * *

The Swiss customs inspector at the checkpoint had been notified that a refugee would make the crossing and was not surprised to see her come through the field, and he had to admire her poise, however fool-hardy. But they had been told to expect the fleeing Duchess of Aoste, a member of the endangered Italian royal family. "[H]e was astonished and annoyed to hear me say that I was Edda Ciano," Edda remembered. Accepting a member of the exiled Italian royal family was one thing. Accepting Mussolini's daughter as a refugee was a problem. The Swiss had already been tricked into accepting the Ciano children, and Edda knew that she could not expect to find a warm welcome in Switzerland. She was as despised as her father, and her presence had the potential to compromise Switzerland's precarious neutral status. The border agents now had on their hands a major diplomatic incident.

They would be up all night dealing with the problem. The phone lines buzzed back and forth between the border post and Bern for hours, and diplomats were roused from sleep for urgent consultations while the Swiss figured out how to manage this very unwelcome arrival. Edda sat on a bench in the customs post under the glare of a flickering light, staring ahead resolutely and unmoving for hours.

Word eventually reached the head of the American Office of Strategic Services in Bern, Allen Dulles, who already had the so-called Ciano Diaries on his radar. "Shortly after Edda arrived here," he noted in his files, "I made enquiry of Magistrati." Massimo Magistrati was the Italian minister in Switzerland, but he was also the husband of Galeazzo's late sister, Maria Ciano, and the man to whom Edda had forwarded Galeazzo's December 23 letters to Winston Churchill and Victor Emmanuel III. "[H]e conveyed, and I believe honestly," Dulles recorded, "the impression that she did not have the Diaries and that they were still in Italy." That was good news for Edda—had she been suspected of having the diaries, her situation would have been perilous even in Switzerland. But it also meant that Allen Dulles let the matter drift longer than he would have liked later.

* * *

The next morning, January 10, the Swiss decided there was nothing else to be done. They would try to hide Edda's presence at all costs, but they could not return her to Italy. The Gestapo was hunting her. She would obviously be executed if deported. The Swiss threw up their hands and processed the refugee application. Then Edda was taken by car to the nearby Swiss village of Neggio and reunited with her children.

Seeing her that day for the first time in months, her son Fabrizio remembered his impression of his mother: She was "[s]mall, very thin, upset, in dire straits and wearing a navy blue short coat. She carried the diaries around her waist." Those who witnessed her bulky figure that day quickly speculated that Edda was pregnant. Her "delicate condition" was the only reason, in fact, that she had not been searched at the Swiss border. If she had been, the diaries would have been discovered. But no one thought to ask if she were hiding something that in that moment to her was equally precious. It was the last chance at Galeazzo's life that she carried with her.

CHAPTER 9

The Trial of Verona

January 8, 1944–January 11, 1944

Galeazzo's trial finally got under way, after all the fits and starts of the previous weeks, on Saturday, January 8. This was the same morning that saw Edda standing bedraggled in Harster's office with the diaries strapped to her waist. The trial was held in Verona's Castelvecchio, an ancient military fortress, where German officials and Galeazzo's most zealous fascist enemies filled the noisy gallery. Galeazzo, dressed in a sports coat and trying to stay calm, was forced to balance before the judges on a rickety wooden chair, while behind him and his five co-defendants, black drapes dramatically framed Mussolini's emblematic *fasces*—the ancient Roman "bundle" of thin wooden branches, from which the word *fascism* comes—and a crucifix.

The trial—talked of as the trial against the traitors to fascism—was both extraordinary and entirely predictable. The morning the trial began, Galeazzo had been informed of the resignation of his chosen defense attorney, he did not doubt under pressure, and he was assigned instead an almost comically incompetent public defender. A good attorney, however, would not have made a difference. The trial was, as Galeazzo had written to the king in his December 23 letter, "nothing else but premeditated murder." The vote at Grand Council had been an entirely legitimate action—indeed, had been explicitly permitted by Mussolini—and there was no legal case to answer for. This was raw political theater. The charges were score settling on the part of his accusers and, for Mussolini, a test set by the Germans to prove his mettle and a chance to display his ideological commitment to fascism to increasingly war-weary Italians.

There was one aspect of the trial, though, that attracted a good deal of speculation and gossip in Verona. Throughout the trial, at every break, a young German woman was seen beside Galeazzo, whispering to him words that seemed to raise his spirits. As soon as Edda and Emilio's flight from the clinic at Ramiola had been discovered, Hilde had returned to Verona and Galeazzo, and they hardly bothered anymore with pretending they were not involved.

* * *

All day on January 9, as the wheels of Galeazzo's "infamous destiny" ground forward, Hilde had been anxiously awaiting word from Emilio Pucci. She had hoped to hear that Edda had crossed the border on the eighth. When she returned home on the night of January 9, to the Hotel Gabbia d'Oro, the Gestapo and SD staff house where she shared a room with some other female agents, she was beginning to worry. Emilio was supposed to come and bring Edda's ransom letters. She had expected him all day and understood that something must have happened. Hilde tossed and turned when she went to bed that night just before midnight.

She would not sleep long. That night, Emilio had waited at the border an hour or two, to make sure that Edda had crossed, before turning south to Verona with the three letters. When he arrived in front of the Hotel Gabbia d'Oro, it was just after one o'clock in the morning of January 10.

He knew where Hilde lived, but, in all the stress and confusion, he remembered her room number incorrectly and gently called into a room a floor below her. As Emilio told the story: "I went into a room where two girls were sleeping....One of the girls told me she slept in Number 70. I climbed to Number 70 and called. [Frau Beetz] came out of her room and I gave her the letters and told her that Countess Ciano had gotten into Switzerland, taking the documents with her; that she must tell Count Ciano this, and hand in the letters as soon as possible and to prevent his execution."

Edda had written three blackmail letters, and Emilio was about to pay an unfathomable price for being the bearer of news that was certain to enrage all of the recipients. They were letters calculated to ignite a firestorm. The recipients each knew Edda well enough to understand that she was not bluffing. She had smashed her room in the clinic. She would bring their regimes crashing down with her if it were in her power. As Mussolini's daughter, she knew a great deal of sensitive information. And she had the diaries.

* * *

To General Harster, Edda had written:

> General: For the second time I have entrusted myself to the word of the Germans with the outcome which you know. Now it is enough. If that is not done which was promised me I shall release against the Axis the most fearful campaign and thereby I shall make use of all the materials which I have and of all that I know. My conditions are: that within three days from the moment at which these letters will be transferred to Frau B[eetz] my husband must be at the Bern railway station, accompanied only by Frau B. between 10:00 and 15:00 hours.

If this should be carried out in a completely loyal way, we will retire into private life and let nothing more be heard from us. The diaries will be turned over to Frau B. by my husband on that same day. I enclose two letters on this same subject, the one to the Führer, the other to the Duce. Turn these over immediately together with a copy of this letter itself. Edda Ciano.

To Hitler, she wrote:

January 10, 1944

Führer: For the second time I believed your word and for the second time I have been betrayed. It is only the fact of the soldiers who fell together on the battlefields that restrains me from going over to the foe. In case my husband is not freed in accordance with conditions which I have specified to your general no considerations will restrain me any longer. For some time the documents have been in the hands of persons who are authorized to use them in case anything should happen to my husband, to my children, or to my family. If, however, as I hope and believe, my conditions are accepted and we are left in peace now and in the future, one will hear nothing from us. I am distressed to be forced to act in this fashion, but you will understand. Edda.

And to her father:

January 10, 1944

Duce: I have waited until today for you to show me the slightest feelings of humanity and justice. Now it is enough. If Galeazzo is not in Switzerland within three days in accordance with the conditions which I have made known to the Germans, then everything which I have at hand in the way of proofs will be used without pity. If, on the other hand, we are left in peace and security against everything from pulmonary consumption to auto-accident, then you will hear nothing further from us. Edda Ciano.

Emilio passed the three letters, each sealed and inside a larger envelope on which Edda had written "General Harster," to Hilde, and in the hallway they debated in urgent whispers. Hilde was of the view that they should wait to give the letters to General Harster. Galeazzo's trial was ongoing. Perhaps at the last moment Mussolini would pardon his son-in-law, making Edda's dangerous threats unnecessary. There was no coming back from Edda's letters, Hilde reasoned. Hilde also reminded Emilio that he needed to flee Italy, that night if he could reach the border again in time. The letters would trigger his arrest warrant and interrogation by the Gestapo. She wanted to give him a head start. Emilio agreed to leave it to Hilde's judgment and departed, intending to set off immediately on the road to Como and, he hoped, from there to Switzerland and Edda.

As Emilio crept down the stairs to his car, their luck failed disastrously. He was spotted by another resident agent, who demanded to know where he had been and why he was in the building. When Emilio replied that he had come to deliver a message to Hilde, the agent let him pass. Emilio drove into the night, thinking he had made a narrow escape. But at the Hotel Gabbia d'Oro, Emilio had unwittingly set into motion a chain of events that would undermine Hilde's plans to stall the delivery of the letters and that would put his life in immediate danger. Hilde would blame herself for it later.

* * *

The agent watched Emilio drive away and then stormed up the stairs to find Hilde and get to the bottom of matters. Hilde heard footsteps on the stairs, then threw the packet of letters to the ground as the door opened on the darkened bunkroom. When the agent demanded again to know who had visited, suspecting a tawdry romantic liaison, Hilde lied, claiming she hadn't heard a thing. Unconvinced, the agent turned on the light to take a good look at Hilde and whomever or whatever else she might be hiding. There on the floor, where Hilde had tossed it, was the packet of letters, clearly addressed to General Harster. They must have been left while she was sleeping, Hilde offered lamely. The agent studied her, and then announced that he would take the packet immediately to Harster.

Hilde leapt forward. They had been delivered to her; she would take the packet herself, as soon as she dressed. When the door closed and with the suspicious agent waiting outside, Hilde tried to put on her clothing as slowly as possible and to stall. The best she could do for Emilio now was to give him time to make his getaway. But he couldn't get to Switzerland in ten or fifteen extra minutes. All hell was about to break loose, and Hilde knew it.

Hilde could not stall forever. Sometime before dawn on the morning of January 10, a clerk roused General Harster from sleep. Frau Beetz was waiting outside with an urgent message for him and Walter Segna. Hilde passed the general the unopened packet of letters, stating that they had been delivered to her at the hotel by Emilio Pucci, along with the message that Edda had fled the clinic at three o'clock the previous morning and was headed for the Swiss border. She had likely crossed over already. General Harster surprised Hilde by laughing. "I guessed it!" he exclaimed.

"However, she has done well," he went on seriously, reading the letters and shaking his head ruefully, "otherwise at this hour great troubles would have begun for her." Mussolini's letter was placed into the hands of a courier, with instructions to take it to him immediately. Someone would need to place the calls to get Hitler on the line. A nervous General Harster read the letter to him over the phone also before dawn on January 10. Hitler ordered an immediate manhunt for Edda. Mussolini, too, received the letter before daybreak. In the morning he rang for his personal secretary, Giovanni Dolfin, who later recorded what the Duce told him:

> Last night a letter was delivered to me from Edda, who has fled. In case Ciano is not free within three days, she threatens to publish a complete documentary account of our relations with the Germans. I had known for some time Ciano kept a diary.... His personal relations with Ribbentrop were never good, and toward the end they hated each other. The publication of this diary which aims to show the continuous German treachery toward us, even during the period of full alliance, could at this time provide irreparable consequences.... It is peculiarly my destiny to be betrayed by everyone, even by my own daughter.

Edda would have laughed bitterly at that statement. She knew precisely who she blamed most for this betrayal: her father.

* * *

For days, there had been fresh rumors that at any moment Galeazzo's trial would be suspended, and on January 10, as the case entered its final stage, Hilde, sleepless and on edge, was still half expecting some sudden turn in the direction of their fortunes. Edda's blackmail letters to Hitler and Mussolini had been dispatched by General Harster sometime after 3:00 or 4:00 A.M. Hilde dared to hope that there would be some kind of amnesty as the two dictators weighed the problem.

Hilde had gone to Galeazzo's cell that morning as usual, and she had told him that Edda was on the run. Hilde and Emilio assumed that she was safely over the border, but there was as yet no confirmation from the German police. In fact, at that moment Edda was still sitting in the station at the border, waiting for the Swiss diplomats and police to decide whether to process her refugee application. Galeazzo cried tears of relief when Hilde told him of Edda's flight. He hoped desperately that Edda made it. He missed his children.

Galeazzo began his morning, as in previous days, in the prisoner's dock, and both he and Hilde expected the trial to continue for at least another day. They were anxiously waiting to see whether Edda's ransom demands would trigger a delay or perhaps even a modification of the charges. Instead, after a break for lunch, the judges returned to the courtroom and abruptly announced a shocking verdict: guilty. No one in the courtroom was prepared, least of all Hilde or Galeazzo. Hilde broke down at the back of the room, crying heaving sobs that, more than anything else, said she was not just a run-of-the-mill German intelligence agent.

Galeazzo sat rigid and unmoving in shock at the unexpected announcement. Six men had been tried. Five of them—all of whom had voted against Mussolini at the Grand Council—were condemned to death for treason: Emilio De Bono, Luciano Gottardi, Carlo Pareschi, Giovanni Marinelli, and Galeazzo Ciano. Only one indicted man, Tullio Cianetti, was spared the death sentence. He was sentenced to thirty years in prison, his reward for having shrewdly written Mussolini an abject and early letter of apology.

In fact, there could have been no other decision, no matter what Hilde or Edda had hoped for. If the eight judges had voted to acquit Galeazzo, they would have been shot along with the defendants in a volley of machine-gun fire in the courtroom. The fascist police chief covering the trial, Major Nicola Furlotti, confessed two decades later that an attack would have taken place that afternoon if there had been any attempt at a pardon: "We were determined not to allow Ciano to escape." The party-run police were prepared for extrajudicial action. Assassination or execution were the only two outcomes possible.

* * *

The verdict came at 2:00 P.M. The sentence was for death by firing squad the next morning. After the sentence was announced, the prisoners were returned to their cells, and behind the scenes there were frantic efforts throughout the day to secure from Mussolini a last-minute commutation. Galeazzo's old friend Zenone Benini, still incarcerated on other charges, was permitted to see Galeazzo that afternoon in prison. As Galeazzo entered his cell, Zenone could not help but start crying.

Galeazzo chided his friend. "Ah, I come to see you so that you can give me courage and you burst into tears!"

"Sit down," Zenone invited, politely gesturing toward the single chair.

But Galeazzo was full of black humor. "Oh, no, you sit down, I shall have all the time in the world to rest."

Zenone remembered how, after he had dried his eyes, Galeazzo "spoke of his children, of his wife, who had tried everything under the sun to save him." Galeazzo spoke of his love for Hilde, "that noble creature whom the Germans set to spy on me." "To her," Galeazzo confided to his friend, "I have entrusted my political testament and other correspondence of great importance."

* * *

Hilde came to Galeazzo's cell too that evening. She brought him the only gift that in the first days of January either Hilde or Edda could think to procure for him that now could matter: a small vial of poison. It had been Edda's idea. Edda had been determined, if she could not save her husband, to put a painless death within his power. Galeazzo was ready. He would take it, with Hilde beside him.

Galeazzo unbuckled his watch from his wrist and slipped from the hem of his overcoat a diamond ring that he had hidden. He passed the mementos, along with his fountain pen, to Hilde, asking that she safeguard them for his wife and children. Galeazzo lay down on his narrow prison cot, said a last prayer with Hilde, and drained the vial of cyanide. Hilde wept quietly. With her hand on his arm, they waited together for Galeazzo's passing.

Galeazzo's heart began beating violently. Panic swept him. The work of the poison had started. "But then I became aware: my heart was beating normally. This was dying? What, I was alive, very alive": Something had gone wrong with the formulation. He wasn't dying after all. The poison was strong enough to make him nauseous, weak, and miserable. But the cyanide was not strong enough to kill him. Galeazzo was devastated. It meant there was no escape.

Thus began, Hilde said, the "most terrible night of my life." She and Zenone sat with Galeazzo in his cell all that evening and throughout the long night ahead of them. Later, when the Germans suspected that Zenone knew the location of the diaries, revealed to him in a dying man's prison-house confession, Zenone would also pay for his loyalty to his old schoolmate.

Hilde and Zenone talked that night of clemency, still daring to hope that Edda's letters or Mussolini's loyalty to his daughter might change the outcome. As night fell, the five condemned men signed a joint request for pardon to be delivered to Mussolini. Surely Mussolini would not allow the father of his grandchildren to face execution. Galeazzo, sick from the attempted poisoning, dismissed these cheerful words. "Forget about the plea for mercy: Let us speak of serious things," he said. "When you return among men, and this cursed war will have finished (and it will finish soon) do not abandon my children and my wife: they are the only things that I still have. Edda has conducted herself admirably toward me." He did talk to Zenone of the diaries, as the Germans suspected, saying they "have stripped me of my possessions. I am poor now. But there is one treasure they have not taken which is of more value to me than all the rest: my Diary, now in the hands of my wife."

The confirmation of Edda's safe escape just before dawn was the one bright spot in an otherwise harrowing night. Sometime before six o'clock, the prison chief, Dr. Olas, came with the news from the prefecture for Hilde: German intelligence had evidence that Edda was in Switzerland and had been granted refugee status. "The German lady again was there," Zenone recorded, and "Ciano's face radiated satisfaction when he got that news." They passed the hours that remained talking and reading Seneca on Stoicism. Galeazzo had ceased to hope, and he would soon also cease to fear.

* * *

Neither Mussolini nor Edda's mother, Rachele, slept that night either. Rachele remembered seeing the light on under her husband's door all night and hearing him pacing. Edda's furious letter, threatening revenge and speaking of betrayal, bothered her father. She also had to be stopped from publishing the count's papers. Their publication would damage him with Hitler. More than that, though, Mussolini was desperate for some reconciliation with his daughter. She was his favorite child. He spent hours vacillating. He loved Edda. She would never forgive him for the death of Galeazzo.

Mussolini that night expected the request for a reprieve to come. Just after 1:00 A.M. on January 11, Mussolini asked his secretary if there had been any news, and a rumor began to spread that he had called a cabinet meeting to discuss a possible pardon. But it was nothing more than a rumor. Mussolini was told there had been no update, no correspondence.

Had the clemency appeal come at that moment, he may even have signed it. He was torn. Mussolini, awaiting the possibility of a plea, telephoned General Karl Wolff, the head of the SS in Italy, to broach the subject of a pardon. General Wolff advised him that Hitler's instructions were that the matter was "an exclusive and absolute internal Italian" decision. But General Wolff hinted slyly that Hitler did not believe that Mussolini had the resolve to carry out the sentence. Mussolini was stung. "A failure to execute could harm me in the consideration of the Führer?" Mussolini asked. "Yes, very much so," the general advised him.

Mussolini was determined in that moment. He would not intervene. Or maybe he would. But he didn't think so. There was, in any event, still time to consider the best course of action. He expected to receive a petition of mercy at any moment, and he would decide on its merits. What Mussolini did not know was that the clemency appeal, submitted hours earlier, had been stalled. The appeal had fallen into the hands of Minister Alessandro Pavolini, an ardent Fascist party loyalist, and Minister Pavolini had no intention of placing before Il Duce any such temptation. Minister Pavolini welcomed Galeazzo's execution. He intended to see that it went off without any interruption.

* * *

In the prison cell at Scalzi, the ringing of the monastery bells told Galeazzo and Hilde that it was 6:00 A.M. There had been no response to the appeal for mercy. Galeazzo expected to be shot at dawn, but by seven thirty, the sun was rising. For half an hour, Hilde dared to believe that the sentence had been postponed. By 8:00 A.M., her hopes were dashed, and the prefect confirmed that the execution was moving forward.

The five condemned men were driven through deserted streets to a local shooting range outside of town, established in the courtyard of a nineteenth-century military fort at San Procolo. The morning was cold and wet, and in the prison van Galeazzo raged against the perfidy of his father-in-law. But the moment he stepped into the compound he set his jaw in defiance. He would not let them see him beg or grovel. "I shall not give those who wanted my death the pleasure of seeing me die a coward," he had confided to Zenone during that long night reading the Stoics. Hilde stood in the corridor of the fortress, sobbing against a wall and fingering tenderly Galeazzo's gold watch, which she wore on her wrist throughout the morning. In the yard, German journalists armed with film and cameras jostled for position, while a firing squad of young men dressed in black and army green ranged themselves in two tiers, one standing and one kneeling. Their commander, Nicola Furlotti, one of Galeazzo's implacable enemies, paced quietly in anticipation. Among the twenty-odd witnesses were the prison director, Dr. Olas, a priest, Father Chiot, and a physician, Dr. Caretto, who would certify the executions.

* * *

Just after 9:00 A.M. on January 11, with Mussolini still waiting for the clemency petition and unaware that the execution was proceeding, the condemned men were handcuffed. Father Chiot led them out into the courtyard where flimsy wooden chairs were lined up facing a wall. Hilde turned toward a corridor wall, unable to watch what was happening. De Bono was led out first, followed by Ciano and then Marinelli, who, hysterical and fainting, had to be dragged to his execution. Galeazzo, still light-headed from the aftereffects of the cyanide, was unsteady. The sky was gray, and the photographers fiddled with their cameras as Galeazzo was led to his chair. He slowly took off his overcoat and scarf and asked the prison director to see that his son received them. Pressed to sit, Galeazzo threw himself at the chair in anger, fell over, dizzy, and sat again, while a soldier tightly bound him. The prisoners were placed with their backs to their executioners. When the soldier tried to put in place a blindfold, Galeazzo twisted his head in defiance. The soldiers shrugged. The count could die watching if that was what he wanted.

In the silent courtyard, the swish as the guns were raised and the bullets clicked into chambers seemed louder than one could have imagined. De Bono defiantly called out in the instant before the shots fired, "Viva! Italia! Viva! Duce!" Marinelli in raw terror screamed, "Don't shoot!" Galeazzo said nothing.

Galeazzo Ciano had seen—and even done—terrible things. He had witnessed firsthand the infernal, bitter machinery of the fascist regimes spreading death across Europe and had been part of that engine. He had tried to find a way out of that heart of darkness in July 1943 when he renounced Mussolini and voted to depose him. He had tried to preserve his diaries as a testimony. This was the price. At the final instant, just as the volley exploded, Galeazzo made his last decision. He flung himself against the ropes that bound him and turned to look over his shoulder to face the firing squad, eye-to-eye with his executioners. It was a horrible moment, caught forever on film in the flash of cameras.

Perhaps his young executioners were rattled by the burning gaze of a condemned man. De Bono, struck cleanly, died instantly. The other four were struck but alive. Galeazzo had been inexpertly struck with five bullets in the back but remained conscious. A German SS officer who witnessed the execution was contemptuous. It was complete incompetence. "The men lying on the ground had been so inaccurately hit that they were writhing and screaming," he reported. The squad reorganized and a moment later a second round of shots was fired.

Another bullet this time grazed Galeazzo's neck, sending blood in a long cascade with each heartbeat. He was now, among the prisoners, the only one still living. He lay on the ground, moaning in pain, and the firing squad balked at a third volley. Dr. Caretto and Nicola Furlotti walked to where he lay in the dust and gravel. Furlotti leaned forward. Then he fired a shot from his revolver into Galeazzo's temple. Still Galeazzo lived. Furlotti shot point-blank again. Only with the second shot did Galeazzo expire.

The executions and the events that had led Galeazzo to his death that morning would be known in Italian history afterward simply as the *processo di Verona*—the trial of Verona. But those who had witnessed the firing squad that morning knew that it had always been about murder and not about justice.

CHAPTER 10

Emilio

January 10, 1944–February 15, 1944

It was 9:25 A.M., and the trial was over. A German diplomat who witnessed the execution said in disgust, "It was like the slaughtering of pigs." Winston Churchill later said that it had been an act of "calculated vengeance" and a family vendetta "in keeping with a Renaissance tragedy."

By 10:00 A.M. a shocked Mussolini learned that his son-in-law was dead. Only that afternoon would he come to understand that the expected appeal for pardon had been withheld from him. His son, Romano, remembered his father crying. Mussolini was also surprised to learn that he would be blamed for having refused that commutation. An American nun who spent the war in Rome recorded in her diary the next day, "Ciano is dead. They shot him as a traitor yesterday morning.... Whatever animosity may have been roused by his extremely colourful career, there is nothing but sympathy now, for him and for his family; sympathy coupled with growing indignation at the behaviour of his father-in-law and the Fascists. Ciano's wife made every effort to persuade her father to spare her husband's life, but Mussolini was adamant."

* * *

Galeazzo Ciano's suffering was over. Emilio Pucci's terrible ordeal was just beginning. On January 10, leaving the Gestapo apartment at the Hotel Gabbia d'Oro just before two o'clock in the morning, Emilio fled for the border as Hilde had urged him.

He had been hoping to make the crossing near Sondrio, in the mountains about 150 miles northwest of Verona. But Emilio was exhausted. "I was on my way to Sondrio, where I hoped I could make arrangements to get through. But since the night of January 2d (eight days before) I had been up driving," he said later, "and after my recent illness I was in very bad shape. So I fell asleep. I woke up shortly before four." When he awoke and tried to start his car, the engine wouldn't turn over. Car troubles had plagued this entire sorry adventure. On the roadside, Emilio considered. He had passed a small house a few miles back, and there was nothing to do but ask the farmer for help getting the car started. The farmer obliged, and Emilio was soon back at his car.

But the border was being watched. The Gestapo was hunting for Edda and Emilio, and the Germans did not yet know for certain on the morning of January 10 that Edda had already fled to Switzerland. As he stood at the roadside, a German patrol car passed and demanded to see his papers. Emilio, unfortunately, did not have false papers and was traveling under his own identity. The agent looked down, saw his name, and, in an instant, "Four machine guns were stuck against my throat and I was shoved against a wall. They asked me to tell them where the countess was."

Emilio was caught. The agents screamed murderous threats, demanding that he talk, but Emilio was afraid that if he said anything it might put them on the trail of Edda. He knew she had tried to cross the border, and he assumed she had made it safely to the Swiss checkpoint. But if she had not been processed as a refugee and admitted into Switzerland formally, political pressure from Germany might be enough to have her claim rejected. Indeed, on the other side of the Swiss border that morning, as Edda sat on the bench waiting, the Swiss might well have welcomed the opportunity to rid themselves of an unwelcome and politically difficult arrival. Emilio had no doubt that, if Edda was returned to Italy, they would kill her.

Emilio tried to bluff the Gestapo agents and said that he had been on his way to Sondrio to meet Edda. His primary concern was that they believed Edda was still in Italy. The Gestapo men threw him into the back of the car and roared off in the direction of Sondrio, eager to apprehend Edda. They spent most of the day waiting at the rendezvous, but Edda, of course, was a no-show. Now his interrogators were angry. Again the agents demanded an answer: Where is the countess? They counted down the seconds of the one minute he had to tell them. "I stiffened to receive the blow, but it didn't come. I was kicked around, then shoved into a car and taken to Gestapo headquarters in Verona."

On January 11, Hilde learned of Emilio's arrest just before the execution started. When she was certain there was no help left for Galeazzo, she rushed to Gestapo headquarters. Emilio recorded later that he saw Hilde that morning a "few minutes after Count Ciano had been shot." Hilde was as powerless to help Emilio as she had been to save Galeazzo. She hoped that Emilio would keep all their secrets. Her own life was in danger if Emilio broke down during interrogation. When Hilde's role in helping Edda escape with the diaries came to light, she would be the next one in prison. Hilde hoped, but she was not optimistic. She had a pretty good idea of what awaited Emilio in Gestapo custody. Most people talked, in the end. It was the only way to stop the torture.

First his Gestapo interrogators would try the easy way: psychological terror. Emilio was led into a cell, and he waited there from midmorning until four o'clock that afternoon, a tactic meant to rattle him. At 4:00 P.M. guards escorted him in to see General Harster, who politely counseled him that it would be best now to be forthcoming. But Emilio was still afraid that anything he said might compromise Edda's chances of having her asylum application accepted. He was resolutely silent.

Emilio was driven by the Gestapo back to the Ramiola clinic, and now interrogated along with Dr. Melocchi, who had unhelpfully shared with the Gestapo his view that Emilio was anti-fascist and anti-German. Thankfully, Dr. Melocchi did not reveal the presence of the papers that only days before Edda and Emilio had left in his safekeeping and were still hidden at the power station. Again, Emilio said nothing, although General Harster was certain the marchese knew where to find the countess and the papers. Emilio's identity had been confirmed by the hotel at the border, but he still refused to talk about the countess or her escape mission.

It would be the hard way, then. Emilio was next delivered to the Gestapo headquarters in Milan, at the Hotel Regina, for pressured questioning and, ultimately, torture. "[W]hat struck me," Emilio said later of the colonel who questioned him, "were his hands, small well-manicured hands, which seemed incapable of hurting a fly. Nevertheless, the appearance of the room told me directly that those hands were responsible for a lot of dirty work."

Inside the interrogation room stood three men: the colonel, an aide-de-camp, and a major. An elderly woman sat at a typewriter recording a transcript of the interview. Emilio noticed that she kept her eyes studiously on the paper in front of her. The colonel and his chief interrogator, the man with the delicate hands, was Walter Rauff, the head of the secret police in northern Italy and a Nazi known for his cool brutality and "political gangsterism." Among Colonel Rauff's ignominious contributions to the Nazi war effort was his design of a mobile gas chamber. Emilio did not speak German, so the interrogation took place in broken English, followed by broken French, and Emilio refused to tell them anything, in either language. He had no way of knowing still whether Edda had been accepted in Switzerland, and he was afraid of placing her in danger.

At last, exasperated, Colonel Rauff said something to the major that Emilio couldn't understand. The typist jumped from her seat and rushed from the room, eager not to witness what followed. That scared Emilio. Colonel Rauff walked slowly, deliberately, to a storage cupboard and removed three leather riding crops, one for each of the three German officers. Approaching Emilio with a leisurely stroll, suddenly in a rage all three men began to beat Emilio in the face and around the head with whiplashes, screaming abuses. "The worst thing," Emilio remembered later, wasn't the pain: it "was the dreadful feeling of humiliation."

The beating went on until Emilio mercifully fainted. He awoke to find that he had been propped up against a wall. German words seemed to come from somewhere far away, and he could not understand the meaning of what was happening. Blood from wounds on his forehead filled his eyes and blurred his vision. Suddenly hysterical, it all seemed to Emilio very funny, and, when Colonel Rauff told him to clean himself up, Emilio took a handkerchief and made a comic show of daintily patting himself and arranging his hair. "Is it alright?" Emilio asked, giggling. The colonel was not amused.

Tying Emilio to a chair next, the men took steel vises that twisted his fingers and wrists. "I felt as if my bones were going to split and a cold sweat ran down my back," he remembered later. Again, Emilio fainted in pain. He came to again to find he was still being beaten with the riding crops, looked up at his tormentors, and gave in once again to the darkness. On it went, Emilio coming to and then passing out again every few minutes until midnight, resolutely saying nothing. The three men came back next with guns, threatening to shoot him point-blank, but Emilio just wilted.

He drifted in and out of consciousness and realized that he was lying down now, shivering, on the cold floor of a prison cell. Through a small window he could see the stars in a clear winter sky: "I thought of the clear nights in Africa, when I used to fly over the desert, and I tried to imagine the wonderful feeling of being again free and a human being." Then the darkness took him.

The next morning, January 12, he awoke in the San Vittore Prison and was transported back to the Gestapo headquarters, where the torture resumed, and he was promised that it would go on day and night until he told them where they could find Edda and the diaries. Colonel Rauff's beatings were increasingly brutal and indiscriminate. By day's end, when Emilio was returned to his cell, handcuffed and half conscious, his skull was fractured in several places and he was bleeding internally. That night, Emilio decided there could be no alternative. He couldn't bear the pain. He knew this ended with the Germans killing him. Better to end it quickly. He didn't have a vial of poison. But he had hidden a razor blade in his underwear before setting off with Edda for the border, intending to give her his loaded weapon. The Germans had not discovered it. Wriggling in his handcuffs, having to stop for long moments with his vision blurry and his joints swollen, riding the waves of pain that coursed through his body, he finally managed to pry it free.

Holding the cold thin bit of metal in his teeth, Emilio hesitated. He hoped that Edda had made it. He had done his best to save her. Then, with the blade cutting his lips and tongue, twisting and contorting to reach, he began to run the razor along his left wrist as sharply as he could, hoping to cut his wrists deeply enough to start the bleeding.

Handcuffed, it was impossible. He maneuvered the razor to one hand and lifted the cuffs toward his face. "I tried to slash the veins in my neck" instead, he remembered. "But I was too weak." The fractures in his skull left him dizzy. When he came to again, it was to the sound of the guards in heavy boots, fetching him for another day of torture.

Emilio's third day of torture was January 13, and he survived to be thrown back into his cell by evening. On January 14, he was surprised when no one came, and they left him there, with the fractures in his skull and his face swollen. By now, word of Galeazzo's execution and

Edda's escape had reached Berlin. Hilde's intelligence director, Wilhelm Höttl, arrived that morning in Verona, to oversee in person the hunt for the diaries, which the Gestapo still believed were hidden in Italy. The Germans were determined to make Emilio talk, one way or the other.

* * *

Hilde knew, of course, that Edda had fled with the foreign-office diaries that her office was hunting. She did not yet know that Edda and Emilio had hidden another packet of papers—"the chocolates"—with Dr. Melocchi in Ramiola, but she did know enough to suspect that some papers may have been left with the Pessina family in the rush to the border. Hilde, however, continued to say nothing. More than that, she reported to Nazi supervisors that the diaries were definitively gone.

In order not to place Edda or the children in danger in Switzerland, Hilde told a new story, a tale that she and Galeazzo had agreed upon in those last days in prison. The diaries, she reported to Harster and Höttl, *were* in Switzerland. But they were *not* with Edda, she lied. They had been moved earlier to a bank safe held by one of Galeazzo's friends, with instructions to move forward with the publication of the diaries following his execution. Hilde already understood, even if Edda did not yet, that the Gestapo would soon be making its presence felt in Switzerland and would be looking to question and then liquidate her.

The ruse might offer Edda a little protection, but the Germans were determined to prevent publication of the diaries at any cost and immediately planned to deploy in Switzerland. Wilhelm Höttl told Hilde that there was a new mission. She was to go to Switzerland undercover and find the papers and this diplomatic friend. She was also to make contact with Edda and to persuade her that she had better keep quiet about what was in the count's diaries and about how the Germans had double-crossed her. The Germans assumed that Edda had the power to authorize (or not) the publication of the count's papers. Walter Kaltenbrünner was afraid that if Edda knew where the manuscripts were and if she could make contact with Galeazzo's unnamed friend, she would release the diaries, just as she had threatened Hitler and her father.

Hilde agreed to the covert mission in Switzerland now on one condition—she wanted Emilio Pucci to go with her. Emilio and Edda were lovers, Hilde explained to her boss. Edda would trust him, as she would not trust a German. Emilio would be critical to finding out what Edda knew and to persuading Edda to stay silent. Wilhelm Höttl saw the sense in her argument and agreed to her strategy. He ordered that Emilio Pucci's interrogation should be paused, and this was the only reason the marchese remained unmolested in his cell on January 14.

Hilde had not shared with Wilhelm Höttl the real reason for her request: She was tormented by guilt. She had passed the ransom letters to General Harster too soon, not giving Emilio enough time to make it over the border. She wished that she had stalled, even if there had been consequences. Taking Emilio Pucci with her now on the mission was the only way to prevent him being killed by the Gestapo. It also might be the only way to prevent Emilio from cracking under pressure and talking. She could save him. Maybe she could save her own skin too.

When Hilde arrived in Munich, she learned that there was just one problem: Emilio wanted nothing more to do with Galeazzo's pretty Nazi spy or this vile assignment.

CHAPTER 11

Refuge in Switzerland

January 14, 1944–January 27, 1944

Emilio was being held in the notorious San Vittore Prison in Milan, routinely used as a staging point for transports to the death camps at Auschwitz and the site of gruesome abuses. Hilde knew it. But, when the heavy door to his cell opened with a creak, Hilde still gasped at her first sight of Emilio. His bloodied, broken face was unrecognizable. He struggled to lift himself from the floor. Hilde had cried a lot in the past few days, and she started crying again at what they had done to Emilio.

She sat with Emilio in the cell and explained to him that she was a German spy and needed his cooperation to save him. Emilio would need to agree to be smuggled across the border into Switzerland. In exchange for his life, he would need to agree that, once in neutral territory, he would pass to Edda the Gestapo's warning: If she spoke of Galeazzo's diaries or made any effort to have them published, German intelligence would liquidate her and the children. When Hilde explained that the bargain was, in effect, his help in terrorizing Edda into silence and suppressing Galeazzo's testimony of war crimes, Emilio gallantly and stubbornly refused. He wanted no part of that mission. He would not do anything that would harm Edda, he insisted, and he had no interest in helping the Germans. Hilde pleaded with him. The Germans would kill him. Emilio just looked at her through eyes half swollen shut with bruises.

Hilde put her head in her hands. She "said that she didn't care what I did," Emilio said then. She told him that "she only wanted to get me out of prison and into Switzerland because she felt personally responsible for my life since I had been arrested because she turned the letters in too soon." For her to save him, he had to accept his role in the German mission. He could do whatever he wanted once he was safely in Switzerland. Finally, Emilio agreed that he would pass to Edda the message. It had dawned on him that Edda's life was already in danger from the Gestapo. And if that was the case, someone did need to warn her.

* * *

On the day that Hilde and Emilio met in Milan, Edda was coming to terms with her new reality in Switzerland. She had been accepted as a refugee, on the condition that she agree to live incognito and not draw any attention to her presence in the country. If she made a nuisance of herself, the border officials warned her sternly, she would be expelled, and she could take her chances back in Italy. That would be a certain death sentence. If she remained, she would also be placed under strict house arrest for her entire stay in their country. Her de facto prison in those first days was a convent in the village of Neggio, where she lived with the children. Orders were that Edda Ciano should have no outside contact and should be permitted no political information. The local corner shop had been barred even from selling her a newspaper.

But on the morning of January 14 she was allowed to have one official visitor from the Italian consulate. The man—likely Franco Bellia—was an old friend of Galeazzo and had offered to be the one to come tell Edda the news that she was not allowed to read: Galeazzo had been executed. Edda was seated at a small table with a pink-and-white-checked table-cloth. She traced out the checkered pattern with her fingertip while the diplomat spoke. After he had said the words, she thanked him for the courtesy of coming in person. Her face showed no emotion. Back in her room, alone, she howled in grief and fury. But Edda had closed in on herself now. She no longer trusted anyone.

After she composed herself, Edda summoned the children. "Come, let's go for a walk," she told them. Her daughter, Raimonda, could see that their mother had been crying. Despite the bitter cold, the children walked with her to the top of a hill in the village, where a large wooden cross with flowers marked a convent sanctuary, looking out a long distance over the valley. Fabrizio was thirteen, Raimonda not quite eleven, and Marzio turned six that winter. "Papa is dead," she said simply, looking out over the mountains: "They shot him."

The children walked quietly back with Edda. Raimonda locked herself in the convent bathroom. Her brother remembered later that "she shouted with an incredible force for a girl ten years old. She shouted words that could not be understood, broken by sobs, and she beat her head against the wall." Edda begged her to open the door. The convent gardener had to be called to break it open. Fabrizio said of his grandfather's role in the execution of his father that winter, "everything got mixed up, crossed together and fought together: hatred with affection, the obvious with the incomprehensible, great certainties with great doubts…I cried many nights following. As did Edda."

Edda and the children had not yet begun to comprehend the Gestapo danger. The Swiss police had, however. The next week, on January 18, Edda and the children were moved under police escort to a new location in Lugano, where surveillance was tighter. By February, they had been moved again, farther north and well away from the Italian border, to the remote village convent of the sisters of Santa Croce in Ingenbohl.

* * *

In Lausanne, Switzerland, Galeazzo's old friend Susanna "Suni" Agnelli also learned that week that she had foreseen his fate correctly that summer afternoon in Rome when she and Prince Raimondo had visited Galeazzo at his apartment. Susanna and her sister Clara had managed to get across the border in the fall of 1943, and she was now a medical student at the university. "The day came when Galeazzo was tried, then sentenced, then shot in the back while tied to a chair in a courtyard in Verona," Susanna remembered: "I could not talk to my fellow students about being struck by Ciano's death. They all hated him; he was the symbol of fascism; they all said it served him right. I saw him as Galeazzo, a friend, weak and good, credulous and childishly vain. I imagined him disbelieving to the last, hoping in some magic charm that would save him."

* * *

In Italy after the "trial," the bodies of the executed men were displayed to the public, and then Galeazzo's bruised and broken corpse was placed in a coffin and buried in Verona. Locals wondered later at the identity of the mysterious young woman who came, her face covered in a veil, to place a bouquet of red roses on the site. "As long as his tomb remained in Verona, it was covered in flowers—difficult to find there during the winter months of the war," locals remembered.

Hilde, determined that Galeazzo's last personal objects—his watch, his fountain pen, his overcoat—should reach his family as she had promised him, delivered them to his mother, Carolina, who was by then in a hospital in Varese with heart troubles, before departing for Switzerland with Emilio. Hilde too felt her heart was bruised and broken that January. "I loved Galeazzo, Countess. And I still love him," Hilde confessed tearfully to Carolina Ciano. "It was the great love of my life." She had only realized it when it was already too late to save him. But like Edda, Hilde was now determined that there would at least be justice and a reckoning. Galeazzo had wanted his diaries turned over to the Allies and published, as an indictment of fascism. And she had vowed to him that she would try to protect the lives of Edda and his children. Hilde was going to do whatever it took to keep both promises. She would do it for Galeazzo.

* * *

It took a few days for the German intelligence office known as Amt VI to arrange the details of Hilde's mission and to smuggle Emilio into Switzerland. With her intelligence director Wilhelm Höttl on the ground in Verona to oversee operations, her cover story was processed by the German consul in Switzerland the next morning, January 15. She would travel as a diplomatic employee and as an office secretary at the German mission in Lugano. Two days later Emilio Pucci, alive but in bad shape, was transferred north; the following night, January 18, German intelligence smuggled him by boat across Lake Lugano into Switzerland. He landed ashore on January 19, at four o'clock in the morning. The Swiss were not aware of his clandestine arrival. Later that day, Hilde entered Switzerland at the official border checkpoint on her diplomatic visa.

Hilde checked into the Hotel Alder, a lake-view villa in Lugano, where she would stay for the duration of her time in Switzerland, and the plan was for her to reunite with Emilio at the hotel immediately on the afternoon of January 19, as soon as she had entered the country. She was not supposed to see Edda in person—that would break her cover—but she would assist Emilio in acting as an intermediary in Lugano, where German intelligence knew Edda and the children had been relocated a day earlier. Emilio's presence in Switzerland was unknown to anyone outside Amt VI. With Hilde's help as an undercover Nazi agent, he would secretly make contact with Edda in person in Lugano and convey to her the German messages and warnings.

Emilio, however, was not in any condition to be making clandestine boat trips. His skull was badly fractured, and he was suffering from terrible headaches and nausea. His face was black and blue, and his features were distorted from internal bleeding. On his first day in Switzerland, he collapsed on the street before he could reach the Hotel Alder, and anyone looking at him could tell that here was a man in serious medical trouble. He was rushed to a hospital in Bellinzona, north of Lugano, and admitted to the emergency ward, where his status as an undocumented active-duty Italian military officer in Switzerland was quickly discovered.

Emilio's undocumented status was the first official confirmation that American intelligence had that Edda had entered the country, and it set off chatter in Bern. Spymaster Allen Dulles fired off an immediate telegram to Washington: "We have learned from a source…that Edda Ciano was…permitted to enter Switzerland with her children. We are attempting to have this verified." A few hours later, he followed up with a second report to the State Department: "News of Edda's arrival has now been received by our newspapermen who say, however, that they have been absolutely forbidden to send out this information."

* * *

Emilio Pucci's role as an involuntary German agent was over before it started. Emilio would spend the next several months in recovery at the hospital. When he was finally released, he would be interned and placed under police surveillance. Internment was part of the Swiss policy for managing the risk of foreign nationals. Switzerland, a small, neutral nation caught in the middle of war on all sides, was in a difficult position when it came to refugees like Emilio and Edda.

Edda, as the daughter of the putative Italian head of state and as the widow of a man recently executed, was a clear political case and also a security risk. There was no question she would need to remain under house arrest in the convent and under constant police watch. The US diplomatic service noted in internal messages that "steps [were] taken to intern Countess Ciano in a convent so that she cannot cause trouble for Switzerland or make herself talked about," but even her being placed "under rigid surveillance, in the cloister at Ingenbohl," didn't prevent the press complaining about the Countess Ciano being given the benefit of asylum few thought she merited.

Emilio Pucci, on the other hand, was an active member of the Italian air force, and internment rules for soldiers were equally strict. Swiss "neutrality" depended on all refugees with military status being interned. The authorities in the case of Emilio Pucci stretched the rules as far as they could, in light of his aristocratic status as a marchese and his obvious Gestapo beating, ultimately offering a compromise solution. Once his hospital stay was over—which in January 1944 was still many weeks away—Emilio could be released from internment with the payment of a bond, surety that he would not attempt to return to Italy until the war ended and would not engage in any military or political action. The price, fourteen thousand Swiss francs, was not a vast sum for a man of his considerable means, but the funds proved impossible to obtain once he had fled Italy. Hilde—who, of course, could not visit Emilio without breaking her own cover as an agent—was determined to raise that bond and free Emilio. She needed him as part of the team to work with Edda. They still had some diaries to pass safely to the Allies, just as Galeazzo wanted.

* * *

Locked away in the convent in the winter of 1944 and struggling to process the death of Galeazzo and the family betrayal that it represented, Edda meanwhile was falling apart. Edda couldn't even help herself. She certainly couldn't have helped Hilde that winter, even if Hilde had been able to reach her. But no one was allowed contact with Edda, apart from clergy and the children. Fabrizio shared a room in the convent with his mother and was an eyewitness to her devastation. "From her eyes ran a river of tears: it seemed never to finish," he remembered, "[a] continuous, silent crying, but without a sob. Only her shoulders trembled. Poor Edda: at that time she was really reduced to a rag. All skin and bones."

Soon the Swiss authorities became concerned with reports that Edda slept until noon and passed the day in bed, chain-smoking cigarettes and binge-drinking cognac while the Ciano children ran feral. When an inspector came to interview the children, he was shocked when Fabrizio, asked about his father's death, simply shrugged and advised him without the least trace of emotion, "So it goes, in the destiny of men." None of them were going to school. Edda couldn't be bothered with dressing. The police removed Raimonda and Marzio from their mother's custody and placed them as boarding students at Theresianum school, a convent-associated school a few hundred meters away, where they could visit Edda on weekends.

Fabrizio, however, was sent to a high school in the nearby Schwyz canton. Frightened to leave his mother alone, he promptly ate a bag of tobacco on arrival at school to make himself sick. They sent him to the infirmary rather than home to his mother. He crawled out the infirmary window in his pajamas and walked half dressed through the winter snow back to Edda. The police gave up and let the boy stay. The family was clearly too traumatized to worry about a teenager's education.

* * *

By the end of January, Hilde was in Lugano and frustrated. There was no way to reach Edda or Emilio reliably without blowing her cover as a diplomatic secretary. Both were effectively incarcerated. She had managed in those first ten days to see Emilio in the hospital just once and speak with him for a few minutes, but he was still too sick to be released and his communications were under constant surveillance. She was still working to arrange his release from internment and the bond, when the doctors did discharge him, but so far that had been a dead end. And now with her mission interrupted by Emilio's discovery, other Gestapo agents and spies had already been deployed to Switzerland to hunt for Edda and the diaries—"the competition." German intelligence felt certain now that Edda knew where the diaries were hidden, and Hilde had lost control of the mission. Those other Nazi spies were not acting as covert double agents, and Edda and the children were in terrible danger.

Hilde tried to warn her. She wrote a letter, urging Edda to keep quiet and to try to get herself and the children to Britain as quickly as possible. Hilde didn't think Switzerland was safe enough any longer, not with the Gestapo actively looking to silence Edda. Edda was desperately broke and, depressed, talked now of wanting to die in Italy. Hilde tried to warn Edda that Italy would indeed be a death sentence. But she couldn't just send Edda a letter directly. Someone had to take it to her. Emilio promised that he would try to find a friend who could carry the letter to the convent. If he could not, he would find a way to slip the message into one of his communications.

Some of Emilio's letters to Edda had made it through. His writing to his paramour was, in and of itself, not going to set off alarm bells with any intelligence service, and neither Edda nor Emilio was any longer in Switzerland covertly. As Swiss police files show, however, Edda's correspondence was very much under surveillance, and the authorities reported on all her visitors and actions. Guessing as much, Emilio's letters to Edda were carefully generic and full of euphemisms to avoid censors.

Edda used during her time in Switzerland at least two different false last names: Pini, the family name of Galeazzo's mother, and Santos. And it is clear that either Emilio or Hilde did take the risk of sending to Edda at least one of Hilde's messages immediately on landing in Lugano. On January 21, 1944, a woman signing her name as Emilia Santos—the cover name that Edda had used entering Switzerland at the border and at the clinic in Ramiola—wrote to Hilde a curious and clearly coded letter. "My dear lady," the letter reads, "I send you the piece of soap you asked me for. If you should need other things please let me know. The children are well and I am quite well too. I thank your [*sic*] for all things and am with cordial wishes Emilia Santos." Whether the "soap" was a pretext for the letter or whether some parcel went with it no one knows any longer, but the existence of the letter strongly suggests that Hilde and Emilio did manage to get at least one warning letter through to Edda. Edda, who had no illusions about Hilde's relationship with Galeazzo, welcomed the help.

* * *

By the end of January, fretting about Edda's safety and the safety of the diaries, Hilde and Emilio resolved on a new plan. Hilde thought that Edda needed to flee to London, where she would be outside the reach of German intelligence. She and Emilio would attempt to contact the British intelligence service, hoping now to exchange the diaries for the safe removal of Emilio, Edda, and the children out of Switzerland. The Gestapo posed a constant and real danger to Edda. After all, if Hilde could get into the country to act as an Amt VI agent, so could— and so *had*—any number of her colleagues.

Galeazzo had wanted his diaries given to the Allies, and he had not cared whether that meant the British or the Americans, but his diplomatic connections were stronger in Britain, and in his final letters he had written directly to Winston Churchill. Their new plan was to sell the diaries to Churchill's government and to use the funds to support Edda and the children in a new life in the United Kingdom. If the rumors are true that Christine Granville had helped Edda safeguard some of the count's papers in the autumn of 1943, that may have been another reason for reaching out now directly to British intelligence.

On January 27, Hilde made contact in Switzerland with a British intelligence agent named Lancelot de Garston. Officially, Garston was the vice consul in Lugano, but covertly he was an operative for MI6, in foreign intelligence, and, as Hilde was in a position to know, was being actively targeted by the Gestapo. Hilde passed to Garston a letter, written by Emilio on Edda's behalf, offering to sell the Allies the diaries for publication. Such contact with British intelligence was for Hilde hugely complicated, because she had to assume that all their messages were intercepted. She forwarded to German intelligence all her communications with Emilio and Edda so as not to get caught as a double agent, informing Höttl of her attempt to make contact with Lancelot de Garston in her intelligence briefings, playing it as an attempt to gain Emilio and Edda's trust and tricking them into revealing to her the location of the diaries. She was playing so many sides against the middle that Swiss and Allied intelligence began to wonder if Emilio was working for Amt VI. The mission was in shambles.

Hilde was the only one who knew it, though. Her boss at the RSHA messaged her through an intermediary—her "runner"—on January 31 with only positive words about her mission. The Germans still considered Hilde a loyal, crack agent. This message instructed the runner to "[i]nform Felicitas"—Hilde's code name—that:

> she has behaved well and that her main aim is to keep Frau R. [Rio di Savoia, a German code name for Edda] convinced to be politically inactive.…Emil [Emilio] is to influence Frau R. and to not let her get in contact with the other side. If it is possible without risk to Felicitas, it remains interesting as to

where the documents are located and the technical possibility to keep them should be preserved.

The "other side," presumably, was the British and the Americans.

Another week passed, and then two. Nothing. British intelligence appeared to be spectacularly uninterested in the diaries of Galeazzo Ciano. If Christine Granville really had managed—unknown to Hilde or Emilio—to obtain copies from Edda, it would explain the deafening silence, but it also may have simply been that Lancelot de Garston, wary of being drawn by a pretty German "secretary," assumed he was being set up by a Gestapo "sparrow."

* * *

In the beginning of February, waiting to contact British intelligence or waiting for Emilio's recovery and release from the hospital was no longer an option. News arrived that panicked Hilde and changed everything. Mussolini, wanting to persuade Edda to keep quiet and perhaps to return to Italy, had reached out to her confessor, a priest in Rome named Father Guido Pancino, who, as Hilde was also in a position to know, was working as a spy for the Germans out of Hilde's office, reporting, as she did, to General Harster. Mussolini was almost certainly being played, and Hilde saw instantly the danger a priest reporting back to German intelligence posed both for herself and Edda.

* * *

Father Guido Pancino is a murky character, and unsurprisingly his account and the account of Hilde Beetz tell different stories. What history can agree upon is that Father Pancino was not a physically imposing man. He had balding hair and wore thick, round glasses; he stood a mere five foot four and weighed 145 pounds according to OSS documents. Hilde did not doubt that Edda would trust the priest, just as she would have trusted Emilio had their plan gone smoothly. The Pancino family and the Mussolini family had been neighbors in the 1920s, and Father Pancino said later, "I was friends with [Benito Mussolini's] children, especially Edda, who was three years younger than me. She was a thin, nervous girl with two big eyes. I got along well with her, we played and enjoyed being together." The childhood friendship had been renewed in 1941 when Edda and Father Pancino had ended up stationed in the same Red Cross field hospital during the Italian campaign in Albania.

Now, in the first months of 1944, Mussolini wanted to prevent the Germans from locating Galeazzo's diaries at any cost. His grasp on power was tenuous, and he could not afford to lose face with Hitler, who had long thought that Mussolini needed to take a firmer hand with his unruly daughter. He missed Edda and his grandchildren. He felt some guilt, too, about Galeazzo. Mussolini turned to Father Pancino as a trusted emissary, asking him to travel to Switzerland to persuade Edda to come home and to keep quiet about the diaries. In mid-February, assisted by the Vatican and Joseph Goebbels, the priest's papal authorization to travel to Switzerland at Mussolini's request was in process. General Harster assigned his second-in-command, Walter Segna, to escort Father Pancino personally and to ensure that Mussolini's financial enticement to Edda—a gift of four million lire—made it safely across the border.

This was all bad news for Hilde. What if Edda, confiding to an old friend and her priest under what she would believe was the seal of confession, revealed that she had the diaries with her? Just as terrifying: What if Edda revealed that Hilde had helped her to flee by double-crossing the Nazis? Suddenly it was no longer just Edda's life that was in danger. If Hilde was discovered, she would be executed for treason. Hilde now had to get to Edda, somehow. And she had to do it quickly.

CHAPTER 12

Father Pancino

February 15, 1944–May 5, 1944

Hilde needed to warn Edda: Father Pancino was a German spy. The problem was that there was still no good way to get to her a secret message.

Hilde was sick with worry. But she was also indignant. Or she decided, at least, that it was better if her bosses thought so. She was hoping that if she was insulted enough at another agent stepping into her mission, Wilhelm Höttl might cancel Father Pancino's assignment. That would be one solution to what otherwise appeared to be an intractable problem. Clearly, she wrote in a chilly letter to her boss, she had lost the confidence of her superiors, or they would not be sending Pancino to interfere in the operation. She asked to be pulled from Switzerland.

The gambit worked. Wilhelm Höttl took the bait. He replied on February 15, urging Hilde to calm down and to be strategic. Pancino was coming at Mussolini's insistence to try to persuade Edda to return to Italy and her father's control. The mission was bound to fail. Edda would be a fool to return to Salò after her father had executed her husband. Mussolini had already put a bounty on his daughter's head, and he was hunting her as surely as the Gestapo. Hilde's mission was different, and she remained in complete command. He had talked to "the boss," Höttl assured her, urging Kaltenbrünner to direct General Harster specifically to leave Hilde in charge of the Swiss operation. He had described her in "glowing colors," he wrote wonderingly, and now she asked to be removed from the mission? Höttl warned her to think of her reputation as an agent: "use this chance, you, who rule over all men anyway, and get this old man of God under your thumb."

It was meant to be reassuring. But it didn't solve her concern: Father Pancino was still coming. Hilde realized, too, that there was another looming problem. Her Swiss visa was going to expire shortly. There was no guarantee she would be allowed to remain in Switzerland, even if General Harster left her in command of the mission. The Swiss had a say in that matter, and her regular contact with Emilio Pucci, whose hospital discharge was now imminent, had raised some eyebrows. She really needed Emilio to talk to Edda in person. He could warn her. And that meant she really needed to raise the funds to release Emilio from refugee camp internment the moment he was released from the ward. They had to hurry.

* * *

Who, she wondered to Emilio, could they mobilize to help with the money? Emilio's thoughts turned to Susanna Agnelli, as much his old friend as a friend to Edda and Galeazzo, now studying medicine in Lausanne. The Agnelli sisters had fled to Switzerland in 1943, along with most of the Italian royal family and the country's aristocracy, and Susanna was living with her sister Clara in grinding poverty in a small flat at 11, Avenue de Gramont, despite the fact that Clara, through marriage, was now the Princess von Furstenberg. Their mother, Virginia Agnelli—whose father was an Italian nobleman but whose mother was an American socialite—had been arrested in Rome after the fall of Mussolini's government as an American. Managing a daring break from house arrest, Virginia had arrived in Switzerland as a refugee but had been persuaded to return voluntarily to Italy, where the family had left behind vast assets. That had been a tragic mistake. Virginia now found herself in serious difficulties in Rome. It was a good warning for Edda.

Emilio telephoned Susanna and asked her if she would come visit him. As Susanna remembered that telephone call later, Emilio told her when he rang that he had escaped from prison after being tortured by the Germans and having his head cracked open. And, he told Susanna, he had tried to bring Galeazzo's diaries into Switzerland. Just as Emilio was about to say more and ask for Susanna's help, the telephone clicked ominously. The line went dead. Susanna didn't doubt that the police, listening to the call, had broken the connection. She waited for Emilio to call back in the next several days, but the call never came.

A few days later, a letter arrived. Emilio was not allowed to telephone anyone now, he wrote. He had been discharged from the hospital and moved to a rehabilitation clinic in the countryside. He needed her help. "Would I try to get a permit to come and see him? He was desperate," Susanna recalled. Leveraging all her contacts and her considerable charm, Susanna managed to get permission to travel to see him. What precisely was said between the two old friends when they met is not recorded, but from that moment forward the Agnelli clan—Susanna, her sister Clara, and, on her return to Switzerland later that year, their mother Virginia—were part of the circle of conspirators in Switzerland trying to protect Edda and the diaries. They were up against Germany's state intelligence network. Soon the Agnelli women would draw into that circle another of their friends, an American socialite named Frances de Chollet.

* * *

Emilio had not warned Susanna about the Gestapo.

Coming home from classes on February 21, a Monday, in the early evening, Susanna was stopped as she was walking down the stairs into the Place de l'Université. The dusk had fallen and there was a mist in the evening air, making everything gray and solemn, Susanna remembered later. "I saw a woman walking toward me, the figure of a plump girl with a drawn, terrified face."

"Are you Suni Agnelli?" the woman asked, tumbling over the words.

"Yes," Susanna said, hesitating.

"I must talk to you at once," the woman insisted, "it is important, it is urgent. We can't talk in the middle of the street. Give me your home address, I will come and see you." Susanna gave the address cautiously, and the woman slipped away into the milling groups of students.

"I was slightly anxious as I waited for this strange woman," Susanna recalled. The woman when she arrived sat uncomfortably on a chair in Susanna's apartment, and Susanna could see that her hands were shaking. The woman clenched her hands tightly to try to control them. She said simply, "My name is Hilde B. I am German. I work for the SS." It was a terrifying introduction. Susanna remembered later how the sweat trickled along her body in fear when she heard that. A Nazi agent in her apartment could only mean the worst kind of trouble.

"I was in charge of Galeazzo Ciano until his death," Hilde went on through tears. "I got him a vial of potassium cyanide. They had sworn to me that it would work. He did not die, he was only sick, so they had to practically carry him to the execution." Hilde's shoulders shook as she sobbed. When she regained control, she continued: "Galeazzo told me about you. I was with him all the time he was in prison in Verona. I was supposed to make him talk; instead I became fond of him. I wanted to help him, to try to arrange his escape—at least to spare him the execution. I didn't even manage that." Hilde was sobbing again now as she said the words: "You must help me." After a moment of silence, Susanna said simply, "Yes, what can I do?"

"Get me a vial of real cyanide," Hilde said, "one which you will guarantee is going to kill me instantly. I have to go back to Italy. If the Germans discover me, if they kill me I don't care, but if they torture me—I know what it means—I know I will not be able to resist, I can't face it. I know you study medicine. I know you can get it. Please get it for me, do it for Galeazzo."

Susanna paused. Was this some kind of trap? She couldn't see what the game might be. Why? she asked Hilde. "But why don't you ask the Swiss for asylum? They won't refuse now that you are here, if you explain."

Hilde blushed. Because of her husband. "My husband is a general on the Russian front," she explained. Susanna knew Galeazzo well enough to guess what being "fond" of each other meant. Hilde had been a newly-wed when she was first sent to spy on Galeazzo at the castle outside Munich, and her husband had also been a friend of Galeazzo. Gerhard Beetz certainly knew that his wife worked for Amt VI as an agent. But Gerhard was probably not fully aware that Hilde had fallen in love with the count. He certainly was not aware that his wife was risking both their lives working as a self-appointed double agent for the Allies. If she defected, the Germans would take revenge on her family. She couldn't do that to Gerhard. And, Hilde explained to Susanna, she was worried too for her elderly mother and younger brother in Weimar. Susanna accepted that those were valid worries. She agreed to find Hilde poison.

Hilde had a second request as well. Could the Agnelli riches be spared to pay the bond to release Susanna's old friend Emilio from internment? Susanna here could not be as encouraging. In Switzerland as refugees themselves, even the Agnellis were impoverished. But Susanna promised to ask a friend who might be able to access some money.

And Hilde asked one more favor. Hilde was desperate to get a personal letter to Edda, telling her Galeazzo's last words and begging her as a matter of urgent safety not to publish the diaries until after the war. She needed to warn Edda to trust no one with the secret of the papers. Susanna promised that she would try to see Edda and deliver it to her. "Your husband died with calm," Hilde had written in her letter. "He wants the world to know everything about him, but more than this he wants you and the children to be safe. Therefore he wanted to say to you that until the end of the war and the beginning of a life without risks you should not do anything which could make your own position more difficult."

Hilde was right to fear that Edda was in danger. There was a price on her head. Mussolini had offered a bounty when she first fled and had sent her brother Vittorio after her to stop her. By the spring of 1944, the Gestapo was making active plans as well to kidnap Edda and the children from the convent. She and the children were under Swiss police protection, but snatching one of them during a walk might be workable. They believed that if they could simply get her a few miles from the convent, they would be able to apply sufficient pressure to get the information they wanted. Any car journey Edda might take would be a welcome opportunity. Once the Gestapo had ascertained from their hostage the location of the count's papers, the files were ominously silent on what the agents were to do next with Edda or where to take her. On the one hand, Hilde's message to Edda to not risk exposure was in the best interest of Edda and the children. But encouraging Edda to keep her head down and stay silent was also a message in keeping with Hilde's intelligence mission. It was precisely what she had been sent by the Nazis to accomplish.

* * *

By the end of February things were getting desperate. Susanna Agnelli had tried to see Edda to pass her the letter and had been refused permission. Hilde's visa was expiring in a matter of days. Her visa extension was delayed, and something had alerted the Swiss to the unusual nature of this consular secretary. She would be required to leave Switzerland. Father Pancino, meanwhile, had made initial contact with Edda and soon was sure to be permitted access to the convent, since his authorization came from the Vatican. He was a priest. The nuns were not going to prevent him seeing a parishioner.

Hilde made one last effort to see Edda in person herself and, failing, accepted the inevitable. Emilio and Susanna would be left to take over their unofficial "operation." On February 27, resigned but worried, Hilde wrote to Emilio to put in place contingency plans. "My dear friend," Hilde wrote,

> I was in I[ngenbohl]. The convent is situated amongst the other houses and you can stay nearby the buildings as long as you like it without being sent away…I saw none of the family. Then I continued on my way to your friend in L[ausanne]. I am really an enthusiast of her. I found her address at the University and waited for her in the little apartment she is sharing with her sister. Her mother is in Italy. The trouble she spoke of to you is rather serious: her mother was arrested by the fascists.…Of course the daughters have to be very cautious in all their [doings]. But S[usanna] will do for you all she is able to do. First of all she will try to get you free, with the help of a friend of hers. She hopes to succeed though she too has not much money. She will write to you and perhaps come personally after the beginning of the university-holidays (8th or 10th March).…The Swiss allow nothing, no correspondence, no visits and not even to go outside the door of the convent. So S[usanna] too is not able to see her, but she will try to let her have the letter. Perhaps S[usanna] can in some way warn her not [to talk]. Do you know her confessor? What sort of man is that?…It is impossible for you to go

back. Your safety was the most important thing of our action. I am sure they would not have you enter the army but arrest you once more. You can't go back. For our communication there are two ways: you can write to my name, Consolato Germ. Lugano, and they will send the letters to me or you can write to my address in Germany, Weimar, Belvedere Allee 14. Please, write in Italian and use some German words if you have [heard] that she [is] better and things are well and some English words if she is in communication with the English. We will name her "my friend"...After every letter I receive I will write a postcard with "molti salute" to S[usanna]. You must tell her about this.

By the time Hilde was preparing to leave Switzerland, there was one other wrinkle. Wilhelm Höttl, Hilde's spymaster, joked that Hilde "rule[d] over all men." By February 1944, Emilio was also falling in love with Hilde. As Hilde said later, his "feeling of gratitude for his safety was rapidly changing to a feeling of affection and love." Although Edda in her convent-prison didn't know it yet, her affair with Emilio was over. Poor Edda: first her husband and now her boyfriend, their hearts conquered by Hilde. She knew about Galeazzo, but she would not learn about Emilio's infatuation for months, perhaps longer.

Hilde was not completely forthcoming in her letter to Emilio. She asked what he knew about Father Pancino. She did not share with Emilio that she already knew he was a German spy in the employ of General Harster. Hilde knew that all her correspondence would be read by Amt VI. She knew because she was providing her bosses with copies of all her communications in her briefings. Working with Emilio to gain access to Edda had always been part of the mission. Breaking the cover of a fellow spy would have been unforgivable. Unfortunately, the consequences were disastrous. Emilio, blithely unaware and assuming that Father Pancino shared the goal of keeping Edda safe, promptly waded into a mess, placing Hilde in mortal danger.

* * *

The loyalties of Father Guido Pancino were complicated. He had been sent by the Duce to prop up the Italian fascist state, not the German one, and his personal fealty was to Mussolini. This was precisely why General Harster had thought it a good idea to send Walter Segna to Switzerland with him as a minder—or, perhaps more accurately, as a *reminder* of his additional obligations to the German intelligence mission. The priest reported to two fascist states, and where Mussolini's interests aligned with Hitler's, the arrangement worked smoothly. But those interests did not always align, and General Harster was perfectly clear: Father Pancino was loyal just to one man: himself. As a result, he was a man with whom one could bargain.

The arrival of a man of such flexible principles delighted the other German intelligence and security agents in Switzerland—with Hilde as a notable exception. Everyone had a different motive for wanting Galeazzo's diaries. Mussolini, fearing Hitler's wrath, hoped to destroy them. The Germans, worried about their publication, hoped to prevent them falling into the hands of the Allies. Ribbentrop, who stood to lose the most from the diaries, would have readily burned the papers. Kaltenbrünner and Himmler, still hoping to destroy Ribbentrop in an internecine Nazi political battle, wanted those diaries on the desk of the Führer. All those factions of agents and enforcers deployed to Switzerland, looking for Edda and the papers. Now came Father Pancino: a man for all seasons. The race was on to see which party the priest would favor.

Father Pancino did not face the same obstacles visiting Edda in the convent as Hilde or her friends from Italy. He was her confessor, and he had come to try to persuade Edda to return to her father's protection in Italy. The Swiss would have been delighted to be rid of the sensitive political complication Edda and the children represented. First, however, Father Pancino visited Emilio, to hear from him the story of their escape from Ramiola and perhaps to ferret out the fate of the family papers. Emilio, taken in and unaware of Father Pancino's role as a German informant, having not been warned by Hilde, promptly shared too much information. It must have seemed innocent enough. Father Pancino was ostensibly there as Mussolini's personal envoy and a spiritual family counselor. Hilde had confided to Emilio, unwisely, that she had taken notes on some of Mussolini's diaries, which had been in Edda's possession. Emilio mentioned this to the priest in passing.

Father Pancino found that extremely curious. It meant that Frau Beetz had *seen* papers that she knew to be in Edda's possession and had not confiscated them? The Germans were actively seeking Mussolini's wartime diaries, along with Galeazzo's papers. Why had Hilde not disclosed this information to General Harster? The priest asked Hilde directly. Hilde, when pressed, simply shrugged, said Emilio was wrong, and that she supposed he must have some brain damage.

Father Pancino was not convinced. He said nothing more. But he began to have an inkling that Frau Beetz was playing a double game in Switzerland. He did not like this young woman. As soon as he could prove it, he planned to turn her in to General Harster.

* * *

By the time of Father Pancino's first in-person visit to the convent in early March 1944, Edda had seen no one she could trust for nearly two months. She was essentially a prisoner in Switzerland. She was thin and sick and depressed. Spilling everything to an old friend—to her confessor, no less—was a mighty temptation. "Edda was in Ingenbohl, in the Heiliger Kreuz convent," Guido Pancino said of his visit:

I carried with me the last letters of Galeazzo Ciano, his personal objects and a long letter from Mussolini. It was a humble, sweet, affectionate letter, a letter from a father afraid of losing the affection of his favorite daughter. Edda was in a state of terrible despair. Each word was an accusation against the father and a threat of revenge. If I tried to tell her that Mussolini was asking for her forgiveness, Edda's hatred turned against me. I stayed with her for about twenty days trying to comfort her, but without achieving anything Mussolini had asked me for.

Edda was broken in spirit. She was also broken financially. Father Pancino had brought a generous cash gift from her father. *What else could her father do?* the priest asked her. Edda softened. She did have a favor to ask of her father: that Galeazzo's body be moved from Verona and interred in the Ciano family vault in Livorno, with his parents. Her father, looking for a gesture, quickly acceded. But Edda, wary, did not give the priest the diaries. Father Pancino was patient. He would keep trying.

* * *

By the beginning of March, Hilde had received the anticipated bad news about her Swiss visa. She would be given a brief extension, until March 20, just long enough for her to make plans to exit the country. She would have to return to headquarters in Italy. She could try to persuade her German intelligence supervisors to renew her visa and send her back to Switzerland, but she was beginning to wonder whether it was worth the effort—or the personal danger. Father Pancino had ongoing access to Edda at the convent by March 23 and had already challenged Hilde on the subject of Mussolini's papers. She didn't doubt that Edda would be tricked into handing over the diaries.

The diaries, though, were the least of Hilde's problems. She had helped Edda flee Italy with the papers, contrary to orders. Her life depended on one of two things: Edda keeping her secret, or her supervisors considering Edda unreliable. Hilde, judging the first scenario unlikely, confided to Wilhelm Höttl in her intelligence briefings that she wasn't sure investing more time in trying to see a "hysterical woman who at times, is not quite normal" made sense any longer.

Hilde returned to Italy in the last week of March, and she was assigned to wait in a safe house in Cernobbio, near Como, owned by a German banker, where she resumed desk duties while her bosses considered. A report to her superiors noted frankly that the mission in Lugano had not produced results. She had not been able to reach Edda in Switzerland, who was being held essentially incommunicado. Emilio Pucci was recovering, but he would remain interned and under observation. Susanna Agnelli was still working to secure his bond and to see Edda.

On the other hand, her bosses considered, Hilde had obtained for the Germans a large portion of the diaries before Ciano's execution, including the materials most likely to be damaging to Ribbentrop. Hilde's chain of command in Amt VI went as follows: Harster, Höttl, Kaltenbrünner, and Himmler, and in the internal Nazi struggle she was part of the anti-Ribbentrop operation. She had done good work on her first clandestine assignment. Hilde was rewarded with a month of vacation time, from April 7, to coincide with the leave of her husband.

Unfortunately, by the time she returned from that holiday in early May, Hilde was in grave trouble. Father Pancino had returned to Italy convinced that Hilde Beetz was acting as a double agent. He took immediate steps to report her to her intelligence superiors. He hoped he was signing her death warrant.

* * *

After the war, there were those who wanted to rehabilitate the priest; some still claim that he was not, in fact, a Nazi agent. Those who hope to rehabilitate Father Pancino note that, back in Italy, as a village priest at the end of the war, in 1945, he worked with the partisans against the Germans and fought to save his parishioners from violence. The facts of the spring of 1944, however, can only point in one direction: Guido Pancino, knowing that Hilde had worked to save the Ciano family and knowing what would happen to Hilde if she were discovered, turned her in to the Gestapo. While Hilde was on vacation, Ernst Kaltenbrünner was informed that, according to the intelligence of Father Pancino in Switzerland, Hilde Beetz had assisted her "targets" and had harmed the German intelligence mission. The penalty for treason, as everyone knew, was execution.

Her holiday ended May 4. Hilde returned to work at the German Amt VI main headquarters on May 5. On May 6, Hilde was called into Ernst Kaltenbrünner's office. If she had been discovered, she would not survive the outcome.

CHAPTER 13

Germania

May 6, 1944–August 24, 1944

Ernst Kaltenbrünner was a terrifying man. He stood six feet four inches tall, and his long, thin face had an unsettling skeletal aspect. He was known for possessing a dangerous temper. His power as the "big boss" in the state security sector, answering only to Himmler and Hitler, was essentially unchecked. Life or death was entirely in his power. But most disturbing was the deep, angry scar that ran from his ear to his chin and pulled menacingly at the features of his face when he talked. It was said that he had earned the scar in a dueling ritual, part of some university fraternity in his native Austria, where he had trained in another life as an attorney, but it added to his fearsome reputation.

Hilde's heart pounded. Here was the head of division asking her with a penetrating glare if she had betrayed the Reich by helping Edda Ciano flee Italy with the count's diaries. The truth was, of course, that she had, and Hilde had no way of guessing what part of the story was already known to her superiors. To be caught in a lie would be worst of all. But even a fraction of the truth would be enough to see her shot by her fellow agents. A word from Kaltenbrünner would see her dead within the hour.

What could she do except steadfastly deny all of it? The report, she assured Kaltenbrünner, was untrue. She had never worked against the Amt VI interest. Anything Edda said was unreliable. Emilio had brain damage. Ribbentrop had sent in his own agents, who would naturally try to undermine her. She had obtained successfully from Galeazzo Ciano several volumes of his diaries. If she seemed to have had an emotional interest in her target, it was because her mission had been to seduce Galeazzo. She had continued to attempt to contact Edda in Switzerland. Emilio was smitten and would do as she instructed. Naturally, she had pretended to Edda and Emilio Pucci that she was on their side and working to help them. How else would they trust her? She had reported it all to her superiors in her intelligence filings. She was confident that, had it not been for Emilio's unfortunate collapse and his injuries sustained in Milan, she would have succeeded.

Ernst Kaltenbrünner considered Frau Beetz. Hilde was undeniably smart and pretty. She spoke with calm assurance, and nothing about her suggested duplicity. She had an open, transparent face, and she had pressed to join Amt VI when the war started. He could see why his deputy, Wilhelm Höttl, defended her so passionately. And in the face of these charges and the internal investigation, Höttl had defended her.

Kaltenbrünner did not know, of course, that Wilhelm Höttl's letters to his agent sometimes sounded a bit like a man who was smitten himself. In one of their communications in December 1943, a handwritten note added to the bottom of one of Hilde's letters read, "Dear girl, I've got much to do but I will still take care of you, so I don't want to hear any accusations of you being neglected." What gets lost in the translation of that sentence to English is the striking use of *du* in writing to Hilde—the familiar form of "you," reserved in German for intimate relationships. Hilde had her supervisor wrapped around her finger.

Kaltenbrünner snapped shut the file. Höttl had vouched for the girl. She had done good work. He had investigated the reports. Her accuser had wanted the mission for himself but had been ordered to report to Hilde as the "line" operator after Hilde complained to her boss about the chain of command on the mission, weeks earlier. Kaltenbrünner was confident the accusations were false, "motivated by personal jealousy." Nothing but a celibate priest and peripheral agent, threatened by a pretty woman with a formidable career track record. The matter was settled. She was to report to the office for a new assignment. And with that, she was dismissed.

* * *

Her new assignment, though, took her right back into the heart of the danger. She was assigned to return to Como, make contact with their agent Father Pancino, and, using his influence, continue trying to make direct contact with Edda. Hilde did not yet know the source of the anonymous accusations. Even if she had, there was nothing she could do except hope that Emilio and Edda kept quiet.

Father Pancino was not fooled. He would be watching Frau Beetz carefully. If there were any evidence of Hilde misstepping, Father Pancino would relish the chance to report it. A second time, Kaltenbrünner would not be so believing. The priest planned to wheedle from Edda her confidences. He was on the brink of receiving the diaries from her in Switzerland.

* * *

Ernst Kaltenbrünner's dismissal of the allegations against Hilde reflected a broader distrust of the cleric, and not without some reason. The Germans were not completely confident that the priest was reliable, and that had worked in Hilde's favor. "[M]y mission," Father Pancino remembered, "was getting complicated." As he described that mission:

> Edda Ciano was in possession of the famous diaries of her husband, which were tempting to Himmler, head of the

SS. Himmler knew that in the Ciano Diaries he had transcribed lengthy talks he had with Ribbentrop. The German foreign minister had expressed negative judgments on Hitler. Himmler wanted to accuse Ribbentrop in front of the Führer and was willing to do anything to get those diaries.

Father Pancino was ostensibly working with Amt VI, contrary to the instructions of Mussolini, to deliver those diaries to Kaltenbrünner and Himmler. What no one quite knew was whether the priest's loyalties lay with Himmler or Mussolini. Mussolini wanted control of the diaries no less urgently than Himmler. There were concerns within the German intelligence services that Father Pancino might hide the diaries—or parts of them—if their contents were damaging to Italian fascism.

Himmler's agents attempted to turn him, offering the priest, first, handsome sums of money—one hundred million lira—and a ticket to anywhere he wanted in exchange for delivering the diaries to them directly. The modern equivalent of more than five million dollars and safe passage out of wartime Europe was tempting. When Father Pancino insisted on staying in Switzerland and continuing to make contact with Edda, taking a wait-and-see attitude, Gestapo agents were assigned to tail him, in the hope that he would lead them to the diaries. If they had a chance, their instructions were to kidnap Edda.

"Once, Edda and I, to escape the German spies," Father Pancino said, "met on top of a large oak tree. We were forced to use secret words to make appointments." Whether it was a ruse to reassure Edda that Father Pancino was on her side or whether the subterfuge was evidence of the double mission that Kaltenbrünner suspected is unclear. But the result of feeling that she and the priest were engaged together in evading Gestapo surveillance had one very convenient effect: It affirmed for Edda that she could trust her confessor.

By late spring, Edda was ready to take Father Pancino into her secret—

or so Pancino told the story. On May 15, Edda and the priest met in the hilltop convent in Ingenbohl where she remained incarcerated. There, according to Father Pancino's post-war version of the story, Edda passed to the priest at least some of the original manuscripts. The priest carried them out of the convent that day, and for a few days he kept them hidden in his hotel room.

"You were in possession of the Diaries of Ciano?" he was asked after the war. "Yes, those famous notebooks remained in my hands for several days. Edda gave them to me in the Heiliger Kreuz [Holy Cross] convent to take them to safety. I kept them hidden in my room for a while, and when the opportunity arose, I went to Bern and deposited them with Credit Suisse. Only those who had pronounced a password with the three numbers of Edda Mussolini's date of birth could withdraw them." The box was registered in his name and in the name of Emilia Conte Marchi. He promised that, if Edda were killed, he would publish the papers after the war and use the proceeds to support the orphaned Ciano children. And if he had any sense—and he surely did—he would have made copies of the diaries in those several days that they were in his possession.

Did Edda give to Father Pancino all of the diaries or only a small, now lost portion of the papers? No one is quite certain. It is believed today that some of Galeazzo Ciano's private diaries are still missing—perhaps destroyed in Rome in the days after the vote in Grand Council, left behind by Edda in her flight with the Pessina family, or perhaps a portion of these papers Edda gave to her confessor. Father Pancino insisted later that the papers he deposited in Credit Suisse remained there until Edda picked them up—or someone picked them up for her. "It was then Edda who picked up the Diaries," he insisted. As we shall see, even this is not so certain.

* * *

Hilde knew nothing of this in May. She established contact with Father Pancino, as Kaltenbrünner had instructed, but her return to Switzerland was delayed by visa troubles. The Swiss had flagged something unusual, and her application for a visa to reenter was delayed and then, finally, denied. Any chance that Hilde would be able to see Edda in person now was over. At first, it might have seemed that Father Pancino had won: He would take charge of the mission. But by early June, Father Pancino himself was the victim of cautious Swiss scrutiny and also forced to return to Italy without a visa. Back in Italy, he continued to make trouble for Hilde. He pestered her with questions about Edda's escape over the border and pointedly said that he knew she had known about it. He hinted that maybe he should sit down with Edda and Hilde together so they could get to the bottom of it. Then, as good luck would have it, the priest, returning to his local parish in the north, found himself trapped when partisans in the Italian resistance closed the roads to travel.

It was a brief reprieve for Hilde. Guido Pancino was determined to bring her down, and sooner or later Hilde knew that he was likely to get a visa to return to Switzerland. Hilde felt sure Edda would talk. She was not the kind of person one could rely upon not to act impetuously. And Edda did not have all the papers with her in Switzerland. Emilio, infatuated with Hilde and trusting her completely, had revealed to her in Lugano the secret that only he and Edda knew: There were more papers and some of Edda's jewels hidden away in Ramiola with Dr. Melocchi. What would happen when Father Pancino was alerted to *their* presence by Edda?

* * *

It was not Hilde's finest moment. But she was young, and she was very frightened. Hilde decided that she had better make a show of "discovering" the papers and jewels in Ramiola before Father Pancino learned about them from Edda and had the chance to use them against her with Kaltenbrünner. Hilde would have liked to have been loyal to Galeazzo and to have saved all the manuscripts, but she needed something to try to prove that she was still a loyal Nazi agent. She couldn't face the kind of "interrogation" Emilio had suffered. Turning them over would harm no one. Edda still had the foreign-office diaries to publish. Hilde felt sure that it was her life now that swung in the balance.

She would have to put on a good show of obtaining new evidence, because, as late as March, Hilde's intelligence briefings had assured Wilhelm Höttl that no papers remained in Italy, while those in Switzerland were already in the hands of neutral third parties. The trouble was that Höttl—her protector—was no longer her supervisor. He was transferred to an assignment in Budapest and replaced by Dr. Klaus Hügel, a Swiss-born intelligence specialist with the Nazi security services, assigned to join General Harster and his lieutenant, Walter Segna, in Verona. Dr. Hügel was not smitten with Hilde.

Hilde arranged to receive a "tip" on June 22 about the location of some previously unknown papers in Ramiola. She promptly reported the tip to Segna, requesting permission to follow up, and when the request was approved Hilde considered. She needed as a partner the stupidest agent in the office. Someone too dense to ask the obvious questions. She decided on an unfortunate Italian officer whose name is recorded only as Radice.

Hilde and Agent Radice traveled by car to Ramiola to gather preliminary evidence that same afternoon, and they spent the following day chasing down leads connected to the clinic. Hilde confessed that she took pains to make it all "look difficult." Unsurprisingly, the lead was solid. Hilde reported the good news back to General Harster on June 24 in person and reported more promising developments to the general two days later, on June 26.

It all seemed to be moving along smoothly. Then, on June 27, on a return visit to Ramiola, Hilde misstepped badly. She had learned about the papers and about a code word from Emilio. She knew that Edda used the pseudonym Countess Santos. But Emilio wasn't expecting Hilde to attempt to retrieve the papers, and Hilde did not know that Edda and Dr. Melocchi had agreed in advance that any request for the papers with the code word would come only in writing.

Hilde might be recognized at the clinic as a German agent, since she had been there before, so the feint was to send Radice in alone. He announced himself as the nephew of a renowned gynecologist in Milan, Professor Fossati. He was there as Edda's friend and courier. When Radice asked the doctor for the papers on behalf of the countess, Dr. Melocchi, caught off guard, asked to see the letter. Radice looked startled, and the doctor instantly realized he'd made a colossal blunder.

A few days later, Hilde and Radice tried again. This time, Radice returned with a "letter" from Edda. The doctor, a seasoned partisan, was fast on his feet. Pretending to believe the letter was genuine, he smoothly explained in his best conspiratorial manner that the papers were no longer in Ramiola. Tell the countess, please, he added, that Emilio Pucci has taken them to an empty family house in Florence for safekeeping.

Hilde had to admire the doctor's cool thinking. She knew perfectly well that it was a tall tale. The papers remained safely hidden in the electrical power plant, where Dr. Melocchi had stashed them before Edda and Emilio fled for the border. Hilde's problem was that she needed those papers "discovered." Dr. Melocchi was going to have to be persuaded. It took a few more days back in Verona for Hilde to "develop" suspicions and put together a file on the doctor and his partisan activities. This time, Walter Segna decided he would go with Hilde himself to oversee the operation for General Harster.

When they arrived back at the clinic in Ramiola on Friday, June 30, with an SS interrogator in tow, both Edda's accomplice, Dr. Elvezio Melocchi, and his brother and business partner, Dr. Walter Melocchi, were advised to consider their position carefully. Hilde informed the brothers that she was a German agent and, keeping up the ruse, confided that the countess's emissary, the fictional nephew of Dr. Fossati, was already under arrest and being "questioned." The doctors demurred. They were escorted to Parma by the Gestapo.

A ride to Parma with the Gestapo was enough to convince the doctors that enough was enough. Dr. Elvezio Melocchi promptly turned over the manuscripts—which included Mussolini's diary from 1914 to 1918, Edda's diary of her wartime service, some of Mussolini's personal but politically sensitive letters to his daughter, and a large cache of diplomatic materials documenting the lead-up to war on the Continent—in exchange for the promise that Dr. Melocchi would not be prosecuted for his support of the partisans. "Why should I suffer torture to protect the papers of a man in whom I had no interest and to whom I had no obligation," Elvezio Melocchi said in explanation. He owed Galeazzo Ciano nothing.

* * *

Hilde, already flying high in the eyes of her superior, now had another victory to her credit. She had found a second major cache of the Ciano papers and delivered them to her Nazi bosses. When Hilde realized what was in the packet, she was startled. "In trying to protect the papers," American intelligence reports recorded in post-war interviews, "Frau Beetz said she knew of one set, those at Ramiola, which she had thought were the least significant; when they were found, she realized to her horror that they were the most important, since they contained information from Germany."

The Germans now possessed—thanks almost entirely to Hilde's work as an agent—more than two-thirds of the Ciano papers. In January, she had delivered up to General Harster and her superiors the down-payment papers, before Galeazzo and Edda were double-crossed with the cancellation of Operation Conte. Those comprised the five or perhaps six volumes that Edda and Galeazzo called the Conversations. Now the Germans recovered from the electrical power plant in Ramiola the two foreign-office diaries from 1937 and 1938 that Edda and Emilio had been forced to leave behind when she fled, the papers Edda and Galeazzo called Germania, the personal family documents, and the valuable jewels that Edda had been relying on financially. Hilde had double-crossed the Nazis when she helped Edda flee with the majority of the actual diaries. But she had delivered up the rest of the manuscripts to the Germans precisely because Galeazzo and Emilio, two men in love, had trusted her with their locations.

Certain references in the Ramiola papers now put the Pessina family in hot water. Hilde, feted as a star agent and crack translator, was assigned to do a quick summary of the papers for her superiors. The result was of electrifying interest. Hilde was to hand-deliver the papers to Zossen, south of Berlin, immediately. Hilde's intelligence synopsis provided the Germans with the first connection between Edda and her friends Tonino and Nora Pessina. Walter Segna and two agents made an unwelcome visit in the weeks following the recovery of the manuscripts to the Pessina home. The terrified family steadfastly denied all knowledge of any papers and survived the encounter, but they were on the radar screen now of the Gestapo. If Edda had left any final papers with Tonino Pessina on her flight for the border, they have never been recovered. If there were any, the Pessina family could be forgiven for having burned them all in 1944, although on this the history is resolutely silent.

All Edda had left with her in Switzerland were those crucial last five foreign-office diaries, from 1939 to 1943, out of three large bundles of original papers. If Father Pancino is to be trusted, at least part of *those* rested in a safe-deposit box in Switzerland in Bern—and he had the pass code. It looked very much as if the diaries of Galeazzo Ciano were not going to make it to the Allies.

* * *

The Ramiola papers, like the down-payment papers, were not destined to survive German custody. Hitler wanted to know the contents of the count's touted manuscripts, to assess the danger and to decide what scores would need to be settled. If Edda Ciano thought there was something in those documents to risk blackmail over, that would need to be investigated. Then the papers would be destroyed.

Hilde requested and was assigned now the job of translating the Ramiola cache into German for the Nazi leadership. With her husband at the front in Russia and her reentry to Switzerland impossible, she received permission to return to her family home in Weimar, Germany, and to complete the translation work there under tight Gestapo surveillance while caring for her elderly mother. Hilde was also given the task of translating a second part of Mussolini's diary, which had been discovered in Gran Sasso when he was liberated and had been copied before being returned to him. No one in Germany cared about Edda's Red Cross service recollections. Her diaries had no political relevance.

From late June or early July until August 24, 1944, when the work was completed, Hilde remained in Weimar translating the papers. Hilde's orders in Weimar were that under no circumstances should copies be made of the papers or the translation. Each afternoon, when her translation progress was completed for the day, she returned the papers to the Gestapo headquarters in her hometown, where they were placed in the safe until the following morning.

CHAPTER 14

The Banker's Wife

July 30, 1944–August 15, 1944

It would take Hilde until the end of August 1944 to complete work on the most important materials. Hilde was now officially sidelined from the hunt for Edda and the remaining diaries. But the search was heating up in Switzerland in earnest. Her Amt VI mission was placed in the hands of other Gestapo agents just as a new party joined in the espionage hunt for what were now being called the Ciano Diaries.

The international race to find the diaries of Galeazzo Ciano that summer started with a curious newspaper article. The Allies entered Rome on June 4. On July 30 a tantalizing note appeared in the *New York Times*, reporting on a recent article in the Italian press. One of the last people Galeazzo had spoken with in prison was an Italian journalist, who claimed to have received a copy of at least a portion of the count's diaries and his permission to publish. "Interested parties are deliberately holding back the publication of the late Count Ciano's diary, the Communist newspaper *Unita*, charged today," the *New York Times* recorded:

> The diary, which Ciano kept from the beginning of the war until his arrest last summer, is said to be one of the most

important historic documents of the Second World War. It was believed that his wife had taken the only copy with her when she fled to Switzerland, pursued by the orders from her father, Benito Mussolini, to get her, dead or alive. However, *Unita* said that the diary was in Italy and had been hidden or suppressed by some who feared its revelations.

Was it true? Galeazzo and Edda insisted at various times that copies of the diaries had been left with friends in both Italy and Switzerland, perhaps with the Pessina family and perhaps as well with contacts connected to the Vatican or with the Spanish embassy. There are those tantalizing suggestions that copies were given to Delia di Bagno and Christine Granville and couriered to British intelligence. Those claims may have been a desperate bluff. Or the Cianos may have taken the necessary precautions to circulate multiple copies. On the one hand, given the importance Edda and Galeazzo placed on the papers, it would not be surprising if they had had the foresight to make copies. On the other hand, there is no public record of any copies having been found. But the fact that some extracts of the diaries *were* published in *L'Unità* with the article that summer, while the originals remained in Switzerland, suggests that Galeazzo did share some material during his last days in Scalzi Prison, when he was drafting his posthumous preface to his future readers.

The *New York Times* article percolated through the intelligence community. Suddenly the Ciano Diaries were on the radar of American intelligence operations. And that summer, there was an American woman—a banker's wife—who was about to find herself pulled into one of the war's most astonishing rescue missions: a mission to outwit the Nazis and save the last surviving portions of Count Ciano's diaries.

* * *

The American intelligence mission as it related to the diaries of Galeazzo Ciano was vague and haphazard that summer. There wasn't a lot to go on, other than that odd *New York Times* article and the Italian press copy, and so it floated down the list of priorities. Then in the middle of August, there was an intelligence break that suddenly put the Ciano Diaries front and center. Allied troops moved as far north as Florence that month and were pushing the retreating Axis toward the mountains. Zenone Benini—the Fascist party friend who had been with Galeazzo Ciano in prison on the night before his execution, along with Hilde—was picked up and arrested. During his interrogation, his relationship with Galeazzo and Edda quickly became a crucial factor. He knew about the diaries and could vouch for the importance of their contents.

Zenone Benini's account of the diaries and their contents impressed the US State Department: "the Diaries...appear to be the most important single political document concerning recent Italian foreign affairs in existence," internal files noted. The American ambassador, Alexander Kirk, and the War Department were now pulled into the matter. Diplomatic overtures in Switzerland were the topic of interdepartmental discussion. The hunt for the diaries of Galeazzo Ciano was on. The questions now: Where were the Swiss keeping Edda? Where were the diaries? And how to persuade Edda to give them to the Americans?

Zenone Benini, arrested in Italy and finding himself in a difficult position as a fascist, was eagerly looking to demonstrate his cooperation with the Allies. He agreed to help and to act as an intermediary with Edda if a letter could be delivered to her. "Benini is convinced that, as a life-long friend of Ciano and as financial manager of both Galeazzo and Edda," intelligence reports noted, "he can persuade the latter to make the document available to Allied authorities. He is equally convinced that Edda Ciano...has not turned the diary over to the Germans, since she regards it as an instrument of eventual security for herself and children after the collapse of Germany and the Italian Republican Fascist government." This was welcome news for the Allies.

At the request of the Americans, Zenone wrote a letter to Edda on August 15. "I was in the Verona prison from the 30th November to the 30th of January and I was able to get in touch with Galeazzo in spite of the strict guard kept," Zenone told Edda. "I spent the last tragic night…with him, and I am burning with the desire to bring you his last wishes, his last words, and his advice." The US government hoped that Edda would open up to her husband's old friend and, ultimately, agree to turn Galeazzo's diaries over.

The trouble was that no one—not the Germans and not the Americans—knew as yet precisely where the Swiss, who determinedly did not want trouble with their unwelcome political refugee, were keeping Edda or how to get the letter to her. The Germans were hoping to locate Edda so they could arrange her permanent disappearance. The Gestapo had been plotting to kidnap Edda since the spring, and agents mused ominously that "it would be sufficient to have the Countess go about 10 kilometers from the convent" to dispose effectively of the problem of Edda. The only thing that had saved Edda so far was that she was locked up still in that convent. The Americans now were determined to locate her too, and obtain the Ciano Diaries before the Germans could destroy them.

* * *

Locked away incognito for more than half a year, while competing intelligence services hunted for her, and despised by her Swiss guardians, Edda's mental health was collapsing by the summer of 1944. She lived— not unreasonably—in terror of the Gestapo harming the children. She was depressed and anxious. She was financially strapped and homesick for Italy. The Swiss federal authorities too were increasingly concerned about security risks that posed the potential for an international diplomatic nightmare. Perhaps she knew by now that Emilio had fallen for Hilde. One hopes for Edda's sake she didn't. But she was cracking up under the cumulative pressure.

Edda was tough. Her courage, in fact, had been throughout the entire ordeal nothing short of astonishing. But the psychological burden was immense. Edda had lived since January as an unwelcome guest, impoverished, under house arrest inside a convent. Her bank accounts and assets in Italy had been seized, and she was living as a virtual prisoner in Switzerland. She was still processing the complex emotional repercussions of Galeazzo's execution and her father's role in it; she found herself isolated from everyone in the outside world except her father's agent, the duplicitous Father Pancino; and her children had been removed from her custody due to her failures as a mother. And everyone hated her: She was Mussolini's daughter.

Sometime in July, just before the news story broke in the *New York Times*, she was transferred from the convent to a high-security mental hospital, an inpatient psychiatric clinic near Monthey that her son Fabrizio described bluntly as the "provincial insane asylum." The decision to move Edda to the Malévoz Psychiatric Hospital, under the direction of renowned psychiatrist Dr. André Repond, was intended by the Swiss federal authorities, in part, to place her in a more secure facility, where the Gestapo could not reach her. But it was also a tacit admission that Edda was not coping.

* * *

At Monthey, despite the luxurious nature of the private clinic's amenities, Edda was even more miserable than before. The conditions were highly regimented, and, although he was still interned and prevented from seeing Edda in person, Emilio was determined to help her. He might have fallen for Hilde, "rule[r] over all men," but he was chivalrous and considered himself a gentleman. And Edda was in real trouble.

Emilio was living by the end of the summer of 1944 in Fribourg, a walled medieval city perched on a rock promontory above the Saane River, some twenty miles southwest of Bern, the Swiss capital. Susanna Agnelli and her friend must have come through with the funds to free him from internment camp, because, although Emilio was under police surveillance, he had been assigned to tutor schoolchildren as a wartime work contribution.

The Swiss could not decide what to do about the problem of Emilio Pucci. One day, he was assured that he would be allowed to join Edda and the Ciano children in Monthey. The next day, there would be intelligence concerns that Emilio was working either as a German or as a British spy, either of which would preclude his having any contact with Edda. As late as August, Emilio, Susanna, and Hilde, in stealthy communication and unaware of the growing American interest in the papers, were still trying to broker a deal that would see Galeazzo's diaries passed to the British in exchange for the safety and financial security of Edda and the children, and one can understand why the Swiss were wary. While the Swiss debated, Emilio remained under surveillance by a team led by a man named Werner Balsiger, a high-ranking police official in Bern, whose wife, it was said, spied for the Americans.

If this all sounds complicated, this was the reality of intelligence in wartime "neutral" Switzerland. Switzerland was the natural nexus of espionage, because it permitted the pretense of indifference. If the darkest place in Dante's hell was reserved for those who in times of moral crisis stayed neutral, here was an entire country caught up in the inferno—or working to keep up appearances. Because not everyone in Switzerland was neutral at all. The Allies and the Axis both ran essential operations out of the country and out of Bern especially. Those who found themselves in the country during the war seemed to always have nuanced national and international connections. If they were European refugees living at large, they generally had titles. If they were Americans, they inevitably had deep pockets or government positions. Often, their ties were transatlantic. To wit: Emilio Pucci was an Italian nobleman who had been educated at Reed College, in Oregon. Susanna Agnelli was the daughter of an Italian business mogul and the daughter of an Italian princess—whose mother was an American.

For the moment, at the end of August 1944, the pressing issue for Emilio and Susanna was the fact that Edda Ciano was unfairly locked up in an insane asylum in Monthey. Her friends agreed that this was completely unacceptable. Of course poor Edda was miserable. The Swiss simply needed to permit better accommodations. Emilio and Susanna turned now to a formidable ally: Susanna's mother.

Virginia Agnelli was a force of nature. Like her mother, the American-born Jane Campbell—a grandmother whom Susanna remembered as someone who "said atrocious things at which people trembled, but she could make anyone's life fun if she decided to look after them"—Virginia had been astonishingly beautiful in her twenties. As a middle-aged widow—she was forty-five that year—Virginia was confident, imperious, rich, and downright sexy. She had been tricked once into returning to Rome, with disastrous and dangerous results. Eugen Dollmann had also played the role of her knight in shining armor, helping her to flee, and she would not make the mistake again of returning to fascist Italy. Virginia was now safely ensconced in Switzerland as an aristocratic refugee, reunited with at least three of her daughters—Susanna, Maria Sole, and Clara.

Virginia Agnelli was a social luminary in Switzerland, as she had been in Italy, and was extraordinarily well connected. She was determined to help her daughter's friend Edda Ciano. Because of her American mother, Virginia was a natural point of contact between the American expatriate community in Switzerland and aristocratic Italian circles. And at the center of the fashionable American expatriate community in Switzerland was a banker's wife named Frances de Chollet.

* * *

Frances de Chollet was born Frances Winslow in 1900, to a patrician New England family, and she found herself in Switzerland in the midst of World War II in a somewhat roundabout fashion. Frances had married, as a younger woman, Boies Penrose II, a formidable, well-connected man with a firmly fixed square jaw and oversize political influence. Theirs had been a *New York Times* society-column wedding, and it had been an equally high-profile divorce in 1936, at a time when being a divorcée still amounted to a minor scandal. Frances and Louis de Chollet, a Swiss banker and a title baron, married in short order thereafter.

Although the Penrose divorce settlement granted custody of a teen-age daughter to Frances and gave the father custody of a young son, the family was soon back in the society scandal pages. Boies Penrose objected strenuously to the refusal of Frances and Louis, who by now also had their own toddler, to return to America when the war started in 1939. Taking matters into his own hands, he abducted his daughter. The child custody case with her ex-husband—which Frances lost decisively— set off an international manhunt for the "Penrose girl" and was again splashed across the papers. Police searched incoming transatlantic liners with warrants in hand, trailed by journalists and flashing camera bulbs, amid great speculation and drama.

Penrose's misgivings were perhaps not entirely misplaced, though his methods were distressing. Louis de Chollet, working in Paris on behalf of his former employers in New York City, the celebrated stockbrokerage of Halle & Stieglitz, was helping move funds—Jewish funds especially—out of the French capital in advance of Hitler's blitz-krieg, under the cover of operating an "information bureau." The family returned to Paris from the custody trial in New York City, arriving only days before the fall of France, and their second daughter was born during the Nazi occupation. When Louis's financial activities became too dangerous in 1941, Louis, Frances, and their two young daughters fled France at the urging of the Swiss consulate, making the last part of the border crossing by foot. They returned to Fribourg, Switzerland, the seat of the aristocratic de Chollet family for centuries.

There Frances and Louis de Chollet took up residence in a run-down but sprawling family-owned country house known locally as Le Guintzet. Unlike Susanna Agnelli and Edda Ciano, Frances had not arrived as a refugee. She arrived as the baron's American wife and promptly set about refreshing the estate and the neglected gardens. Then the couple started hosting spectacular parties.

They were glittering, wonderful parties. Frances drew around her at Le Guintzet a raucous wartime "salon" frequented by artists, international refugees, Allied commanders, and other Americans and expatriates. The locals shook their heads at that house. There were always people laughing and swapping partners. There were stories of socialites doing intoxicated stripteases. Frances and Louis's marriage was already falling apart, and Louis had a roving eye that rivaled that of Galeazzo Ciano. Overnight house parties did nothing to ease those tensions.

There were also other, more serious whispers. Many of those who came and went had connections—known and unknown—in the Allied intelligence sector. Le Guintzet was known as the house of spies, and, perhaps inevitably, it was not long before Frances de Chollet found herself drawn into the world of espionage, run by Allen Dulles as an accidental agent. Her assignment: the Ciano Diaries.

CHAPTER 15

The House of Spies

August 14, 1944–October 15, 1944

It was Susanna Agnelli's mother, Virginia, who unwittingly drew Frances de Chollet into the hunt for the Ciano Diaries.

When Frances and Louis were forced to flee occupied Paris in 1941, Le Guintzet was a huge, shuttered estate with more than a dozen bedrooms spread out across two vast wings, set upon cavernous working cellars. Perched on the top of a hill outside the village of Fribourg, with views of the snowcapped Alps in the distance, the location was remote and private.

Virginia Agnelli had foolishly found herself in Italy in the winter of 1944, arrested by the fascists. When she had a second chance, she fled to Switzerland, aided by the same Eugen Dollmann who had helped Edda and Galeazzo arrange their ill-fated flight to Munich. Virginia managed to cross the border that summer—the summer of 1944—with only her jewels, which were famously splendid. She needed someone willing to mortgage the gems, advancing her the funds to live in Switzerland until her vast Italian assets as part of the Fiat dynasty could be liberated. Louis de Chollet, who had made his wartime career in Paris moving funds across borders, was working in Switzerland as a banker. He agreed to advance Virginia funds and to hold the jewels. Jacqueline de Chollet, the older of Frances and Louis's two daughters, was six years old in 1944, and she remembers her mother wearing the Agnelli jewels during the war.

A fast friendship sprang up at the end of that summer between Frances and Virginia. They may well have met before the war, in some high-society watering hole like Deauville or Paris. Such a connection between the two families would have surprised no one. They ran in the same social circles. In Switzerland in the summer of 1944, the two women connected following Virginia's flight across the border. The pair, both middle-aged, had a good deal in common. Virginia's mother was American, and, like Frances, Virginia had fought a vicious and highly publicized custody battle, in her case with her wealthy father-in-law over her seven children. At least three of Virginia's now grown daughters, Clara, Maria Sole, and Susanna, were in Switzerland, and all three were frequent visitors to Le Guintzet. Frances and her daughters also spent long afternoons in the Agnelli family garden, where there were parties for the children.

* * *

Virginia and the three Agnelli daughters quickly became part of the salon at Le Guintzet, but the house, staffed in the grand country-estate fashion with gardeners, cooks, maids, nannies, liveried staff, and a solemn butler, was full of guests, some who came and went and others who stayed on as semi-permanent, occasionally immovable, residents.

Visiting artists sketched the gardens and painted serious-faced portraits of the two de Chollet daughters, who suffered under the iron rule of a particularly unkind English nanny. The family housed other children, as well, including a string of young wartime refugees from the Swiss camps. These were mostly orphaned girls whose parents had worked for the resistance and who had been separated from them in their flight across the border, or girls whose parents were Jewish and had perished in the concentration camps.

Upstairs, in the bedrooms, were the aristocrats. To Frances's considerable ire, Marie Thérèse, the Countess de Monléon, moved into one of the bedrooms and declined to vacate, passing her days drinking vodka martinis in bed and chain-smoking. Accompanying the countess was her thirty-one-year-old daughter, Princess Roselyne Radziwiłł, the wife of Polish nobleman Prince Stanisław. The countess hated Frances, a fact that was, perhaps, not unconnected to the liaison that sprang up between Roselyne and Frances's husband, Louis. Frances, humiliated, suffered not only a younger mistress in the house but also the mistress's imperious pro-German mother, who calmly warned Frances that, when the Germans came, she would happily denounce her.

There were a dozen bedrooms, and they were rarely vacant. Frances and Louis kept a guest book at the estate, and five or six couples coming for cocktails or weekend house parties was common. But nearly all those who came and went had some connection, in one way or another, with the Allied military command or with its espionage operations. Frances's daughter Jacqueline put it simply: "most of the visitors…were affiliated in some way with British or American intelligence," although many of the most senior among those spies signed only fanciful nicknames or refused to write anything. The guest book at Le Guintzet recorded the comings and goings of well-connected men and women like Victor Seely, Rudolph de Salis, Colonel George Banshawe, Colonel Younghusband, Donald Bigelow, Phyllis B. Legge and Barnwell R. Legge, and General Raymond Duval and his wife, Jeanine.

Sympathetic experts of other sorts also passed through those doors, with their own connections to the intelligence service. Swiss psychiatry then was dominated by Dr. Carl Jung, who had close ties with American intelligence through an OSS agent named Mary Bancroft, his patient. During the war, Mary was the acknowledged mistress of American spymaster Allen Dulles, one of the visitors to Le Guintzet who declined to record his presence but whom Jacqueline remembers. Allen Dulles later said of Carl Jung, whom the Americans code-named Agent 488, "Nobody will probably ever know how much Professor Jung contributed to the Allied Cause during the war, by seeing people who were connected somehow with the other side." The guest book at Le Guintzet from the war period includes a cryptic reference to "the doc," whom the family thinks may have been Carl Jung. Certainly the guests included other of the doctor's famous patients.

Among the guests too were Swiss authorities who were sometimes less than entirely neutral. Another guest-book regular was the friendly chief of police for the Swiss Federal Public Ministry, the same Werner Balsiger who was charged with oversight of Emilio Pucci's internment. Frances de Chollet told her daughter after the war that Werner's wife provided intelligence for the Americans.

Little surprise, then, that this house of spies, with its walled gardens and odd visitors, garnered raised eyebrows.

* * *

Frances was drawn into the affair with the diaries sometime in the late summer of 1944. That summer, Edda was still incarcerated in the psychiatric hospital in Monthey and desperately unhappy. Emilio Pucci was still interned as a school tutor not far from Fribourg. Hilde was back in Weimar, translating the cache of Galeazzo's diaries for the Reich, and Emilio and Susanna were still working together to try to keep Edda and the remainder of the diaries safe from the Gestapo.

The introduction between Frances and Emilio Pucci took place sometime at the end of that summer, and it was her "great friend" Virginia Agnelli who arranged for them to meet in Morat, a little lakeside hamlet just north of Fribourg village, where Emilio was interned. The purpose of the introduction was specifically so Frances could meet Edda Ciano.

Was Frances de Chollet simply curious to meet the infamous daughter of Benito Mussolini? Did Virginia, who knew Edda from Rome, simply wish to make the introduction because she thought Frances—who considered police chief Werner Balsiger a friend—might be better positioned to help Edda arrange more sympathetic terms for internment? Or was it not a coincidence that Frances, the society hostess of the house of spies, was drawn into an emerging intelligence drama?

The case for Frances being an established, if casual, operative in Switzerland before August 1944 is circumstantial but fascinating. Allen Dulles arrived in Switzerland in late 1942 and during his time as spymaster in Bern routinely pulled into his intelligence network well-placed Americans, especially women. Was Frances one of those women from early on? Her daughter Jacqueline remembers being sent throughout the war on strange errands by her mother. On one occasion, Frances sent her as a small girl down to the train station to collect a gentleman who, she was told, would be carrying a particular briefcase. Refugees-in-hiding frequently resided in the de Chollet mansion.

Jacqueline also remembers clearly that her mother would bike each day to the train station with her beloved dachshund Badsy in the front basket, and travel to Bern and back on some unexplained business. Frances had acquired Badsy in 1937, when the family was living at the Ritz hotel in Paris, and they were inseparable. Once, when her mother could not take the dog, Badsy trotted down to the station alone and hopped the train to Bern, where it turned up expectantly at the fashionable Schweizerhof Hotel looking for its mistress. That the dog was immediately recognized in the lobby gives a hint as to at least one of Frances's frequent destinations.

There in Bern at the luxury hotel, Frances was part of a group of American friends who enjoyed long lunches. That group included three men who were at the center of the US intelligence service: Allen Dulles, the head of the OSS, and his two colleagues, Donald Bigelow and Gerald Mayer.

Frances knew Allen Dulles and his wife, Clover, from before the war, and it appears that it was another mutual American friend in Switzerland, Jane Cabot, who reconnected him and Frances in Bern not long after his arrival. Allen was an undeniably charismatic and attractive man who exuded sexual energy, and Frances at least felt there was chemistry. Clover, though, was a fellow Bostonian, and Frances considered her an old friend, which meant that any liaison herself with Allen Dulles was out of the question. Frances knew too well the pain and shame of a philandering spouse, and Allen's extramarital affair with Mary Bancroft was anything but a state secret.

Gerald Mayer, Allen Dulles's close associate and right-hand man with the War Office and at the OSS, regularly signed the guest book at the house of spies from at least spring of 1944 forward. Allen never signed the book. But he too joined the house parties.

Was Frances drawn into the matter of the Ciano Diaries by chance or by design? The question remains unanswered and perhaps unanswerable. Freedom of Information Act requests have turned up no OSS declassified files related to Frances or Louis de Chollet, a fact that is not, in and of itself, determinative. Personnel files are frequently sealed for sixty or more years after the death of the individual, which might mean researchers won't have answers—if they exist—until sometime after 2050.

What is known is that Frances de Chollet met Emilio Pucci in Morat sometime in the latter part of August or, at the outside, in the first few days of September. And immediately following, the Le Guintzet guest book records on September 4, 1944, an extraordinary meeting that can only have been part of a coordinated plan to address the matter of Edda's safety and the fate of the Ciano Diaries.

* * *

On that evening, the guests at the home of Frances and Louis de Chollet included Emilio Pucci and representatives from the Italian and American delegations, from the US intelligence services, and from the Agnelli family. Allen Dulles's lieutenant Gerald Mayer was present. Allen, with his reluctance to sign the ledger, may also have been an unrecorded attendant. On the Italian side was Giorgio Bombassei Frascani de Vettor, considered reliably anti-fascist by the Americans, and his wife, Eli. Phyllis Legge, the wife of the US military attaché in Switzerland, attended (and her husband is another likely unrecorded person present), as did Clara von Furstenberg, Susanna Agnelli's sister and housemate in Lausanne. Clara was the wife of the German-born Prince Tassillo von Furstenberg, and his name appears in wartime OSS files as assisting the Allies.

It was a small, strategically select party, and each of them had either established connections to the OSS in Switzerland or established connections to Edda Ciano. Such a gathering cannot have been accidental. Emilio and the Agnelli women, Susanna especially, following Hilde's pleading and dramatic visit to Lausanne earlier in the year, had been working, as yet fruitlessly, to arrange the transmission of the diaries to the Allies as part of a deal to improve Edda's financial and domestic situation and to forestall a Gestapo kidnapping. After they'd been stonewalled by the British agent in Bern, nothing was more natural than that they might reach out next, using Virginia Agnelli's American connections and her friendship with Frances, to the American intelligence service. There, they found a receptive audience. The Americans were actively working to establish personal contacts with friends of Edda by August, following the publication of the *New York Times* article. Emilio later said that when he first met Frances de Chollet that summer, the Americans already seemed to him very interested in the Ciano Diaries.

From that first meeting in early September at Le Guintzet, things progressed quickly. There were more meetings among Frances, the Agnelli women, the Americans, and now also the British representatives in Switzerland. On September 11, Frances passed the evening with Virginia Agnelli and another of her daughters, Susanna's younger sister, Maria

Sole. On September 26, Frances passed the evening with Catharine Cabot, the mother-in-law of her friend Jane Cabot Reid, who had connected Frances with Allen Dulles in Switzerland. With the party again that night were H. Norman Reed, with the British legation, and Phyllis and Barnwell Legge, with the US military.

And as always, there were those shadow guests who came and went from the house of spies unrecorded. Frances de Chollet was about to take charge, whether she was ready or not, of one of the Second World War's most consequential covert recovery missions.

CHAPTER 16

My New Found Friend

October 15, 1944–December 9, 1944

The mission began to heat up in October.

Edda was miserable and remained locked away in the clinic in Monthey in the autumn. By October, Emilio Pucci had managed to have his internment transferred, with the direct or indirect support of Frances's friend Swiss police chief Werner Balsiger to the lakeside hamlet of Estavayer-le-Lac, just a little west of Morat, on the shore of Lake Neuchâtel. Emilio was residing some twenty miles north of Fribourg. Edda's clinic-prison was some sixty-odd miles in the other direction, south of Fribourg.

Nothing about the geography made contact easy. Virginia Agnelli, determined to assist them, approached Walter Balsiger for a change. Surely, she pressed the Swiss official, he could help to arrange to move Edda to "a house or apartment somewhere in French Switzerland" where she could have her children with her? The clinic director, Dr. Repond, recognizing Edda's "deep depression" and the pressures of long-term internment, threw his weight behind the request and went so far as to travel with Edda to Lausanne to the Agnelli home, where, for a short period in October, Edda—still incognito for her safety—was allowed to stay on a family visit.

There Edda and Emilio were reunited in person. They had not seen each other since that night three-quarters of a year earlier when Emilio had handed Edda his loaded gun and left her to flee across the militarized border. Since then, Galeazzo had been executed, and Emilio had been captured and tortured.

In those few days together, able to talk freely at last, Edda and Emilio considered what to do about Galeazzo's diaries. Should Emilio attempt to negotiate a deal with the Americans? he asked Edda. He explained that he and Hilde had already failed to interest the British secret service. Emilio had only met Frances de Chollet a handful of times, but he assured Edda that the Americans were keen. Should he return to the house of spies in Fribourg and attempt a transfer? Edda was uncertain about what to do with the diaries and whether she could trust the Americans. But she agreed that Emilio should test the waters. She was curious by now, too, to meet this woman Frances de Chollet, the spy hostess.

By the end of October and Edda's short stay with the Agnelli family in Lausanne, Allen Dulles was involved officially in the matter. It is not impossible that Frances, a frequent guest at the Agnelli home, was first introduced to Edda during this visit and alerted Dulles. Cables passed back and forth across the Atlantic, and Dulles received formal instructions to attempt to obtain the diaries in Edda's possession. The official request to Bern arrived via telegraph on October 22, 1944. "We should very much like to have this diary, or a negative of it," the cable advised agents in Switzerland. "Can you make arrangements to get it[?]"

Franco Bellia was the Italian consul and knew Edda personally. When queried, Bellia now advised Allen Dulles that he thought that Edda probably was keeping the diaries with her. This was a change from the views of Italian diplomat Magistrati, Edda's brother-in-law, and surprised

Dulles. By now, American intelligence knew that Edda was being kept at the clinic at Monthey and were confident of access to Edda. What they needed was someone whom she trusted. Someone who would be able to persuade Edda to hand over the diaries to Allied intelligence quietly.

* * *

It was a tricky political and intelligence mission. Switzerland was a small place, the nexus of spy operations in wartime Europe, and it was difficult to operate in any official capacity without other intelligence services noticing. Edda Ciano remained for many—the anti-fascist Italian resistance helping the Allies behind the lines in northern Italy, in particular—very much persona non grata. The Americans could not be seen or suspected of being in direct contact with Mussolini's daughter, especially when the reason for the contact could not be discussed openly, because the networks of trust were too fragile. Even contacting Edda was fraught. The Swiss government was taking steps to ensure that her location was not publicly circulated. At the same time, the Allies were already looking ahead to Nuremberg and the post-war trials that would be inevitable. The Ciano Diaries seemed very likely to include smoking-gun war-crimes evidence.

Allen Dulles needed an intermediary for this now official mission. Emilio's relationship and communications with Hilde had not passed unnoticed, and, although Emilio might have been able to persuade Edda to release the diaries, neither the Swiss nor the Americans were confident that he was not working with German intelligence. The OSS needed someone else, someone who could operate in elite social circles without raising suspicion. An American. Preferably a woman.

Allen Dulles's first thought was to pull in a young American intelligence operative in Bern named Cordelia Dodson, recently arrived in Switzerland—who conveniently had attended university with Emilio

Pucci at Reed College in Oregon before the war—to find out where matters stood with Edda and the diaries. A graduate student in Austria in 1938 when the country fell to Nazi control in the Anschluss, Cordelia spoke fluent French and German and witnessed firsthand the events depicted in *The Sound of Music*. American citizens were allowed to leave, but Austrian citizens were trapped. After she and her siblings helped an Austrian classmate flee across closed borders, Cordelia was quickly recruited first by the military intelligence department and, ultimately, was assigned to the fledgling OSS office in Bern as a spy under Allen Dulles. Cordelia contacted Emilio—"having heard, by chance, that I was in Switzerland," as Emilio remembered—and Cordelia reported to her superiors that "I saw Emilio quite often in Switzerland. He was having headaches. The Gestapo had put his head in a vise, and his head had been cracked."

While Cordelia was able to report back on Edda's mental state and on Edda's fears about Galeazzo's diaries, Allen Dulles still needed someone who could befriend Edda and gain her confidence. Cordelia, although a crack operative, was considerably younger and came from a different world than Edda, and it was hard to see that there were many points of common interest between the two women. Dulles also didn't want to blow Cordelia's cover by having her tapped as an American intelligence agent. Fortunately, he had a robust informal network. "According to Cordelia Dodson Hood who worked in the Bern station during the latter half of the war," historical records note, "the Bern office usually had less than eight aides and never more than twelve. When his operations expanded, Dulles could not obtain American aides because the Germans had blocked the borders. Therefore, Dulles explained that he sought out 'Americans who had been living privately in Switzerland for various reasons.'" Women, in other words, like Frances.

* * *

Frances de Chollet was eminently well positioned. She, Edda, and Emilio had mutual friendships in Virginia Agnelli and her daughters, especially Susanna. Edda would trust Susanna, who had been a loyal friend to Galeazzo in Rome. Frances knew Allen and Clover Dulles from before the war, she was an American, and she was the society hostess at an estate frequented by the international Allied intelligence network.

Frances was also bored and restless. She had reached the stage of middle age when she was not entirely sure any longer what she was doing or why it mattered. She was the mother of four children. She had lost custody of two of them and not seen them now in five years because of the war and the closed borders. Her marriage was floundering, she was forty-four, people were coming and going at all hours, and she spent her days dealing with Countess de Monléon—the unwelcome and hostile houseguest that she could not get rid of. Frances was not political. She had never flirted with fascism. Whatever her sins, they were the minor sins of an occasionally frustrated society hostess. But Frances also knew at midlife what it was to not be sure of the way forward and to find that unsettling.

So when Allen Dulles asked her to do something for him, Frances didn't hesitate. She asked Virginia Agnelli to introduce her to Edda Ciano. Dulles just wanted her to meet the countess and be friends with her, as a service to the Allies. Either at the Agnelli home in October or somewhere near Monthey not later than early November, the banker's wife met Mussolini's daughter. Edda was warmly receptive. Edda needed a friend. She was lonely and frightened.

The friendship deepened quickly. From mid-November onward, Frances and Edda were in nearly constant contact, with calls or notes flying between Fribourg and Monthey daily, and the two women quickly agreed to a standing lunch date on Thursdays near the clinic. The train services were slow and inconvenient, and because of an accident when she was six or seven, Frances walked with a limp that, while it didn't stop her from skiing or dancing, did make walking long distances impossible.

Allen Dulles wanted to make sure that nothing interrupted Frances's visits. Frances, a keen amateur mechanic, loved driving and had tried her hand at long-distance automobile racing. He promptly arranged for Frances to have a car—a sporty little Fiat Topolino—so she could drive the mountain roads to Monthey. Private automobiles were an unheard-of luxury in Switzerland in 1944. Gasoline, like nearly everything else, was strictly rationed. Frances was thrilled to be back behind the wheel, speeding toward the clinic.

After each luncheon with Edda, Frances recorded careful notes for Allen Dulles, summarizing what she clearly understood was intelligence information. Her primary assignment was to gain Edda's trust and establish a friendship, but Frances also understood that information about German and Italian political personalities had value to the State Department. She reported in one early note:

> On Thursday I went to see my new found friend Edda; we met in the buffet of St. Maurice station—this has been our meeting place of late. She was gaily dressed in a Swiss idea of a Scotch plaid…her eyes are big & brown—she had liberally used green on the lashes—it was rather pathetic as she must have been very smart & well groomed—I notice that she always enjoys my clothes & so I rather take pains to be more than presentable when I go to see her—an interesting side of her character is the lack of envy or jealousy over the fact that she no longer has nice things & that I have. She began the conversation by asking me had I seen the newspaper the Nation from Bern….She had read the article [on Badoglio] fearing to find something nasty about herself—i.e., she is very vain & very afraid of adverse criticism—wants to be liked & what is interesting wants publicity but only complimentary, which would indicate that she is honest at heart and would

only do wrong convinced that she was doing the opposite. I asked her why Mussolini when in 1939 had a very good future ahead if he stayed out of the war—joined in the fray—she said she could not say but that he had made a bad mistake & that all great people made mistakes—she agreed that it has been a great tragedy for Italy—that had Italy remained neutral her father today would have been very strong.

The following week, Frances reported:

Again Thursday and I have been to see my friend Edda.... We arrived at Aigle and had lunch there for a change and a most excellent one. She was more quietly dressed today.... [W]e were all gay and we talked of many things—we discussed dictators and she was very certain that a dictatorship was the only form of gov. for Italy—She also gave the reason for Ciano's dismissal—It seems that a year before she had told her father that the affair with the P[etacci] sisters had gone too far—that they were making a fool of him etc. her father promised her to stop the affair, but of course the P. Sisters were too much for him and finally they succeed in putting him against his son in law.

For all the insistence it was a "gay" conversation, the subjects seem weighty enough. "She is of the opinion that Hitler will kill himself & that the others will do nothing, not even try to come in to Switzerland, but that they might try to send their families," Frances noted, though she observed that Edda also had more personal concerns. "She is bored to tears...refus[es] to eat the food saying it is disgusting...then she stays in bed because she is bored & only gets up because they refuse to bring her the tray," Frances also reported.

By November 17, Frances had brought Edda around to the subject of the diaries. Edda confided to Frances not only that she did indeed have several volumes of the diaries with her in Switzerland, but also that more manuscripts remained hidden in Italy. Edda—afraid that, if she turned over the diaries to British or American intelligence, she would have nothing left as leverage with which to buy her family protection—tantalizingly referred to the papers in Ramiola as "the chocolates" throughout her negotiations with the Americans. Edda had no idea that Hilde had already discovered those papers, now in the hands of the Gestapo.

* * *

Frances's spy "mission" was to befriend Edda, but it was not a deception. The two women liked each other, and they understood each other's motives. A genuine friendship flourished. Edda was lonely, but so was Frances. Raucous house parties didn't change that she suffered. Edda knew that emotional terrain intimately. Edda's youngest boy, Marzio, was only a little older than Frances's eldest, Jacqueline, and both women also found motherhood sometimes exasperating and exhausting. And Edda, too, was far from home. She was in Switzerland and alive only because Hilde, a German spy sent to seduce her husband, had instead fallen in love with Galeazzo. Perhaps Edda already knew or guessed that Emilio, too, was smitten with that same younger woman and that his passion had cooled for her. There were certain things that Frances didn't need to explain to her.

Frances, for her part, felt sympathy for Edda and admired her stoicism. Edda was warm and witty and funny. As Frances put it, "I adore her because she never complains & her present life is not bright....[H]er character is a delightful mixture of childishness, love of beauty, laziness—a dreamer, an extremely good mind—probably very [a]cute & smart but I must always admit honest—a strong mixture but on the whole a delightful one—and a charming companion."

Edda would have returned those compliments. In time, she would tell Frances so in intimate letters. But in the fall of 1944, Edda was not yet ready to relinquish control of the manuscripts or to tell her new friend the secret of their precise location. She was cagey and suspicious about anything having to do with Galeazzo's diaries. Frances reported in her notes to American intelligence, "I gave her some help and told her as her business manager that I felt she did not realize that she must give me the rest of the chocolates as her means would be soon at an end and she merely shrugged her shoulders."

By early December, as the friendship deepened, Edda was softening. Emilio Pucci and Susanna Agnelli were assuring Edda that she could trust Frances and the Americans. They were afraid that it was only a matter of time before the Gestapo snatched Edda—or one of the Ciano children—by force and compelled Edda to give them the papers. The trouble was that Emilio still found it difficult to communicate in private. He remained under tight surveillance as an Italian military officer and did not enjoy freedom of movement. He certainly was not permitted to join the house parties at Le Guintzet, where the Allied spies gathered on the weekends.

But in early December, suddenly, Emilio needed urgently to get a private message about the diaries to Frances. So he came up with a bit of subterfuge. Emilio was tutoring schoolchildren north of Fribourg. The first week in December was the traditional occasion of a large Christmas procession in Fribourg, where a holiday market culminated in an evening torchlit procession with St. Nicholas, dressed in white robes, being driven through the streets on a donkey. St. Nicholas would alight from the donkey at the cathedral and on the balcony deliver his annual comedy roast of the town's prominent citizens in a sort of living pantomime. Emilio was generally not thrilled to be looking after children, but he volunteered to chaperone the students at the festival and was granted a travel pass to Fribourg. He watched carefully. When he found a moment to slip away amid the excitement over St. Nicholas, he placed an urgent telephone call to Frances at Le Guintzet, hoping to be able to speak with her amid the crowds at the procession. But when the call went through, Frances was not home. Emilio could only leave a message. He needed to see her urgently. There was something he needed to tell her. A message from Edda.

When Frances learned that Emilio had called, she knew it must be something important. Emilio risked internment or, worse, deportation back to fascist Italy if he were caught passing messages on political documents. Frances considered. How to best arrange a meeting? Contacting Emilio discreetly would not be easy. On December 7, a chance opportunity presented itself, and Frances grabbed at it.

A Swiss newspaper ran a report that morning announcing—erroneously—the marriage of Edda and Emilio. Edda's arrival in Switzerland and her internment continued to be a subject of speculation, including the rumor that Edda was pregnant. The diaries she had carried with her were bulky, and Edda blamed her girth when she crossed the border as the source of the rumor. Someone had put together two and two and come up with five, and the Swiss journalist speculated about a hasty marriage to legitimize a child.

Paul Ghali was a journalist connected to the Allied circle at Bern and Fribourg, and although there's no record of his name in the guest book at Le Guintzet, he certainly knew Frances. The article intrigued him. He was curious whether there was any truth in the story. Paul knew that Frances saw Edda. So he did the obvious thing: He asked her.

* * *

Paul Ghali was in his late thirties, having been born in France to a French mother and an Egyptian father. In 1944, he wore his hair severely parted and slicked back in the old-fashioned style of the Roaring Twenties. His face was square-jawed and a bit chubby. Paul wasn't new to the foreign-service beat. He wasn't particularly progressive in his views of women, either, which frustrated Frances.

Paul had been a foreign correspondent for the Chicago-based *Daily News* since before the start of the war in 1939, first in Paris, then in Bordeaux and Vichy, and lately, when that got too hot for Allied reporters, based out of Bern. Most important, he was already working with Allen Dulles at least informally, and on many occasions had served as a point of contact between the OSS and French citizens fleeing occupied Paris or Vichy with information that might be useful to the Allies.

Paul Ghali recounted his version of the hunt for the Ciano Diaries in a breathless book called *Scoop*, written by a fellow journalist named James H. Walters, in which Paul claimed he had been visiting Edda with Frances on a regular basis "for several months" by early December. That can only have been possible if Edda and Frances first met at the Agnelli home in October, during those few days that Edda stayed with the family, and not in mid-November when Frances's intelligence reports to Allen Dulles started. Few of those early reports suggest that the lunches included anyone but the two women either. In fact, Paul Ghali's story was later called a great journalistic coup, accomplished through his individual efforts, and parts of his story gloss over the role of the OSS—and therefore of Frances—presumably because after the war his need to operate as a foreign correspondent during the Cold War made disassociating himself from US intelligence highly desirable. The result, however, was that Frances's role in retellings of the story in the public version of events was reduced quickly to "my blonde friend from Fribourg."

Paul had probably not been joining Edda and Frances at their girls' lunches for months. But Paul probably *had* been part of the informal team assembled by Allen Dulles from back in September or October. According to intelligence files, "Mr. Dulles enlisted the services of a few people, a team, so to speak, in the quest for Edda and the diary. These were Cordelia Dodson, Mme. Louis de Chollet, an American woman married to a Swiss, and Paul Ghali, correspondent of the *Chicago Daily News*." To this list, Allen Dulles later added two other names: a glamorous OSS spy named Tracy Barnes, sent in late in the mission as a boy-toy to charm a nervous Edda, and the intrepid Susanna Agnelli.

* * *

They were a strange team, and only Cordelia Dodson and Tracy Barnes were professional agents. Cordelia was a dark brunette with the air of a movie starlet, and she and her old friend Emilio Pucci had been on the ski team together at Reed College in the late 1930s. Her work with the OSS would involve transporting prisoners on secret flights and work with the Enigma machine in code breaking. Her role in the Ciano mission was simply to make contact with her former classmate Emilio on behalf of American intelligence, and to open up the channels of communication. But Emilio did not need to be persuaded that it was in Edda's best interests to pass the diaries over to the Allies in exchange for protection from the Gestapo. He did not need to imagine what would happen to Edda if she or one of the children were kidnapped. His fractured skull was still healing.

Susanna Agnelli had been pulled into the affair by Emilio and Hilde when they were desperate for help—and she had found Hilde that cyanide. She had been Galeazzo's friend, and she had tried to save him with her warning in Rome that summer. She was an old friend too of Emilio and Edda. It was Susanna who connected them all. Susanna, in fact, was the only person, apart from Edda herself, who knew all three of the "sisters in resistance." She was in direct contact with Edda, Hilde, and Frances. Susanna's role was simple: to vouch for each of the players and assure them that they could trust one another.

Along with befriending Edda, Frances had been given the task of carrying messages back and forth between Edda's isolated world of the psychiatric hospital and the house of spies of which Frances was the hostess. As US intelligence briefings noted, Frances, "the wife of a Swiss baron and investment banker….ha[s] the community standing and relative freedom to facilitate communication between Edda Ciano, Pucci, Ghali and Dulles." Edda was panicked about money, and Frances especially helped negotiate with her old friend Allen Dulles some of the most difficult details. She ferried multiple messages back and forth between Allen Dulles and Edda Ciano as negotiations proceeded in earnest, sometimes concealing letters tucked inside books that she took with her to Monthey and their girls' luncheons.

The financial negotiations were tricky. The United States could not pay Edda for her manuscripts. Any quid pro quo and Galeazzo's diaries would not have the same moral weight as evidence of war crimes. But the Allies *could* allow Edda to sell the publication rights, once the papers were declassified, and no one doubted that Galeazzo's diaries would be a bombshell story and an instant bestseller.

That was where Paul Ghali, journalist, came into the picture. His job was to assure Edda of a ready and willing publisher.

* * *

Frances considered what to do. Emilio had tried to connect with her on December 6 with his urgent telephone message, but she had missed speaking with him. On December 7, Paul had some questions he wanted to ask Emilio about his reported marriage to Edda. Paul Ghali was already part of Allen Dulles's loose network in Switzerland, and he'd more or less been tapped to publish the Ciano story for American intelligence. Both Frances and Paul wanted to help the OSS get the papers. Frances saw a perfect cover story to arrange an important meeting on December 8.

How about Paul come to Le Guintzet to meet with Emilio? Frances suggested. He could ask Emilio about the news article for his paper—and he could reassure Emilio and Edda that there was a robust financial market for the diaries. It can only have been an OSS-directed meeting: Emilio Pucci as a Swiss internee would need the support of Werner Balsiger's office to make the journey back to Fribourg. Emilio agreed immediately to come. Frances called Paul with the message: "Pucci wishes to see you. He will come this afternoon. So hop on the train and be here at four."

The sun set early in Fribourg in December, and it was dusk as Paul arrived at the hilltop estate. A warm fire was waiting in a parlor, and downstairs in the cellar kitchens there were the sounds of people coming and going. After a small chat, when everyone had a drink in hand, Frances, Paul, and Emilio settled in, and Emilio promptly got down to business. No, he explained, he was not married to Edda. As he later said of that meeting: "The day before the papers had printed the news of my alleged marriage with Countess C. [Edda], and Mr G[hali] wanted to know about it. I rapidly dismissed the foolish rumour about the marriage." But, Emilio went on, looking at Frances squarely, he had a message from Edda. She was ready to pass over the documents if American intelligence wanted them. "I was startled by Pucci's offer," Paul said later, "I had come for a trivial inquiry and here was the biggest scoop of my career."

Frances settled back in her chair, relieved and excited. She was not startled. This was what she had been working to make happen. She had done it. Her mission had paid off. Frances knew that Edda would be nervous and indecisive. The information needed to be conveyed to Allen Dulles immediately, before Edda could change her mind. Father Guido Pancino was back in Switzerland in December 1944, at the request of the Gestapo, lingering at the clinic and attempting to coax the remaining diaries out of Edda. It was not at all clear that Edda, in a moment of panic or indecision, might not pass the papers over to the priest who was her confessor.

Paul Ghali, though, started throwing up obstacles. By his own account later, he hesitated to contact OSS headquarters. Sure, he wanted to loop in Allen Dulles. But with a journalist's determination to get the story, he first wanted Edda's commitment that she would sell the publication rights only to his paper. "I would intervene with Dulles only on the condition that Edda agreed to sell the newspaper publication rights to the *Chicago Daily News*" was his position. It was all just bluster. Allen Dulles was not dependent on the largesse of a foreign journalist. Frances was being run by Allen Dulles as an amateur "agent," and she was already reporting to him directly.

Perhaps it was even just some revisionist history when Paul recounted this later. Paul would need to disguise his role as an ad hoc spy for one of the Second World War's most celebrated spymasters, when the Cold War made that a delicate matter for a working journalist. Not a lot of people wanted to give press access to someone whose cover had been blown as an intelligence agent. No one blamed Paul after the war for wanting to massage the history of this story, to make the discovery of the Ciano Diaries sound like a lucky scoop and an accident. But the effect of published accounts like this was the same: They wrote women like Frances de Chollet and Susanna Agnelli out of a story in which they were, in fact, the central characters. In all the essentials, Frances was the spy running this mission for the Americans. Allen Dulles frankly gave her that credit.

* * *

Paul was proposing the sale of Galeazzo's diaries for publication. Emilio, as Edda's representative, said he'd have to ask Edda about selling those rights to the *Chicago Daily News* on an exclusive. The next day, December 9, he then telephoned Paul with Edda's answer. It was a deal. They "told me that they were in touch with Edda," Allen Dulles recorded in his intelligence briefings: She was ready to make the diaries of Galeazzo Ciano, Mussolini's late foreign minister, available "to the American or British Governments." Edda was about to take her revenge on her father and Hitler, just as she had promised.

CHAPTER 17

Lunch at Monthey Station

December 9, 1944–January 8, 1945

Allen Dulles was delighted with the news. This friendship with Edda had paid the hoped-for dividends. Frances had done well—surprisingly well for a socialite with no professional experience in intelligence. But then, being a society hostess and the wife of a complicated man, in a complicated situation, required considerable discernment and discretion. This was precisely why he preferred some of these "accidental" spies in his operations.

He had not been entirely confident she would pull it off. Allen Dulles had been making contingency plans in case Frances couldn't bring Edda around to offer up the diaries to the Americans with girls' lunches. Edda's weakness for handsome young men was well known. Foreign intelligence reports had been monitoring her "nymphomaniac" lifestyle since the late 1930s, and her ski-chalet affair with the young Emilio Pucci had been the talk of Italy when it started. Her predilections—though certainly no better or worse than her husband's or those of any in their circle—were precisely why the idea of Edda managing to become pregnant even in a convent seemed credible to newspaper readers. But Edda, who as noted may already have been aware, consciously or unconsciously, of Emilio's change of heart, was vulnerable to kindness and affection.

Allen Dulles had in mind one particularly attractive agent who might be able to persuade Edda if Frances couldn't. He'd tapped a thirty-three-year-old spy for the OSS named Tracy Barnes for "his looks and charm and the willingness to use them" and on December 3 requested the agent transfer from London to Bern for the offensive. Tracy Barnes was less than delighted with his new assignment.

Tracy Barnes was straight out of central casting. One of his colleagues described him as "tall and blond, with his hair combed back into a pompadour. He was beautiful. Not just handsome, but beautiful." Cordelia Dodson remembered, "We all called him the Golden Boy.... He had those Yale good looks and was athletic and charming." But nobody could begrudge Tracy that. He was too likable. He had already earned a Silver Star for parachuting into France in August 1944 to establish communications with the resistance, and he had ridden into Paris at the liberation a few months earlier "on the back of a tank, holding a big bottle of champagne and catching bouquets from the girls." He was the life of the party, and when the war was over admitted that nothing would ever beat those parties in London or Bern or Fribourg. Allen Dulles had met him that fall in Britain, coming out of a senior-level intelligence briefing, and in early December wrote to his director, David Bruce, asking that Tracy be deployed to Switzerland for a particularly "useful" project. What Dulles had in mind was setting Tracy Barnes to the task of gallantly sweet-talking Edda Ciano.

Allen Dulles was still reluctant to be in direct contact with Edda for political and intelligence reasons. He might be the secret spymaster of Switzerland, but he was in the country on an ostensibly bureaucratic assignment as his cover. He could not risk his role being too broadly noticed and the OSS deported. The work in Bern was just too important. The Allies looked poised now to win the war, but Mussolini remained for the moment nominally in control of parts of Italy. The partisans were helping the Americans in a guerrilla war as they moved north toward the heart of Salò. The last thing Allen Dulles wanted was to jeopardize operations by seeming to be too cozy with Mussolini's daughter. So he deputized Frances and Paul to complete the negotiations, trusting Cordelia to keep Emilio on their side and counting on Tracy to charm Edda. Frances, "nothing" more than a high-society hostess and the "wife of an investment banker," was the least likely to attract attention of all of them. She would report back to Allen Dulles directly.

* * *

It was time for next steps. Frances, Paul, and Emilio agreed that they needed a sit-down in person with Edda to work out the logistics of the contract with the *Chicago Daily News* and the handover of the diaries. Emilio attending would be a red flag for the Swiss police. He would have to return to Morat. Edda trusted Frances, so she would attend, and Paul would come as representative of the newspaper. The little Fiat was small, and they traveled by train to Monthey for a lunch with Edda to discuss the details. One likes to think that Frances balked at a man driving her sports car, and it is hard to believe Paul Ghali would have liked being driven. There in the train-station café, Edda regaled them with stories about Hitler's private life. Frances ventured to ask whether Hitler's "ideas were not quite natural where women were concerned"— a persistent rumor during the war years. Edda cheerfully confirmed it. Paul said after, "I had the impression that, despite her rupture with her father, she remained a Fascist and was proud of being the Duce's daughter."

Edda was already having second thoughts. The diaries were her only asset, and she was afraid of being taken advantage of financially. She was worried, too, about the consequences of betraying the Germans. She wanted revenge on her father and on Adolf Hitler. She also had a pretty good idea of what the Führer's counter-revenge might look like. As Edda said, if "the Germans knew of the dirty trick I am about to pull on them, my life (but that would not have any importance—I am so tired of everything) and that of my children would be seriously endangered." But she was torn. There was something she wanted even more than living: "even if I…have to die, I want first to avenge Galeazzo."

* * *

Frances quickly alerted Allen Dulles that the deal was unraveling. Dulles had one card that he thought they could play that might reassure Edda. Back in August, when the Americans arrested Zenone Benini as a fascist and when the Ciano Diaries were first catching American intelligence interest, Zenone had written that letter for Edda as part of an effort to show cooperation. In his letter, Zenone recorded that Galeazzo's last wishes were for his diaries to be passed over to the Allies and published so the world would know what had happened.

The original copy of Zenone's letter had been forwarded to Washington, DC, but from there Allen Dulles wasn't sure whether it had ever made its way back through the intelligence circuitry and reached Edda. A copy of the letter, however, was still sitting in a cabinet in the US intelligence services offices in Bern, and Dulles decided that now was the moment to utilize it. There had been no way to ensure communications reached Edda safely until her friendship with Frances.

"If she has not already received it, I feel sure she would desire to read it, and, of course, she may keep this copy, if she so desires," Allen Dulles wrote to Frances on December 15, enclosing a copy of Zenone Benini's letter. Allen Dulles was scheduled to travel to Paris the whole next week, and he knew it was difficult timing. He promised that he would come see Frances for an update as soon he returned to Switzerland. And he gave

Frances an extraordinary charge: Her mission was to close this deal for the Americans in his absence.

Privately, Dulles thought that Frances had her work cut out for her. Tracy Barnes noted in an internal telegram that: "Edda is a psychopathic case under [the] influence [of a] Swiss psychoanalyst whose motives and connections [are] dubious. She promises diaries as goodwill gesture one day and the next asks large monetary payment to protect interest children and also some letter of acknowledgment. Naturally matter requires most discreet handling from every viewpoint." Allen Dulles guessed that was probably a pretty good summary.

The letter from Zenone did help to assure Edda, but the strategy also created a new complication. Edda decided that she didn't want to do anything now until she first talked to Zenone, who had been with Galeazzo in the cell on his last night in Verona, about what her husband would have wanted. The Bern office scrambled to pressure Zenone Benini to write again to Edda, urging her to give the Americans the diaries. Zenone refused. He took seriously her concerns about the risk to her life and to the life of the children and would not do anything to pressure Edda to place them in danger.

Edda was now worried as well about a double cross from the Americans: Would the Allies classify the material in the notebooks once they had them translated, preventing publication, or would they release details as part of the war effort, making publication redundant? Both would deprive her of publication income. And how much income would that be? she wanted to know. She and Paul Ghali were still haggling over a price for the publication rights, with Edda sometimes demanding incredible sums. Ultimately, the State Department would agree—off the record—to backstop the payment for the newspaper. But when it had all been arranged and the OSS photographer arrived at the appointed time to make a copy of the papers, Edda had changed her mind again.

She needed, she now insisted, to speak directly to someone in the American government, to get direct assurances. This meant, of course, Allen Dulles. Edda wrote now to Frances to explain: "when your 'important friend' comes I should like to talk with him because, though I am willing with all my heart to carry through the deal the whole thing is too important for me (and I am not thinking of money) to take wild chances blindfolded....Your important friend could come with his car and take me for a ride (not in the American sense of it I mean to say)."

* * *

Edda sent her letter just before Christmas. Frances was busy with holiday preparations at Le Guintzet, where along with managing the children there was a fraught house party, in which pleasure was mixed with some inevitable business. Movie star Drue Mackenzie Robertson— better known after her third marriage as the socialite Drue Heinz—was there for the holiday, along with her soon-to-be-second-husband Dale W. Maher, a senior American diplomat in Bern. Drue signed herself in the Le Guintzet guest book as "Queenie the strip tease Queen," a sly nod to the exotic dancer and spy Mata Hari. Newspapers reported openly after the war that the English-born Drue was working with British intelligence. There were artists, aristocratic Yugoslavian refugees, and a scattering of other Americans. But to Frances's annoyance, among the houseguests was Roselyne Radziwiłł. The princess had already applied by Christmas that year to the Catholic Church for the annulment that would allow her and Louis to marry.

Frances's brief, distracted silence nearly cost them the deal, as Edda began to consider selling the diaries to other parties. Father Pancino had only recently returned to Italy, but he promised to come again to see her over the winter. Edda, cooped up at the psychiatric hospital with three children on school holidays, began to worry she had overplayed her hand when she didn't hear from Frances over the holiday. "Dear Frances," Edda wrote on December 30,

> I was just wondering what had happened to you and everybody else—I suppose everything will turn up O.K. one of these days and just now I don't want to worry too much....[The children] are fine but they certainly tire me out....I wish to God to be, next year, somewhere else, free, with no worries of money and a few friends around me—you, one of them. I'll ring you up on Monday morning and let's hope for the best & otherwise I shall have to try my hand at something else— Happy new year, dear Frances, and lots of love.

The letter must have reached Frances sometime on December 30, a Saturday, or by the following morning, because Allen Dulles, back in Switzerland, quickly got word of it. He may even have been an unregistered guest at Le Guintzet. By Sunday, December 31, 1944, Allen Dulles reported in a hasty secret cable back to Washington on New Year's Eve, "Believe best line to take that Edda should desire [to] make diaries available as generous gesture to help Allies and to present husband's memory in correct light to history....Unless Washington disapproves, prepared [to] pay reasonable amount for diaries, had in mind something between $5,000 to $10,000. Hope [to] arrange this payment through newspapers....Next few days particularly important." It was also clear to Allen Dulles that regardless of the risks, he was going to have to go see Edda Ciano in person.

* * *

Allen Dulles asked Frances to arrange a meeting for January 7 in Monthey. The Swiss were watching Edda—as was the lurking Gestapo—

and the team would need to work carefully to ensure that the meeting was not detected. If any of them were discovered engaged in covert operations to obtain political diaries from Mussolini's daughter, it would jeopardize all their status in Switzerland. And there was the constant risk of Edda being kidnapped anytime she left the clinic.

Frances arranged it with the deft skill that Dulles had come to admire in his unofficial agent. Her plan was simple, she explained. Edda was always allowed to go for a walk at lunchtime around the clinic grounds. There was a gate at one side. She and Edda had agreed that Edda would set out that afternoon for her walk, wearing heavy walking boots and a thick wool skirt, nothing to suggest anything other than a snowy ramble. She would walk where the grounds skirted the road. They would travel down the road by car. Their car would pass and stop near the gate, and Edda would step through the passageway. Inside the car she would find Frances and Paul—both familiar faces—and the "important friend," whose name was not known to Edda but was Allen Dulles.

Switzerland in January can be bitterly cold. The snow crunched under the tires. The team spotted Edda in the distance coming along the road, a thin, tall figure, just as Frances had planned, and they pulled to the agreed-upon spot. It was a clear day, blindingly bright, and Edda was visibly nervous. As the car slowed, she anxiously squinted, looking to see Paul and Frances. She was never certain it would not be the Germans. The Gestapo was watching for any opportunity to snatch her as one means of getting at the diaries. Frances remembered later that Edda, terrified, her hands shaking, got into the car without saying a word, and they drove on to a restaurant nearby at the railway station on the line between Lausanne and St. Maurice where Frances had made a reservation. They would pretend to be four friends dining.

And for the first hour or two, the talk was, indeed, light and social. The team was trying to talk Edda down and relax her. By the second hour, though, Allen Dulles, realizing Edda would never come around to the point and looking discreetly at his watch, finally asked her directly and without preamble: Was she going to give the diaries to the American government? Edda paused. She wasn't ready to answer and instead started to tell them again the story of her trials in Rome and the escape to Switzerland. She repeated that she still wanted to talk to Zenone Benini in person. She wanted to get out of Switzerland and beyond the reach of the Germans before deciding. She was afraid of what the Gestapo would do in retribution. She wanted to be sure she had commercial rights before she proceeded and that there wasn't a trick. She wanted to be certain the diaries would be published. She wanted to think.

The team let Edda talk. Allen Dulles was in charge now, and he had already come to the conclusion that, if Edda talked long enough, she was sure to realize that she was already out of options. When lunch was over, Edda asked if she and Allen Dulles could speak alone over coffee. Frances and Paul waited in the station lobby. For an hour they talked, and Dulles wrote later in his notes of the meeting that Edda:

> was obviously torn between the desire to make the diaries available and the reluctance to part with what she considered was her last asset toward both personal and financial rehabilitation…she wanted assurances regarding the commercial publication of the diaries; she wanted to help restore Ciano's political reputation which she felt had been misrepresented…she wanted to go through with the deal and yet felt that once she had done it, she had put herself largely in our hands.

Dulles afterward admitted his grudging respect for Edda after that meeting. She was difficult. She was traumatized and suspicious. However, she was not wrong: She *would* be in their hands once she passed over the diaries. "I frankly admit she behaved with a good deal of dignity and far more reasonably than I had expected," he wrote. He accepted, too, that Edda was not wrong to be afraid of the danger she was in with the Germans. She and the children would need constant protection.

After that third hour, Allen Dulles had done it. Edda did not look happy, but she was a realist. Dulles explained: The diaries had value to the Americans right now. But the time was coming and soon when the war would end, and then they would not have the same strategic importance. Deciding to abandon her neutrality would have no value once the war was over. Now was the moral crisis, not later. And the Americans would not pay for the diaries. That was not possible, he insisted, maintaining the official line from the State Department. Naturally, a newspaper might, but that was a private transaction. If Edda wished to do the right thing, it would be to her and Galeazzo's credit in the post-fascist world that was coming. She could keep all rights to publication. The Americans had no wish to deprive her of the intellectual property or means of supporting her family once the war was over, although wartime strategy might require the Allies to make some strategic use of portions before then. Strategy might require them to suppress other passages for the time being. But that was all in the future.

Allen Dulles was driving what he and Edda both knew was a hard bargain. Despite that knowledge, Edda agreed that afternoon to let the Americans copy the diaries in her possession. Dulles set up the photography to take place the next day, January 8, at the Monthey clinic. He decided that the "beautiful" Tracy Barnes had better be the agent to handle that mission, as a bit of added insurance.

* * *

On the night of January 8, Tracy Barnes, Paul Ghali, and a photographer—some say an agent named Schachter, although Frances's daughter Jacqueline remembers clearly that it was an agent named Laxton—were smuggled with equipment into Edda's room at the Monthey clinic. They would have to work quickly overnight. There were more than a thousand pages to be photographed, and they had to get it done without being detected by the Swiss police or the staff at the clinic.

According to Father Guido Pancino, who claimed to already have removed the diaries from Edda's possession, it was Edda—or someone acting for Edda and with the password—who collected the diaries from Credit Suisse, where he had deposited them. Perhaps Edda never collected them at all, knowing they were copies. Perhaps Guido Pancino was lying. Perhaps Edda had understood all along that Pancino—who had been in touch again with Edda in December, as Mussolini, seeing the end in sight, grew more panicked—had long since fled with the diaries she had given him, and what she had was only the remainder. But if anyone picked the diaries up from Credit Suisse in Bern, where Frances still traveled with her cosseted little dog Badsy on her curious wartime trips, we can guess that it would have been Frances and not Edda, who was still under intense surveillance. Frances was the one who, above all, Edda now trusted.

That story, however it unfolded, is lost to history. Whatever their route to Monthey, the original diaries of Galeazzo Ciano were at the clinic that night when the photography started. The agent drew the blackout curtains tightly, to conceal the flash of bulbs, and the cameraman fiddled with his equipment. They laid the diaries open on the table, while Edda fretted. Once all the gear was in place, the photo session started. Paul and Tracy would flip the pages, while the photographer worked.

The flash illuminated the room. They were under way. Suddenly, an electric crack and darkness. Nurses filled the hallways, assuring startled patients and bringing lanterns. There were shouts. Someone stumbled and swore. The disaster had struck almost immediately—all the drama of an institutional power failure in a psychiatric hospital.

The photographic equipment and lighting had blown the electrical fuses, sending the Monthey clinic and all their plans into chaos. Edda felt sure it was a sign and wanted to cancel. The team realized that, once the power came back on, any attempt to carry on would only blow the fuses all over again. Sooner or later, their secret rendezvous would be discovered, and then all hell really would break loose. By the time arrangements were made for another day, Edda would have changed her mind. It looked as if the American mission to obtain the diaries of Galeazzo Ciano was destined to fail at the last minute. The operation had gone down, not in flames but in infuriating darkness.

CHAPTER 18

The Ciano Diaries

January 8, 1945–June 25, 1945

Paul found the clinic telephone and discreetly put in a call to Frances with the discouraging update. She would pass the news through channels at the house of spies to Allen Dulles. The operation was a bust. They would need to try again another day and move the operation to a safe location. Assuming, of course, that Edda didn't change her mind again and that they could keep her and the diaries safe a little longer from the Gestapo.

Frances thought quickly. She knew that Edda would refuse to let them take Galeazzo's papers anywhere without her. Edda never let the remaining diaries out of her sight. She was terrified of being tricked and losing them. Why didn't they come to Le Guintzet? They could copy all night at the estate, uninterrupted. Frances would come and collect Edda in person. She had her little sports car, courtesy of Allen Dulles, and she adored driving. Edda would trust her. If Tracy Barnes and Allen Dulles's team could smuggle Edda out of the clinic, she would come and get her and the diaries.

Sources are conflicting on what happened next. Some say that Frances set off that same night. Some say the operation was rescheduled for the next evening. What is not in dispute is that when Frances warmed up the Fiat and took off in darkness for Monthey, to collect Edda and bring her to Fribourg for a late-night photo session, she was well aware that rural mountain roads made her and Edda tempting targets for the Gestapo. The drive was a terrible risk for both of them. Edda was under constant surveillance, and it was a long drive on lonely roads for two women. The journey would take two hours in each direction. Neither Frances nor Edda would ever forget that drive—either the frisson of fear or the excitement. Edda would later talk of it to her friend as their "adventure." Neither of them talked that night of grand ideas and moral choices, but both were aware that they were delivering something important, something aimed at what they each believed was justice.

The convoy to Le Guintzet—Edda and Frances in the Fiat Topolino and apparently an OSS team and Paul in another vehicle—rolled into the gravel drive sometime after midnight. At the estate, they trooped down to the manor's cavernous working cellars, and Jacqueline de Chollet, six years old that winter, remembers the hubbub and seeing them gathered around while a local photographer took shots of the diaries spread out on a kitchen table. She remembers too that her mother, risking both their lives and dreading with every mile the Gestapo, drove Edda back to the clinic in the predawn hours, so her midnight adventure would not be discovered at daybreak and Edda would not face the risk of deportation. At just after 4:00 A.M., on either January 10 or January 11, 1945, while Frances idled around the corner, Edda clambered through a window and back into her room at the clinic, waved, and then Frances was off again, back over the mountain roads she loved driving.

Unfortunately, Edda and Frances's predawn adventure did not go as seamlessly as they had hoped. An intrepid Swiss journalist lurking outside the convent, hot on the trail of Edda's reported marriage and looking for the scoop on another scandal for Mussolini's "nymphomaniac" daughter, witnessed her returning through a window and concluded she had been off meeting a lover. The newspapers were full in the days that followed of unsavory stories about Edda's licentious overnight activities, and it was a stark warning of how easily the Germans might have spotted them had they been looking. And the scurrilous stories in the papers were better than the truth: the breaking story that Edda had just passed over to the Americans Count Ciano's explosive wartime diaries.

* * *

Back in her room at dawn, Edda immediately regretted her decision and panicked. What if the Americans double-crossed her after all? What would the Germans do now to her and the children in retaliation? Hilde Beetz and the Germans had tricked her and Galeazzo. Hadn't the Germans before that promised to take them safely to Spain and instead delivered them into the power of Joachim von Ribbentrop, her husband's sworn enemy, in Munich? What evidence would she have, now that the Americans had copies, that the publication rights were hers? She was desperately broke and saw no other way of restoring her family fortunes. "I have put all my cards on the table and have confidence in you and your government and I expect a fair deal," she wrote to Allen Dulles:

> I am no fool, or dumb, and I can help a lot. Things are not as easy as they looked…I am waiting with great anxiety your answer. Don't make me wait too long or I shall have a second and fatal nervous breakdown. Forgive the mistakes, but it's five in the morning, not able to sleep and too worried to bother about the right spelling.

Edda considered. She did have one other piece of leverage. There were diaries that were still in Italy, hidden at Ramiola—"the chocolates." Edda tried to dangle them now, adding, "Another thing, the rest. The complement of the diaries are still in Italy—if you take me out of here, I am willing to go and fetch them, only Pucci and I know where they are. Pucci does not know that I know."

What Edda did not know is that the diaries they had hidden—which included some of the most damaging and sensitive of all Galeazzo's papers—were already in Germany. Only Edda and Emilio had known their location. But Emilio Pucci had fallen hard for the beguiling Hilde, and he had told her everything. Hilde Beetz had turned them over, not in an act of betrayal but in a desperate attempt to save herself. Though in saving herself she had accomplished her intelligence mission.

* * *

In Weimar, Germany, Hilde was at that very moment working in secret to complete the translation of "the chocolates" for her superiors. Just two days later, on January 12, 1945, Hilde would finish her work on the papers in German possession. That day, she would send the original manuscripts and her translations to Berlin, as were her orders. She had been explicitly instructed to make no copies. Each night, under tight security, she had returned her drafts and the originals to the Gestapo office in Weimar for safekeeping. There had been no breach in security. Once her superiors had read Galeazzo Ciano's manuscripts and taken whatever steps the content required, the documents would be destroyed. Both the down-payment papers and the Ramiola "chocolates" were gone or would be perhaps in a matter of days. Edda just didn't know it.

* * *

Now that Allen Dulles had Galeazzo Ciano's diaries, it was crucial that the material be transferred to the United States under tight security. The American government, already looking ahead to the trials that would eventually take place in Nuremberg, understood that the diaries were powerful evidence especially against Joachim von Ribbentrop, and possibly also against Ernst Kaltenbrünner and Heinrich Himmler. There was also every reason to believe that the materials, in the short term, would work as important propaganda: one more small weight that would, finally, conclusively, tip the balance of the war in the direction of the Allies.

There was no way to send a thousand photographs by telegram. Classified material had to be carried in secret on a flight out of Europe and routed through an Allied base or neutral country. The journey would involve traveling over land through Vichy France and crossing Spain to an air base in Portugal. Someone flying from Lisbon would need to hand-deliver the photographic films to Washington, and it had to be someone prepared to accept that he—or she—might not be able, if the political situation changed, to return immediately to Switzerland. Someone who was an American. Someone US intelligence unreservedly trusted. Allen Dulles could not risk a professional agent like Cordelia Dodson or Tracy Barnes, not in 1945 with the last, crucial stage of the war unfolding. So Frances took the mission.

By now, Frances had not been home to America since that week, nearly five years earlier, when she sailed out of New York Harbor for France with Louis, in the first flush of love and having just lost custody of her teenage daughter in order to protect her marriage. That daughter was now a grown woman. Louis had other pursuits. The children lived in another world, with maids and nannies. Her marriage was collapsing. And this work—her work as a spy, her adventure with Edda—was the most important thing that had happened in her life.

Both Paul Ghali and Frances's daughter Jacqueline remember different parts of Frances's last adventure, her secret flight to carry the Ciano Diaries to America, allowing us to piece together the story. Years later, when queried on whether it had been Frances who acted as the American courier, Paul Ghali's wife went back and looked in her by-then-late husband's files. "You mention the American lady, Mme. De Chollet, whose name Paul used," she wrote: "I was 90% certain she was the lady who got the bottle with the film to the United States but I wanted to make it sure for 100% and unearthed the big file of the Ciano Diary through which I went. Result: Yes, it was Mme. Frances de Chollet who did it. Apparently, she was a good friend of Edda Ciano in Switzerland."

Jacqueline has different but complementary memories of that winter. Her mother hated flying but told her when she was older the story of how she once flew in an "airship" to the United States from Lisbon to take something to America. She would have had to have left Switzerland unseen, have traveled across France and Spain, and she must have done so on a separate passport, because hers is notably silent on any record of her travels. One likes to imagine Frances driving the Topolino fast along the French Riviera, the canisters of film that she and Edda had saved for history on the passenger seat beside her. That part of the story Frances never mentioned. She only told her daughter later that the takeoff from Lisbon in rough weather was a nightmare and the only part that truly terrified her.

And with that last trip to deliver the copies of the diaries of Galeazzo Ciano to the State Department in America, it seems that the intelligence career of Frances de Chollet ended as suddenly as it had started.

* * *

Frances's friendship with Edda Ciano did not end. They had become, through it all, sisters of a kind: a friendship forged in adversity and the sorrows of two middle-aged women not certain any longer where they were going. Frances was determined that Edda would not be double-crossed—or just plain forgotten. She delivered the films, visited family in America, and then returned to Switzerland. Frances took on the role of Edda's financial adviser. She was going to ensure that Edda did receive from the publication of the diaries the funds she needed to secure her family's independence.

Paul Ghali's newspaper, the *Chicago Daily News*, initially offered thirty-five hundred dollars for the rights to publish the Ciano Diaries, which the US Department of State reserved the right to censor if needed for national security. Edda had counted on a much larger sum and was despairing. Ultimately, at Frances's urging as the spy-house hostess, Allen Dulles and the State Department would approve an unrecorded royalty to Edda, paid through the newspaper, of twenty-five thousand dollars for world rights in English. It was nothing more than the diaries deserved. They were clearly a bombshell and destined to become a bestseller. Allen Dulles saw it at once when he received the first translations back from the United States in March 1945. Here was evidence to indict the Germans—Joachim von Ribbentrop especially—of war crimes. Frances also reserved rights in French. Edda assigned to her friend the sole right to negotiate those commercial contracts.

With publication assured, Edda grew increasingly anxious about the fallout. How were they going to get her and the children out of Switzerland and harm's way? There was some talk in Allen Dulles's cables back to Washington of Edda Ciano applying for asylum in the United States, but that went nowhere. None of the Allies wanted to touch the problem of Mussolini's daughter in the spring of 1945, with the war not quite yet over. That left Edda still a refugee in Switzerland and there on suffrage, though her friends had managed now to have her moved to better accommodations in Montreaux. Edda's great fear was angering the Swiss. "[W]e must be very careful," Edda urged Frances. "For God's sake tell

Paul to be very careful…because if the authorities get wind of something off, I'll go to another convent."

* * *

By the end of April 1945, the Allies were on the verge of victory in Europe, and loose ends were starting to get tied up hastily. The Nazis had two important parts of Galeazzo's papers: the down-payment papers, delivered as part of the planned prison break, and "the chocolates"— the papers recovered from Dr. Melocchi at the clinic in Ramiola. Hilde Beetz had been assigned to translate these documents, and some captured personal records of Benito Mussolini, while she was working from home in Weimar, Germany.

When Hilde completed her translations, the Gestapo had sent Galeazzo's original manuscripts and the translations to the Nazi senior command, where the cache ultimately made its way into the hands of Adolf Hitler. Hitler reviewed the materials in German possession, and then sometime in April or May 1945, just before the end, personally ordered the destruction of the Ciano Diaries. Both the originals and Hilde's translations perished.

* * *

Edda's father famously did not survive those last weeks of the war in Europe either. Neither did Clara Petacci, who had tried on that last night in Verona to save Galeazzo. Mussolini had lived in fear of what would happen if he betrayed Hitler. But the danger, in the end, was elsewhere. On April 28, in a small village in northern Italy, partisans in the local resistance, having tracked down Il Duce, lined Benito Mussolini and his mistress up against a wall and mowed them down with gunfire. Their bodies were later strung up, a ghastly image caught on camera. One wonders whether, in those final moments as he faced a vigilante firing squad, Mussolini thought of how his death paralleled the one that he had ordered for his son-in-law that morning in January little more than a year earlier. One wonders, too, whether he thought of Edda, his favorite daughter.

Edda's fury burned as brightly as ever. The Swiss press reported—accurately or not, no one is quite sure—that Edda, when she heard of her father's death and, later, the public abuse of his body, put on a bright-red dress and went for a walk of defiant celebration.

* * *

Benito Mussolini was executed on April 28. Two days later Eva Braun and Adolf Hitler committed suicide in a bunker in Berlin. The war ended officially in Europe little more than a week later, on May 8, 1945, and before the month was out Hilde Beetz's boss Ernst Kaltenbrünner would be arrested, and Heinrich Himmler would be dead from suicide. In June, the Allies would arrest Galeazzo's sworn enemy, the man even the other Nazis hated: Joachim von Ribbentrop.

It was only a matter of time, Hilde knew, before she and her husband would be arrested. She had spent the war as a Nazi spy, working hand in glove with the Gestapo. Gerhard Beetz had been a senior military commander. Hilde retreated to her mother's home and tried to keep a low profile. But she was just waiting for the knock on the door, and she knew she was looking at a prison sentence.

* * *

The Second World War continued, of course, in the Pacific theater until mid-August, but for those in Italy, Switzerland, and Germany there were wild celebrations and other painful reckonings in May. The Swiss wanted to be rid of Edda Ciano. She had never been a welcome refugee, and what to do with her and with Emilio Pucci now were open questions. Emilio wanted to return to Italy, but his status as an officer (and an AWOL officer at that) complicated his repatriation, and he risked facing a court-martial for desertion. A trial would almost certainly end with Emilio in prison too. Cordelia Dodson, his old friend from Reed College and OSS agent, intervened to try to save him.

Without Emilio's heroic efforts, Cordelia argued to Allen Dulles, Edda and the diaries would never have made it to Switzerland. When Allen Dulles was fully apprised of Emilio's role in the preservation of the manuscripts and of his role in Edda's escape from Italy, he agreed that, if Emilio put his story on the record for the eventual prosecutors, something would be done to ease his post-war return to Italy. In May and June, Emilio was debriefed twice by the US government and recorded in two extensive documents the dramatic story of their escape from Ramiola and his torture at the hands of the Gestapo. Emilio also provided detailed information on the location of "the chocolates"—the portions of Galeazzo's diaries that, as far as Edda and Emilio knew, were still hidden with Dr. Melocchi.

As soon as the war was over, Allen Dulles personally traveled to Ramiola to retrieve the diaries and the jewels that Edda and Emilio had left hidden at the electrical power station. There was, of course, no hope of finding them. Hilde Beetz, confronted with the accusations of Gestapo-informant Father Guido Pancino, had "discovered" them in a bid to save her life and passed them over to the Nazis. The Germans, Allen Dulles learned, had beaten them to the cache, and he did not need to be told that Hitler had already ordered their destruction. It was obvious to Allen Dulles that this part of the Ciano Diaries was lost to history. The Americans had received from Edda a small portion of the originals: five slim, papery volumes out of what had once been three small suitcases of papers. The diaries the Allies possessed—saved by the joint efforts of Hilde, Edda, and Frances—were crucially important. But they were only a sliver.

* * *

On May 27, 1945, Allen Dulles held in his hands a package of papers. They were the translations of the diaries that Edda Ciano, with the help of Frances de Chollet, had allowed the Americans to photograph that night in Le Guintzet on the kitchen table. Before Allen Dulles was Robert H. Jackson, appointed by the president as the chief US counsel and the head prosecutor at the war-crimes trials that would come to be simply known as Nuremberg, after their location. The scope of the Holocaust in Europe was so breathtaking in its depravity that the International Military Tribunal would, for the first time in history, attempt to bring the major perpetrators to justice. The charges would be crimes against the peace, conspiracy, war crimes, and crimes against humanity. Allen Dulles personally handed that packet of papers to Justice Jackson. They would indict Ernst Kaltenbrünner and Galeazzo's archrival, Joachim von Ribbentrop, Germany's foreign minister. Hilde Beetz, Edda Ciano, and Frances de Chollet: They had each risked their lives to make that moment possible.

Robert Jackson had looked forward to this moment and noted it in his diaries. He fully understood the importance of the diaries of Galeazzo Ciano, even if he did not fully comprehend that it was three women who had raced above all to save them. Like Paul Ghali, Robert Jackson wrote them, however unwittingly, out of the history. "Dulles," he wrote, "has maintained an OSS post in Switzerland and it is a most valuable one for us. He has…Count Ciano's diaries.…After long negotiation, Dulles personally got the diaries. It contains much said to be very damaging to Ribbentrop." Allen Dulles considered securing the Ciano Diaries one of his major wartime victories.

* * *

By June, Edda's fate had been decided. She would be returned to Italy. As Mussolini's daughter, her position was precarious. Nothing could massage the fact of who her father and her husband had been. Nothing could change the fact that she and Galeazzo had both been, before those mid-war course corrections, fascists. The Swiss, who had never wanted Edda Ciano, were determined to expel her, and Edda wrote a last letter to Allen Dulles, confused and worried about her future. She could not understand why she was being forced to return to a country where she knew she was hated. "I am not a criminal of war (how could I be?)," she insisted. "My government has not asked for me. I have never in my life done anything against the Swiss. Anyway if they send me back to Italy I'll know the meaning of death soon enough." She saw how the story had ended for Galeazzo and her father. It was true that Edda had never served any political role. Her support for Mussolini and for Hitler had been personal and symbolic. But Edda's moral universe was myopic. She would never truly comprehend, even decades later, her culpability as a fascist. All Edda could see was the violence that had been inflicted upon her family and the sacrifices they had made in turning their back on fascism in the summer of 1943 with Galeazzo's vote at Grand Council.

Edda would ultimately be deported back to Italy, tried for crimes that included acting in favor of fascism, the persecution of Jews, and contributing to unleashing of war. In Italy, she was sentenced to house arrest for a period of two years on the small island of Lipari, where she soon found a handsome man to keep her company. The Ciano children were left to stay in Rome for those years with Frau Schwarz, their Swiss nanny.

* * *

For Frances de Chollet, the end of the war was the end of an adventure and a moment of unforgettable and sometimes heartbreaking and bitter clarity. Already newspapermen like Paul Ghali were writing her out of the story of the hunt for the Ciano Diaries, not out of any malign intent, but simply because it was irresistible to be the man who was the hero of such a fine spy caper. She was a wealthy banker's wife and a forty-something mother, and women across America and Europe who had taken part in the war effort, from Allen Dulles's amateur agents and the code breakers in Bletchley to Rosie the Riveter, were expected to retreat back to the domestic, making room for the returning soldiers. For Frances, that retreat to the domestic was impossible. Frances and Louis's marriage by now was frayed beyond recovery. Both had taken on other lovers. Louis would soon file for divorce and eventually marry that fixture from the Fribourg salon at Le Guintzet, Roselyne Radziwiłł. Frances was swept up in a liaison with a French general and traveled with him to Germany in the weeks after the end of the war, where she witnessed and photographed the sweeping destruction of bombed-out cities. She felt afterward that, in her work with Edda saving the diaries, she had participated in the fight to defeat the Nazis.

That participation might not have been celebrated publicly. But Frances was rewarded for her efforts as an amateur spy that summer with the thing she most wanted: her motorcar. Allen Dulles made sure that it happened. When she and Louis fled Paris in 1940, one step ahead of police trouble for Louis's work in smuggling funds out of the occupied capital, Frances had been forced to leave behind her beloved gray Packard sedan. She had parked it in the warehouse of the Cadoricin shampoo factory, owned by a friend of the family. She had no idea if the Germans had discovered it and confiscated her most cherished possession, but she dreamed that, somehow, it still might be waiting for her there under the sheets and amid the stacked boxes. That, she told Allen Dulles, was the thanks she wanted for her part in the spy mission that he considered one of the greatest American intelligence achievements in wartime Switzerland: permission to go to Paris and find out.

Allen Dulles, to his credit, did not write Frances out of the history, at least not in his private communications to the State Department. "[A]n American girl married to a Swiss named Mrs. Frances Cholet [sic] has rendered us very real service," he wrote to officials in the department. "She is now applying through the Consulate for an amendment to her passport for France as she has a house and furniture in Paris....While this trip has no direct military significance, I should like to do her the slight favour of supporting the application....I would appreciate if you would have our State Department liaison man mention this."

Frances was granted that permission. With her visa to Paris in hand, she traveled back to Paris to fetch her Packard, which she discovered dusty and dry after four years in storage, but safe. Jacqueline de Chollet, thinking of her mother, remembers how she went to Paris, fixed the car herself as an able mechanic, and drove it with the windows down, her scarf flying in the wind, all the way home to Switzerland, when the rest of her domestic world was crashing down around her. "That," Jacqueline says, "was my mother."

* * *

On June 25, 1945, Paul Ghali's newspaper, the *Chicago Daily News*, published its first serial installment of the diaries of Count Galeazzo Ciano, covering the years from 1939 to 1943. Each week for the next month the installments riveted America, ultimately becoming, when released as a book in 1946, an instant *New York Times* bestseller. Only those in the inner circle of conspirators, who had fought to save the diaries and to persuade Edda to release them to the Americans, knew to mourn what was missing. Lost in Germany were the early volumes for the years 1937 and 1938, as well as Galeazzo's more fulsome records of his foreign-office conversations and Edda's own wartime diaries. But what was in the official diaries that had traveled to Switzerland with Edda was enough to be explosive—and enough to cause Joachim von Ribbentrop some very serious problems.

Edda and Galeazzo Ciano,
1930s

Wedding photo of Edda
and Galeazzo Ciano, 1930

Edda Mussolini

Galeazzo Ciano, 1937

Emilo Pucci

Raimonda Laza and
Susanna "Suni" Agnelli

Pietro Badoglio

Mussolini and Hitler

Joachim von Ribbentrop

Hilde Beetz, 1943

Ernest Kaltenbrunner
at Nuremberg

Wilhelm Hottl

Zenone Benini

Galeazzo Ciani at his trial
in Verona

Execution of
Galeazzo Ciano
and others

Frances de Chollet

Frances and Louis de Chollet,
crossing the Atlantic in 1940

Le Guintzet

Frances de Chollet
with her children,
c. 1940–41

Frances de Chollet's
passport photo.

Allen Dulles

Clara Petacci, Mussolini's last mistress

Virginia Agnelli with her children

Hilde Beetz, 1953

CHAPTER 19

The Rose Garden

June 30, 1945–October 16, 1945

Heinrich Himmler was dead, part of a wave of mass suicides of senior Nazi officials that swept Germany after Hitler's decision to take his life in his Berlin bunker. Ernst Kaltenbrünner and Joachim von Ribbentrop were in Allied custody, facing trial for war crimes. Wilhelm Harster, ultimately implicated in the murder of more than one hundred thousand Jews, was on the run. When he was finally found, he would also face trial for his war crimes in Holland and Italy. Wilhelm Höttl, arrested in early May, would slip the net. He had cannily reached out to the OSS in Switzerland in March 1945, offering his services as a double agent. In order to save his own skin, he promised to become a Nazi hunter and started naming all known Amt VI operatives.

And this was how on June 19, 1945, the US Army, in the person of a Lieutenant French, arrived at last on the doorstep in Weimar where Hilde Beetz lived with her elderly mother. Hilde had been expecting and dreading for weeks this moment. As a spy and agent for the Nazi regime's intelligence services, Hilde, like her superiors, could expect to be tried and imprisoned for her wartime activities. She was arrested and taken into custody as a German agent, and in the course of her interrogation, thanks to the intelligence previously provided to the Americans by her Nazi-hunter boss, Wilhelm Höttl, she was inevitably asked about her role in obtaining for the Germans the papers of Galeazzo Ciano.

Yes, Agent Beetz had captured the diaries for the Nazis as a spy and had translated them. She confirmed that the originals and her translations, when complete, had been sent to Berlin by the Gestapo. She could not confirm what her superiors had done with those documents, but she had reported to Kaltenbrünner, Himmler, and ultimately Hitler. She did not doubt that the materials had been destroyed. The manuscripts contained damaging information. She had always known they would disappear.

That, she told Lieutenant French, was why she had kept the secret copies.

* * *

Hilde had known she was violating direct orders. She had been explicitly told that copies were not permitted. Every afternoon, when she was done working on the translations for the day, she had delivered the papers to the Gestapo headquarters in Weimar for overnight safekeeping. Every morning, under tight security, she had checked them out again. Had she been discovered making surreptitious copies during those hours when she was alone with the manuscripts, the charge would have been insubordination and treason.

But Hilde had loved Galeazzo. He had been, she had confessed to his mother tearfully, the great love of her life. In translating the manuscripts, day by day, hour by hour, she had lived with his private words and thoughts, sentence by sentence. His voice had been, in a very real sense, with her constantly as she worked on the papers. Galeazzo's diaries were not some cool, detached record of what he had seen. They were intimate and gossipy and wry, just as he had been. He spoke not only of Roosevelt and Churchill, Hitler and Ribbentrop and war, but of intimate matters. How, at the grave of his father, "My youth, too, was buried in his grave," or of his wife "who is intelligent and outspoken." Sometimes his diaries included, too, letters Edda wrote to him, where she wrote of "that idiotic inconstancy which makes mine the most impossible of families," reminding him, "Dear Gallo, let's take it as it comes, chins up!"

Hilde had failed to save Galeazzo. His last wish as he confronted death was to see his diaries published, so the world would know the truth of what had happened in Italy. Hilde had wanted, at least, to keep her word to Galeazzo. Perhaps most important of all, no woman who had lost the man she loved was going to let go, no matter the risk, of the last piece of him. So according to the report that Hilde gave Lieutenant Stewart French, she had done the obvious thing: She "preserved copies of diary entries for the period 22 August 1937 to 31 July 1939, together with carbon copies of her translations."

Lieutenant French was stunned. He wanted to be certain he understood correctly: She had saved copies of the missing diaries of Galeazzo Ciano and copies of the translations of all his missing papers? Where were these papers? Hilde paused. She had buried them, she confessed, in a tin canister in the bottom of her rose garden. She sat there often in the evenings, thinking.

Lieutenant French's official report, telegraphic in style, did not indulge in any scene setting, but the occasion was momentous. These were some of the most important records of the war, and agents across the Continent were hunting for them. All Stewart French recorded was that, spade in hand, representatives of the US Army and Nazi intelligence agent Hilde Beetz tramped out among the flowers. The canister was quickly found. It had only been recently buried, when Hilde became concerned that her home would be searched and afraid that she might lose them. The papers inside were dry and in excellent condition.

Nor were these all of Galeazzo Ciano's papers. "Frau Beetz," Lieutenant

French noted, "now discloses 2 other hiding places of Ciano papers. A. Como Italy with a family named Pessina…B. In Imersago Italy with Pio di Savoia former Spanish Ambassador to Vatican. C. Documents these 2 places believe to be at least equal value to those already in your possession." Lieutenant French wrote up his report—which came to be code-named the Rose Garden Papers—and forwarded the materials back to the Twelfth US Army Headquarters in Germany.

On June 30, 1945, the report of this astonishing discovery reached Allen Dulles in Switzerland. He received Galeazzo's papers not long after. Against all the odds, they had recovered now in Weimar from Frau Beetz's garden not only the missing two volumes of Galeazzo's foreign-office diaries but also the background Conversations and the files the count had called the Germania papers. They had found Edda's missing "chocolates."

But those two other caches of papers that Hilde now revealed, left behind with Tonino Pessina and with the former Spanish ambassador: Those fascinated Allen Dulles. Were those copies—or were they other, fresh materials? Allen Dulles's spy service hunted for them. The Pessina family had been visited by the Gestapo not long after Edda's escape to Switzerland and been subjected to a terrorizing interrogation. The family insisted that they had not passed over any manuscripts to the Germans and knew nothing of any papers. But Tonino could hardly be faulted if he had decided that it was safer to burn the materials. The papers said to be left with the Spanish ambassador disappeared without a trace.

* * *

The Americans had now a dilemma. What to make of Hilde Beetz? If her story was true, she had acted the part, as Allen Dulles saw it, of a self-appointed double agent for the Allies. She was a Nazi party member, had been throughout the war an Amt VI spy, and would normally be prosecuted as a war criminal. She could expect a modest prison sentence and "de-nazification"—a sweeping demotion that would end the career that Hilde had wanted. Yet she had worked to undermine the German mission and had worked to arrange for the diaries to reach the Allies. In her actions she had repudiated fascism no less than Galeazzo Ciano.

The situation was politically sensitive and would require intense scrutiny. Was there any chance the manuscripts in her possession were forgeries? They were destined to bear witness against Kaltenbrünner and Ribbentrop in international trials. To be tricked by a German spy would be a serious embarrassment. "[E]xtraordinary pains to examine the agent's background were taken in this case," the files on Hilde Beetz noted.

What the Americans learned was breathtaking. Hilde Beetz was an exceptional agent. One of the best of the best. And thank goodness it turned out she had been working clandestinely to support the Allies. At the end of the Second World War, with the Cold War already brimming over the horizon, her potential value as a spy in post-war Europe was apparent. Most immediately, here was the agent who could corroborate the information now offered to the Americans by her former boss, the volunteer Nazi hunter Wilhelm Höttl. If he could be vetted, he might be a high-value asset who could lead the Americans to a number of war criminals. But he was also clearly self-serving. Could he be trusted? If Hilde Beetz was brought in as a double agent, Wilhelm Höttl might well tell Hilde, whom he relied upon unstintingly and with whom he was, in all likelihood still infatuated, his real motives.

By July 1945, the Americans had confirmed that Hilde *had* acted the part of a double agent, working against German interests, in her efforts to save Galeazzo Ciano and his papers. A deal was struck. Former German Amt VI agent Hilde Beetz, in exchange for avoiding prosecution, would spy for the Americans in post-war Germany and she would feed them information in the short term on Wilhelm Höttl especially. "[B]ecause of the extremely delicate…project she is undertaking, and the possibility of her association with CIANO might someday lead someone, through misunderstanding, to believe us to be harboring a wicked internationally notorious queen of spies," she was thoroughly investigated. She was assigned, under cover as a secretary, as a "prospective double agent [in] operations against Soviet Intelligence Stations lying outside Berlin."

It was an offer that Hilde could not refuse. It was not simply whether she went to prison and was subject to "de-nazification." Her husband, Gerhard Beetz, had also been arrested as a German military officer, and his post-war fate was pending. She could either continue to work as an intelligence agent—a job she loved and at which she excelled—or she could face a decade of castigation, unemployment, and a possible prison sentence. As the American files on her case bluntly noted, "Our control over her is complete. She can be described as one of the few Germans with genuine anti-Nazi convictions developed prior to and during the war. She has strong westward orientations. Lastly, as insurance, her husband is a German officer now in American custody."

She and Gerhard Beetz divorced in 1947, not long after the war ended, but the American control over Hilde continued for more than another three decades, in one fashion or another. Deployed at first by the CIA, under a new identity, as a "penetration agent," tasked with "aiding current and prospective double agent operations against the Soviet[s]," she had a brief second and failed marriage to an American spy and then tried to rebuild herself and a third marriage as a journalist in West Germany in the 1950s. But as late as 1982, the CIA debated "reactivating" her as an agent. There was just one thing that gave the CIA pause about Hilde: As the file noted, she "is probably better acquainted with the history of our organization and its personnel than any other agent this base has ever run," thanks to a case officer in 1945 who also became "deeply infatuated" with her. That case officer may, indeed, have been the same spy who soon became her second husband. Whomever he was, one feels a twinge of sympathy for any agent assigned to "run" Hilde that first summer as the war ended. Even in her sixties, the CIA decided it was foolhardy to try to think one could control Hilde.

But the truth is also something harder and sadder. Hilde had found herself in the summer of 1943, in her early twenties, in that infernal thicket of moral decision and indecision. And because she had been a Nazi spy, there would never again be for her a straight path forward, any more than there was for Edda. Hilde was the spy who was not allowed to come in from the cold. Edda would always be Mussolini's daughter.

* * *

There is no record that Hilde and Edda ever spoke again after the war. Doing so would have been dangerous for both of them. For Hilde, especially, as an American spy in West Germany, given a "de-nazified" cover, contact with Mussolini's fascist daughter would have raised far too many questions. Nor would contact with a former Nazi intelligence operative have helped Edda, whose post-war life began with a criminal sentence in Italy when the Swiss finally deported their unwelcome refugee.

Frances and Edda did remain in touch after the war, at least for a time. They mourned together in November 1945 when Susanna's mother, Virginia Agnelli, as flamboyant and reckless as ever, died in a car accident in a pine forest outside San Rossore, in northern Italy. According to one of her biographers, Virginia and her chauffeur perished when the car he was driving swerved into oncoming traffic and collided with a US Army truck coming in the other direction. Among the "sisters in resistance" who helped to outwit the Nazis and deliver the papers of Galeazzo Ciano to the Americans and the war-crimes tribunal at Nuremberg, Virginia Agnelli and her daughters deserve to be counted. Virginia's friendship with Frances de Chollet served as an important point of connection between Frances and Edda at a point when establishing trust among strangers mattered. She had fought hard to help Edda when she was incarcerated in an "insane asylum" and was loyal to Emilio. Her daughters Clara and Maria Sole played bit parts in the intelligence drama that played out at Le Guintzet in the autumn of 1944. The role of her daughter Susanna, however, was fundamental.

Susanna Agnelli, perhaps an honorary fourth "sister" in this story, was the one person who connected Hilde, Emilio, Galeazzo, Edda, and Frances in a circle of friendship, and she knowingly took on the risks of defying the Gestapo. She did not go on to marry Prince Lanza or to become a practicing physician. Susanna Agnelli went on to become the Italian foreign minister after the war, the role once occupied by her ill-fated, imperfect, but much-loved friend Galeazzo Ciano, the first woman to hold that position.

The friendship of Edda and Frances endured. Edda never forgot the thrill or the terror of that "little trip" that she and Frances made from Monthey to Fribourg with Galeazzo's diaries or how she sneaked back through the window of her asylum before dawn, when their mission was accomplished, waving goodbye with a smile to Frances. Edda wrote wistfully to Frances, "I miss our talks and mysterious rendez-vous." The two women would always share too that particular solidarity that came from knowing the sorrow of a playboy husband. When the war was over, Frances had already decided that she would go home to America.

From her island imprisonment in Italy, Edda wrote to Frances in February 1946, just as Frances's marriage was in the final stages of its unraveling:

> Frances dear, how is life? Did you succeed in getting away from Switzerland and got to the States? It's a long time since our little trip together and I hope you have had a lovely time and no bothers.... How is Louis? Stepping out as usual?... The death of Virginia has been a terrible blow. It's [sic] seems incredible. Really Death is always at our back ready to catch

us. How is the weather? Here is fine though very cold because there is no heating whatsoever—so write to me: remember me to Louis. Lots of love.

As a postscript, Edda added, "Why don't you come to Italy and Lipari?" Frances never made it to the island. Edda's sentence was meant to last two years, but then, in June 1946, all political prisoners in Italy were granted amnesty. Edda spent, in the end, only ten months incarcerated on the island, returning to Rome and the children. By then, Edda, too, had fallen in love. Her boyfriend was a younger man, an island local named Leonida Bongiorno, who remembered afterward that when he met Edda in 1945 "she looked like a wounded small swallow." Edda begged Leonida to come with her to Rome. "Come and live with me," she wrote in passionate letters, "Don't abandon the happiness that God is offering you." Leonida, though, had already moved on. He had a new girlfriend, the woman whom he would shortly marry. In Rome, Edda spent the next decade staying cautiously out of the limelight. After the war, no one wanted to talk about fascism. Edda was Mussolini's daughter: a living reminder.

Emilio Pucci returned to Italy as well, his health and his fortune ruined. In 1946, broke and still suffering from headaches from his time with the Gestapo in Milan, Emilio signed up again with the new, postwar Italian air force, and tried to live on a small officer's salary. But needing recovery, Emilio met his destiny a year later, in 1947, when he took a leave of absence to take in the cold mountain air in Zermatt, Switzerland. Emilio had led the ski team at Reed College in Oregon. He and Edda had first met on the slopes in Cortina. He had sewn for Edda from her pajamas the belt she used to walk with Galeazzo's diaries across the border, and now he designed for a female friend fashion's first one-piece ski suit. Emilio Pucci's designs quickly took the world of haute couture by storm. By the 1950s he was an international star. By the 1960s,

American celebrity icons from Marilyn Monroe to Jackie Kennedy wore the bold and brightly colored designs from the "house of Pucci."

* * *

With the end of her marriage and the end of the war, Frances de Chollet went home to America. She felt later that in the story of the diaries, the limelight had all gone to Paul Ghali. He was the public-facing intrepid journalist who got the scoop. With Edda, she had risked her life at a moment when the Gestapo was hunting for Galeazzo's diaries and looking to kidnap Edda. With Edda she had driven, risking capture, over the mountains in darkness. She had reported directly to Allen Dulles from the house of spies as an amateur agent. She had flown with the films on a secret flight from Portugal back to Washington. History still made her anonymous. Frances was simply the "American girl" or "my blonde friend": the socialite and "banker's wife" who had stepped in with a "favor." She was too generous to resent it. All that mattered, she told her daughter, was that the diaries had been saved.

Frances had known even before the war ended that it would be a fleeting moment. Susanna Agnelli, a generation younger, might go on to a life on the world stage, might take up the role once held by Galeazzo. Hilde Beetz and Cordelia Dodson, nearly twenty years her junior, might go on to be spies, fighting the Cold War for the Allies. For Frances, forty-five the year that the conflict in Europe ended, World War II and the work she had done was a brief, midlife taste of freedom that soon ended. After the early death of Allen Dulles in 1969, Paul Ghali wrote a letter to Frances that summed up her experience:

> I am sure that Allen Dulles's sudden death was as much of a
> shock to you as it was to me. He was such a good friend of
> ours in Switzerland, and we have so many memories centering

around him....Everything that has been written about him has brought back our own Ciano Diary discovery, and the wonderful and generous help you gave me about it. Even so many years afterwards, I still think it was a great coup for which you and I were little rewarded but for which we have many reasons to be proud. I went through my Ciano files, and almost every page brings back memories of your remarkable ability to keep Edda in line and finally persuade her to let us have the Diaries. How very clever and able you were throughout that story. Of course, as you once put it before we parted, you had started on something so important that everything to follow seemed trivial... Your old friend, Paul."

She *had* started in Switzerland on something so important that everything after seemed trivial. But there was no way for Frances to pick up that thread. She had helped to deliver justice and had served her country. In Paul Ghali's telling of the story, though, he was the protagonist and hero. She was the handmaiden of history and the helper. Decades later, Frances's children would commemorate their irrepressible mother with a bench that still sits in New York City's Central Park. On it is inscribed a quote from Washington Irving that stands alongside Paul Ghali's memory of Frances: "There is in every true woman's heart a spark of heavenly fire, which lies dormant in the broad daylight of prosperity but which kindles up, and beams and blazes in the dark hour of adversity." In the darkest hour of the Second World War, Frances blazed quietly.

* * *

Frances never left a written record of what she thought about the news that broke in the autumn of 1945, in the aftermath of her delivery of Edda and the diaries to Le Guintzet that night when they were copied.

What did Frances think when she read in October of that year that, on the strength of the evidence provided in no small part by the diaries of Galeazzo Ciano, a verdict had come at Nuremberg for Joachim von Ribbentrop?

On October 16, 1945, Ribbentrop—who had done all that he could to destroy Galeazzo, and who was, in the end, undone in part by that enmity—was led to the gallows, hooded and bound, the first of the postwar executions. He would not be the last of the Nazis who had failed to outwit these courageous and complex women, the women who saved the manuscripts on which Justice Jackson based some of his strongest arguments for the prosecution. A year later, in October 1946, Hilde's big boss, Ernst Kaltenbrünner, would also hang at Nuremberg as a result of the evidence these women had provided.

Frances would not have celebrated death. But she had lived in Paris during the Nazi occupation, had witnessed the devastation of the Continent, and knew enough to recognize justice. Decades later, in the 1990s, when Frances thought back on those years, she mused, "moments remain to make me thankful that we were so lucky because so many others were not."

* * *

The trials at Nuremberg did not expiate the crimes that took place during the Second World War. No trial could make right the wrongs suffered in Europe by so many millions from 1939 to 1945. But whatever small measure of justice the trials at Nuremberg amounted to, a circle of intrepid women had made one important part of it possible. "These diaries are unquestionably, incomparably, the most interesting and important Italian memoir material regarding World War II," the CIA notes today in its rendering of the diaries' astonishing history. Frances Winslow de Chollet. Hildegard Burkhardt Beetz. Susanna and Virginia Agnelli.

Cordelia Dodson. And in all her complexity and with all her weaknesses, Edda Mussolini Ciano. These women helped to save those diaries and place them in the hands of prosecutors.

After the war, when the story was overshadowed by the larger-than-life personalities of men like the legendary Allen Dulles or newspaperman Paul Ghali, these women's stories faded into the background. But in the lived moment of what surely measures as one of the Second World War's greatest rescue missions, they were the key actors, sometimes for the first and only times in their lives, and their intelligence, resolve, and courage made some straighter path forward possible. None of them were perfect. All of them struggled in different ways with the complex terrain of betrayal and loyalty. But what they accomplished changed history. After that, what else could seem again as important?

Into Thin Air

1945–Present

About the diaries of Galeazzo Ciano, one other strange story still circulates among the elderly residents of a small village in the Italian Dolomites.

Historians cannot be certain whether all of Galeazzo Ciano's papers were recovered. There are no extensive gaps in the official, chronological diaries that cannot be accounted for, but what was the fate of the papers left with the Spanish ambassador at the Vatican or the documents left behind with their friends the Pessina family when Edda fled for Switzerland? What of the stories of papers passed with the aid of Delia di Bagno to the British spy Christina Granville? Were they simply copies of the originals, left in multiple locations, as Galeazzo always said, or was there another, now lost cache of personal papers? No one knows for certain.

In the village of Erte, nestled in a mountain valley of the Italian Dolomites, though, they tell the story of how, a few weeks after the end of the war, in the summer of 1945, the village priest was a man named Father Guido Pancino, a "controversial, elusive character," rumored to have been a Nazi agent. One day in the small village, two large cars—

they could only have been government cars in 1945, no civilian could get petrol—drew up in front of the church and took from the hands of the village priest two padlocked boxes.

A third locked box the priest kept back in secret. The area around Erte is known for its cliffs. When the men in the black cars departed, Father Pancino called for the boy who was the best rock climber in the area. He asked the boy to hide that box "in a small ravine on a sheer face of Monte Cornetto, between rock crags and narrow ledges." When the boy asked what was inside, he was told a gun, some gold, and a lot of papers.

ACKNOWLEDGMENTS

The author wishes to thank and acknowledge the generosity of Jacqueline de Chollet, daughter of Frances and Louis de Chollet, for providing family recollections; access to the Le Guintzet wartime guest book, her unpublished manuscript, and private photographs; and permission to quote from the letters held in the Frances de Chollet Collection at the Princeton University Library. This book has its origins in a conversation one evening in the summer of 2012 in Provence, where Jacqueline shared the story of her mother's extraordinary wartime adventure.

Doctoral students (and perhaps by the time this book sees print, doctors) Andrew D. Finn and Kristin Starkowski at Princeton provided generous resource assistance, and my thanks to Stef Mills for assistance with translating the archival materials of Hilde Beetz from the German. All translations from Hilde Beetz's German intelligence reports are by Stef Mills; all translations from the Italian are by the author, and the author is solely responsible for any errors or omissions in citations. Citations have been limited here to passages with direct quotations, but the notes provide a complete bibliography of all sources that have been consulted.

My gratitude as always to my literary agent Stacey Glick and to my film agent Lou Pitt for all their intelligence and enthusiasm, to

Lauren Abramo in foreign rights for making sure this book reaches a world of readers, and to my editor at Grand Central Publishing, Karen Kosztolnyik, with whom it has been a great pleasure to work again as an author. Thanks as well to Rachael Kelly, Matthew Ballast in publicity, Alana Spendley in marketing, and the many people at Grand Central Publishing who helped make this publication possible.

Closer to home, generous financial support for this project was provided by the Canada Council for the Arts, and by the gentlemen extraordinaire of the Miles household: my husband, Robert, and my stepsons, Edward and Rory. They have provided a sometimes irascible writer with lots of coffee, long-suffering looks, cheerful questions about even the Gestapo during our long pandemic lockdown, and a general measure of peace and quiet, and I think we can all say in unison that we are, once again, delighted to have survived the experience as a family of another book getting written. My love and, even if I do not say it often enough, my thanks to all three of you, and, of course to Frankie, Francesco, King Rooster (rest his soul), and Widget, whom we shall always remember. My thanks to my mother, Charlene Mazzeo, and to my husband, Robert Miles, for reading the manuscript in process, and to my friend Heidi Davis for long walks on the back of Mount Newton, discussing you know what and you know who. That was what kept a writer going.

ENDNOTES

xiv *"the most important single political document"*: Lorie Charlesworth and Michael Salter, "Ensuring the After-Life of the Ciano Diaries: Allen Dulles' Provision of Nuremberg Trial Evidence," *Intelligence and National Security* 21, no. 4 (2006): 568–603.

1 *Irate housewives muttered words tantamount to insurrection*: Paul Corner, *The Fascist Party and Popular Opinion in Mussolini's Italy* (Oxford, UK: Oxford University Press, 2012), 240, passim.

3 *"The pomposity and absurdity of his manner"*: *The Ribbentrop Memoirs*, ed. Alan Bullock, trans. Oliver Watson (London: Weidenfeld and Nicolson, 1954), xv.

3 *"One could not talk to Ribbentrop"*: *Ribbentrop Memoirs*, x.

3 *"revolting scoundrel"*: *The Ciano Diaries, 1939–1943: The Complete, Unabridged Diaries of Count Galeazzo Ciano, Italian Minister of Foreign Affairs*, ed. Hugh Gibson (New York: Doubleday, 1945), 164.

3 *"completely disgusted with the Germans"*: *Ciano Diaries*, 153.

4 *"set your minds at rest...France and England have accepted"*: Iris Origo, *A Chill in the Air: An Italian War Diary, 1939–1940* (New York: New York Review Books, 2018), quoted in Alexander Stille, "A Chill in the Air" (book review), *New York Times*, September 21, 2018.

5 *inspired a younger and admiring Adolf Hitler*: Adaam James Levin-Areddy, "Thirteen Facts About Benito Mussolini," *Mental Floss* (online magazine), November 1, 2018.

6 *"The Italians having heard my warlike propaganda"*: Ray Moseley, *Mussolini's Shadow: The Double Life of Count Galeazzo Ciano* (New Haven, CT: Yale University Press, 2000), 89.

6 *"I have never met such a pompous and vain imbecile"*: Moseley, *Mussolini's Shadow*, 58.

7 *"has become a nymphomaniac"*: Edda Mussolini Ciano, *My Truth* (New York: Morrow, 1977), 86.

7 *Galeazzo spoke with a high-pitched, nasal twang*: Moseley, *Mussolini's Shadow*, 10.

8 *"I saw [Mussolini] many times"*: *Ciano Diaries*, 278.

10 *"[He] wore a great sable coat"*: *Ciano Diaries*, 443.

10 *"Hitler talks, talks, talks, talks"*: *Ciano Diaries*, 478.

11 *"Hitler looks tired"*: *Ciano Diaries*, 478.

11 *he was also "strong, determined, and talkative"*: *Ciano Diaries*, 478.

11 *"The year 1943 will perhaps be hard"*: "Hitler Still Predicting Axis Victory," *Schenectady Gazette*, January 1, 1943, 13.

12 *"one of the outstanding RSHA operators of the war"*: "Agent

Security—Gambit," November 8, 1946, Records of the Central Intelligence Agency, 608/MG-309 (Hildegard Beetz).

13 *Hilde's office tapped the phone lines*: Katrin Paehler, *The Third Reich's Intelligence Services: The Career of Walter Schellenberg* (Cambridge, UK: Cambridge University Press, 2017), 74.

13 *Helmut Löss had a reputation*: Paehler, *Third Reich's Intelligence Services*, 74.

13 *the "big boss," Ernst Kaltenbrünner, made Hilde's transition*: "Hildegard Beetz," Records of the Central Intelligence Agency, item 71.

13 *People now said that the Italian foreign minister was refusing*: Enrico Caviglia, *I Dittatori, le Guerre e il Piccolo Re: Diario 1925–1945* (Milan, Italy: Ugo Mursia Editore, 2009), 408–09, 420–22; Alberto Pirelli, *Taccuini, 1922/1943*, ed. Donato Barbone (Bologna, Italy: Il Mulino, 1984), 372.

13 *A staunch Republican with a successful legal career*: Greg Bradsher, "A Time to Act: The Beginning of the Fritz Kolbe Story, 1900–1943," *Prologue Magazine* 34, no. 1, pt. 3 (Spring 2002), National Archives of the United States.

14 *The Germans would not discover the existence of the OSS*: Bradsher, "A Time to Act"; also Wilhelm Höttl, *The Secret Front: The Story of Nazi Political Espionage* (New York: Frederick A. Praeger, 1954), 268.

14 *The intercepted telegram was a secret communication*: Neal H. Petersen, *From Hitler's Doorstep: The Wartime Intelligence Reports of Allen Dulles, 1942–1945* (University Park: The Pennsylvania State University Press, 1996), 35; Paige Y. Durgin, "Framed in Death: The Historical Memory of Galeazzo Ciano," thesis, Trinity College, 2012, 50.

14 *Galeazzo Ciano, along with his exiled rival Pietro Badoglio*: "Allen Dulles and the Compromise of OSS Codes in WW2," *Christos Military and Intelligence Corner* (blog), May 23, 2012.

14 *Galeazzo, in fact, had covertly been in contact*: Francis X. Rocca, "Fascism's Secretary of State," *The Atlantic*, July 2000.

15 *"What are you going to do now?"*: *Ciano Diaries*, 579.

15 *"I [chose] to be Ambassador to the Holy See"*: *Ciano Diaries*, 579.

15 *"To leave the Ministry for Foreign Affairs, where for seven years"*: *Ciano Diaries*, 579.

15 *"Galeazzo had fallen into disgrace"*: Antonino Cangemi, "Vita spericolata di un dandy siciliano," *Dialoghi Mediterranei: Periodico bimestrale dell'Istituto Euroarabo di Mazara del Vallo*, January 1, 2019.

16 *"Yes," Galeazzo replied*: *Ciano Diaries*, 580.

17 *In inexpensive, flimsy eight-by-ten-inch calendar notebooks*: Howard McGaw Smyth, "The Papers: Rose Garden," Central Intelligence Agency, Historical Review Program, September 22, 1993.

18 *By July 16, Italy's ambassadors, passing a secret message*: Following the argument put forth by Emilio Gin, "Mussolini and the Fall of Fascism, 25 July 1943: A Reappraisal," *Historical Journal* 61, no. 3 (September 2018): 787–806.

19 *When all the roiling internal discontent was reported back to Germany*: Gin, "Mussolini and the Fall of Fascism."

20 *The villa had been expropriated*: Ilaria Myr, "Villa Giulia: Quando Ciano espropriò la nostra casa," *Bet Magazine Mosaico: Sito ufficiale della Comunità Ebraica di Milano*, July 15, 2018.

23 *He had been weighing this since 1940*: *Ciano Diaries*, 235.

23 *"The darkest places in hell are reserved for those"*: The origins of this quote, more derived from Dante than translated from his work, are generally dated to World War I.

24 *"In a few hours Mussolini will have me arrested"*: Durgin, "Framed in Death," 245.

24 *"My dear Duce," the king told him bluntly*: Patricia Knight, *Mussolini and Fascism* (London: Routledge, 2002), 109.

25 *The king, Mussolini remembered later, "was livid…he shook my hand"*: Romano Mussolini, *My Father Il Duce: A Memoir by Mussolini's Son*, trans. Ana Stojanovic (n.p.: Kales Press, 2006), 17–18.

25 *What Mussolini had not anticipated*: Denis Mack Smith, *Italy and Its Monarchy* (New Haven, CT: Yale University Press, 1989), 304.

26 *If there was one person whom Badoglio despised*: Melton S. Davis, *Who Defends Rome? The Forty-Five Days, July 25 to September 8, 1943* (New York: Doubleday, 1972), 199.

26 *The papers had been a sword over Badoglio's head*: Durgin, "Framed in Death," 249.

27 *"the pederasty of the crown prince"*: "Hildegard Beetz," file dated October 26, 1943, archive file 25, Central Intelligence Agency.

27 *Gossips said that, so strong was his disinclination*: Robert Aldrich and Garry Wetherspoon, *Who's Who in Gay and Lesbian History* (London, Routledge, 2005), 1:453.

28 *"There is a* tramontana *not especially for us"*: Moseley, *Mussolini's Shadow*, 174.

28 *"He probably already knew that my father had been removed from power"*: Mussolini Ciano, *My Truth*, 192.

29 *"Edda was an unusual woman"*: Romano Mussolini, *My Father Il Duce*, 96.

29 *"Stop looking at me with those Mussolini eyes"*: Moseley, *Mussolini's Shadow*, 10.

29 *she had volunteered for the Italian Red Cross*: Rachele Mussolini and Albert Zarca, *Mussolini: An Intimate Biography by His Widow* (New York: William Morrow, 1976), 86, 188; Romano Mussolini, *My Father Il Duce*, 98.

29 *"There was some difficulty in making her realize that the expedition"*: Andrea Niccoletti, "The Decline and Fall of Edda Ciano," *Collier's Weekly*, April 20 and April 27, 1946; these articles are generally considered pseudonymous articles written by Allen Dulles.

30 *"Not yet anyhow," she told them coolly*: Niccoletti, "The Decline and Fall of Edda Ciano," 11.

30 *"[The] children understood," Edda assured herself*: Niccoletti, "The Decline and Fall of Edda Ciano," 11.

30 *Twenty years of dictatorship had ended*: For a survey of context, see, for example, Joshua Arthurs, "Settling Accounts: Retribution, Emotion and Memory During the Fall of Mussolini," *Journal of Modern Italian Studies* 20, no. 5 (2015), 617–39.

31 *"I'm afraid," she told Edda*: Mussolini Ciano, *My Truth*, 189.

31 *"Mussolini Ousted with Fascist Cabinet"*: *New York Times*, July 26, 1943.

32 *"La guerra continua"*: Mussolini Ciano, *My Truth*, 107.

32 *"But they seemed to forget two things"*: Susanna Agnelli, *We Always Wore Sailor Suits* (New York: Bantam Books, 1975), 106.

32   *Three armed police guards escorted them home—a necessary safety measure*: Moseley, *Mussolini's Shadow*, 176.

32   *"We haven't the least chance of survival"*: Mussolini Ciano, *My Truth*, 191.

33   *In the days that followed, nearly a hundred protestors were killed*: Nicola Gallerano, Luigi Ganapini, and Massimo Legnani, *L'Italia dei quarantacinque giorni: Studió e documenti* (Milan: Istituto nazionale per la storia del movimento di liberazione, 1969), 376.

33   *The couple was now under de facto house arrest*: Eugen Dollmann, *With Hitler and Mussolini: Memoirs of a Nazi Interpreter* (New York: Simon and Schuster, 2017), n.p. (e-book).

33   *Edda saw the perils at home clearly*: Mussolini Ciano, *My Truth*, 26.

34   *For visitors to the Ciano apartment, Susanna remarked*: Agnelli, *We Always Wore Sailor Suits*, 108.

34   *Raimondo too was in a precarious position*: Agnelli, *We Always Wore Sailor Suits*, 103.

34   *He surrounded himself with flatterers*: Agnelli, *We Always Wore Sailor Suits*, 109.

35   *"I smiled to make it less terrible"*: Agnelli, *We Always Wore Sailor Suits*, 109.

35   *The Spanish ambassador in Rome had promised*: Mussolini Ciano, *My Truth*, 27.

36   *"I…wanted to help him"*: Agnelli, *We Always Wore Sailor Suits*, 109.

36   *"Warn Galeazzo that he should make sure not to fall into the hands of the Germans"*: Moseley, *Mussolini's Shadow*, 178.

38   *Fit and stylish, in his midforties, with blond hair*: Patrick J. Gallo, *For*

Love and Country: The Italian Resistance (Lanham, MD: University Press of America, 2003), 116.

38 *"What followed," Dollmann wrote*: Dollmann, *With Hitler and Mussolini*.

39 *Edda remembered it as August 21*: Mussolini Ciano, *My Truth*, 193.

39 *"I received a visit from a smartly dressed man"*: Dollmann, *With Hitler and Mussolini*.

39 *"Dear Dollmann," the note read*: Dollmann, *With Hitler and Mussolini*.

39 *"You must be aware, Countess, that Count Ciano"*: Dollmann, *With Hitler and Mussolini*.

39 *"I do not know what the Führer will decide about* him": Dollmann, *With Hitler and Mussolini*.

40 *his diary was reputed*: Mussolini Ciano, *My Truth*, 29.

40 *As Edda would say later that summer*: Mussolini Ciano, *My Truth*, 29.

41 *When Galeazzo's old friend and copilot Ettore Muti*: Paul H. Lewis, *Latin Fascist Elites: The Mussolini, Franco, and Salazar Regimes* (Westport, CT: Praeger Publishers, 2002), 46.

41 *A baby-faced slender man*: Richard Breitman, Norman J. W. Goda, Timothy Naftali, and Robert Wolfe, "The Nazi Peddler: Wilhelm Höttl and Allied Intelligence," in *U.S. Intelligence and the Nazis* (Cambridge: Cambridge University Press, 2005), 265–92.

41 *Though only in his midthirties, he had risen quickly*: "Background of Dr. Wilhelm Hoettl," August 5, 1949, declassified 2000, Central Intelligence Agency Archives.

42 *"Behave normally. Pretend we are going for a walk"*: Moseley, *Mussolini's Shadow*, 182.

42 *Edda walked the short distance west*: Moseley, *Mussolini's Shadow*, 196; letter, Allen Dulles to Dallas S. Townshend, December 3, 1955, AWD 25X1, declassified 2003, Central Intelligence Agency.

43 *The door swung open, Galeazzo threw himself inside*: Smyth, "The Papers: Rose Garden."

43 *At the last minute, Wilhelm Höttl asked Otto Lechner*: Letter, Allen Dulles to Dallas S. Townshend, December 3, 1955.

43 *"The first thing we did," Edda remembered*: Mussolini Ciano, *My Truth*, 196.

44 *The Germans had assured them that they would be taken*: Smyth, "The Papers: Rose Garden."

44 *"The Führer rightly suspects that such memoirs"*: Durgin, "Framed in Death," 253.

44 *If he had been, he would never have embarked*: Dollmann, *With Hitler and Mussolini*.

45 *They were being taken to Munich*: Leyland Harrison to State Department, February 1, 1944, RG 184, entry 3207, box 103, folder 800.2, National Archives of the United States.

45 *Then, of course, the family was reassured*: Mussolini Ciano, *My Truth*, 28; Tompkins, *A Spy in Rome* (New York: Simon and Schuster, 1962), 171.

45 *it had been an "error of judgment"*: Mussolini and Zarca, *Mussolini*, 174.

45 *"My God! I think they count on keeping"*: Mussolini Ciano, *My Truth*, 128.

45 *Priebke had understood perfectly well since leaving Rome*: Smyth, "The Papers: Rose Garden."

46 *there was a flurry of visits and messages*: Mussolini Ciano, *My Truth*, 197; letter, Allen Dulles to Dallas S. Townshend, December 3, 1955.

46 *"I was astonished," Edda confided*: Mussolini Ciano, *My Truth*, 197.

46 *Otto Lechner observed that Ernst Kaltenbrünner*: Letter, Allen Dulles to Dallas S. Townshend, December 3, 1955.

48 *In June, in love, she married Captain Gerhard Beetz*: Moseley, *Mussolini's Shadow*, 186; "Hildegard Beetz," June 14, 1945, United States' classified communication to CO, SCI, Germany, from SCI Weimar, reporting on the interrogation of Hilde Beetz and the RSHA role in the death of Galeazzo Ciano, Central Intelligence Agency Archives.

48 *"He was tall, well-built, physically attractive"*: Moseley, *Mussolini's Shadow*, 185.

49 *eager internal discussion among Höttl and his superiors*: Smyth, "The Papers: Rose Garden."

50 *"signaled the end of Fascism"*: Romano Mussolini, *My Father Il Duce*, 98.

51 *"I had never really hated anyone"*: Moseley, *Mussolini's Shadow*, 200.

51 *Her mission was to beguile Galeazzo*: Paehler, *Third Reich's Intelligence Services*, 228.

51 *Edda, no one's fool, was less than thrilled*: "Hildegard Beetz," June 14, 1945.

51 *Her nickname for her husband was Gallo*: Mussolini Ciano, *My Truth*, 203.

52 *"He had lost his self-confidence"*: Moseley, *Mussolini's Shadow*, 186.

52 *"They were asking for civilian clothes"*: Agnelli, *We Always Wore Sailor Suits*, 113.

52 *Most residents were arrested and deported*: Shannon Quinn, "10 Little Known Facts About the 9 Months the Nazis Occupied Rome," History Collection, May 29, 2018.

52 *Susanna's fiancé, Prince Raimondo*: See Raimondo Lanza di Trabia, *Mi toccherà ballare*, ed. Ottavia Casagrande (Milano: Feltrinelli, 2014).

53 *her half-American, English-speaking mother*: Dan Kurzman, *A Special Mission: Hitler's Secret Plot to Seize the Vatican and Kidnap Pope Pius XII* (New York: Hachette, 2007), n.p. (e-book); Jennifer Clark, *Mondo Agnelli: Fiat, Chrysler, and the Power of a Dynasty* (Hoboken, NJ: John Wiley and Sons, 2012), 68.

53 *In Switzerland, despite the vast Agnelli wealth*: Agnelli, *We Always Wore Sailor Suits*, 122.

53 *drank "boiling soup to keep ourselves warm during the night"*: Agnelli, *We Always Wore Sailor Suits*, 122.

53 *He would soon be returned to power in Italy*: Smyth, "The Papers: Rose Garden."

54 *Edda would have to return to Rome*: Mussolini Ciano, *My Truth*, 203.

55 *Joseph Goebbels confided to his diary*: Moseley, *Mussolini's Shadow*, 189.

56 *The two women set off together*: Domenico Vecchioni, "Quelle due belle spie che si contendono i diari di Galeazzo Ciano: Sono Frau

Beetz per i tedeschi e Christine Granville per gli alleati," *L'Indro*, August 1, 2018.

56 *Unfortunately, Carolina explained*: Mussolini Ciano, *My Truth*, 206.

57 *A few days later, the missing parts of the notebooks*: Mussolini Ciano, *My Truth*, 207.

57 *To this set of papers, they added a fourth loose-leaf collection*: Smyth, "The Papers: Rose Garden."

58 *Her urgent mission accomplished*: Niccoletti, "The Decline and Fall of Edda Ciano," n.p.

58 *Emilio Pucci, born in 1914*: Raymond Rendleman, "Thinker. Tailor. Soldier. Spy. The Kaleidoscopic Career of Emilio Pucci '37," *Reed Magazine* 93, no. 1 (March 1, 2014), n.p. (online reprint); report, Emilio Pucci to Allen Dulles, May 24, 1945, "Edda Ciano Diaries," item 18R, Personal Files of Allen Dulles, Central Intelligence Agency Archives.

58 *"After listening to her story"*: Rendleman, "Thinker. Tailor. Soldier. Spy," n.p.

59 *She would need new reserves*: "Hildegard Beetz," June 14, 1945, 2.

60 *Hilde reported back to her superiors*: "Hildegard Beetz," October 26, 1943.

60 *Galeazzo was surprised to receive a message on October 16*: "Hildegard Beetz," October 26, 1943.

61 *Galeazzo had insisted to his father-in-law*: "Hildegard Beetz," October 26, 1943.

61 *"The Führer alone decides"*: John Gunther, *Inside Europe* (New York: Harper, 1940), 19.

62   *"Ciao, kids, we will not see each other for a while"*: Moseley, *Mussolini's Shadow*, 194.

62   *Galeazzo went out for a brief appointment*: "Hildegard Beetz," October 26, 1943.

62   *"Should he be able, against his expectation"*: "Hildegard Beetz," October 26, 1943.

63   *"[H]e had already told me in conversation"*: "Hildegard Beetz," October 26, 1943.

63   *she had already "taken a strong liking"*: "Hildegard Beetz," October 26, 1943.

64   *"I am aware of that," Galeazzo replied*: Mussolini Ciano, *My Truth*, 210.

65   *"I am determined even now to find out more"*: "Hildegard Beetz," October 26, 1943. The awkward German-to-English translation in this file has been updated to conform to standard idiom.

65   *along with Rachele Mussolini as a passenger*: Mussolini and Zarca, *Mussolini*, 146.

68   *"I was stunned to find that, although back in his own home"*: Mussolini and Zarca, *Mussolini*, 146.

68   *she had come to tell him: "They are safe"*: Mussolini Ciano, *My Truth*, 212.

69   *Mario Pellegrinotti, a sympathetic prison warden*: Moseley, *Mussolini's Shadow*, 204.

69   *Hilde later insisted that she did not "make love"*: Moseley, *Mussolini's Shadow*, 204; "Hildegard Beetz," October 26, 1943.

69   *"Life is sad," he wrote to her in a letter*: Moseley, *Mussolini's Shadow*, 198.

70   *"She gave my husband the letters that I wrote to him"*: Mussolini Ciano, *My Truth*, 225.

70   *For her part, Hilde explained it this way*: "Hildegard Beetz," October 26, 1943.

71   *Christine Granville—better known as Krystyna Skarbek*: Vecchioni, "Quelle due belle spie," n.p.

71   *Files show that her lover, a fellow spy*: Ron Nowicki, *The Elusive Madame G: A Life of Christine Granville* (privately printed, 2014): 218, 234–36.

72   *"My father had a weakness"*: Romano Mussolini, *My Father Il Duce*, 96.

73   *The Gestapo would kill the children*: Niccoletti, "The Decline and Fall of Edda Ciano," n.p.

73   *Vittorio, moved by his sister's genuine distress*: Mussolini Ciano, *My Truth*, 213.

74   *Edda and Emilio had arranged for two old friends*: Mussolini Ciano, *My Truth*, 215; Giovanni Colli, "Confronto drammatico tra Edda e Frau Beetz: Il 'giallo' dei diari di Ciano," *Il Tempo*, June 6, 1989.

74   *They headed north to Milan*: Moseley, *Mussolini's Shadow*, 202.

74   *They had bribed an Italian border guard*: Mussolini Ciano, *My Truth*, 214.

76   *"You must now forget your family name"*: Moseley, *Mussolini's Shadow*, 202.

76   *Emilio waited until morning*: Mussolini Ciano, *My Truth*, 215.

76   *She had another important message for her husband*: Mussolini Ciano, *My Truth*, 223.

77 *they turned to the only avenue either could see ahead*: Mussolini Ciano, *My Truth*, 225.

77 *Hilde—described by one commentator*: Niccoletti, "The Decline and Fall of Edda Ciano," n.p.

78 *Hilde still planned to execute her duty*: Moseley, *Mussolini's Shadow*, 184.

79 *"We practically have two options"*: Paehler, *Third Reich's Intelligence Services*, 228.

79 *She assured her handlers that the diaries*: Paehler, *Third Reich's Intelligence Services*, 228.

80 *"It has been said," Edda wrote later*: Mussolini Ciano, *My Truth*, 225.

80 *He asked Hilde to draft a formal memorandum*: "Hildegard Beetz," June 14, 1945.

80 *Hilde described the feelings*: Corinna Peniston-Bird and Emma Vickers, eds., *Gender and the Second World War: Lessons of War* (London: Palgrave Macmillan, 2017), 80.

81 *Galeazzo put on a great show of irritation*: Moseley, *Mussolini's Shadow*, 204.

81 *Smuggled into Galeazzo's cell by a friendly prison guard*: Mussolini Ciano, *My Truth*, 225; editorial remarks.

82 *"Aside from Frau Beetz, who was acting from selfish motives"*: Mussolini Ciano, *My Truth*, 218; editorial remarks. See also Zenone Benini, *Carcere degli Scalzi* (Firenze: Ponte alle Grazie, 1994).

82 *the German ambassador to Salò and the Italian-based SS*: "Hildegard Beetz," October 26, 1943.

82 *Ribbentrop, it now transpired, had been behind*: Peniston-Bird and Vickers, *Gender and the Second World War*, 78.

83 *"I approach Christmas feeling very sad"*: Moseley, *Mussolini's Shadow*, 207.

83 *"Truly I have moments in which I seem to be going mad"*: Moseley, *Mussolini's Shadow*, 207.

83 *"One man, just one man"*: Moseley, *Mussolini's Shadow*, 206.

83 *"I was never Mussolini's accomplice in that crime"*: Moseley, *Mussolini's Shadow*, 206.

84 *"Within a few days a sham tribunal will make public"*: Moseley, *Mussolini's Shadow*, 206.

87 *Clara, moved by the plea, did what she could*: Moseley, *Mussolini's Shadow*, 211.

87 *"I now realized," Edda said*: Mussolini Ciano, *My Truth*, 227.

88 *Those who whisper that Christina Granville*: Vecchioni, "Quelle due belle spie," n.p.

91 *warning her supervisors that "If [Galeazzo] is shot"*: Moseley, *Mussolini's Shadow*, 212.

91 *"I later learned," Edda said, "that General Harster"*: Mussolini Ciano, *My Truth*, 227.

91 *"It is useless, nothing will come of it"*: Moseley, *Mussolini's Shadow*, 214.

92 *General Harster before his appointment to Italy*: "Ex-Nazi [Wilhelm Harster] Sentenced in 'Anne Frank' Deaths," *New York Herald Tribune*, Europe Edition, February 17, 1967.

94 *"I was…obeying [Galeazzo's] instructions"*: Mussolini Ciano, *My Truth*, 29.

95 *One of those Gestapo men was Walter Segna*: Walter Segna, Interrogation Report, May 13, 1945, XARX-27856, Central Intelligence Agency, declassified 2001.

97 *The packet contained eight volumes, bound in green leather*: Smyth, "The Papers: Rose Garden"; see also Walter Segna, Interrogation Report, May 13, 1945.

100 *The notebooks were large but flimsy*: Smyth, "The Papers: Rose Garden."

101 *"I began to run down the road"*: Mussolini Ciano, *My Truth*, 229.

101 *"Each time a car passed I raised my head"*: Mussolini Ciano, *My Truth*, 229.

103 *"Hitler had at the last moment vetoed Ciano's liberation"*: "Memorandum on Edda Ciano," November 17, 1955, Central Intelligence Agency, declassified 2003.

104 *"No intervention now can halt the course of events"*: Giovanni Dolfin, *Con Mussolini nella tragedia: Diario del capo della segreteria particolare del Duce, 1943–1944* (Milan: Garzanti, 1950), 188–89.

105 *Kaltenbrünner's only reply to her plaintive message*: Report by Hildegard Beetz to RSHA, June 18, 1945, Verona, archive file 71, Central Intelligence Agency.

106 *"She stared at me, incredulous and panic-stricken"*: Mussolini Ciano, *My Truth*, 234.

106 *"Frau Beetz could have taken the notebooks then"*: Mussolini Ciano, *My Truth*, 230.

107 *Far fewer self-disclosures have been known to make strangers*: Arthur Aron et al., "The Experimental Generation of Interpersonal

Closeness: A Procedure and Some Preliminary Findings," *Personality and Social Psychology Bulletin* 23, no. 4 (April 1997): 363–77.

107 *"You are crazy to have come here"*: Mussolini Ciano, *My Truth*, 234.

108 *"You have deceived us in the most despicable manner"*: Moseley, *Mussolini's Shadow*, 216.

108 *American spymaster Allen Dulles would later see*: Peniston-Bird and Vickers, *Gender and the Second World War*, 80.

108 *Hilde would help her*: Report by Hildegard Beetz to RSHA, archive file 67, Central Intelligence Agency.

108 *"I felt an obligation to repair the wrong"*: "Hildegard Beetz," October 26, 1943.

110 *Galeazzo had written in that long day*: Smyth, "The Papers: Rose Garden."

111 *"I decided to go to Switzerland"*: Mussolini Ciano, *My Truth*, 230.

112 *Kaltenbrünner had sent a warning telegram*: Moseley, *Mussolini's Shadow*, 218.

112 *Lieutenant Hutting immediately set off for Ramiola*: Walter Segna, Interrogation Report, May 13, 1945.

113 *The doctors confirmed that she had asked for sleeping pills*: Moseley, *Mussolini's Shadow*, 218.

113 *Placated by these reassurances, the SS returned to their posts*: Walter Segna, Interrogation Report, May 13, 1945.

114 *Then, taking advantage of the lull*: Report, Emilio Pucci to Allen Dulles, May 24, 1945, item 18R, "Edda Ciano Diaries," Personal Files of Allen Dulles, 8; Roman Dombrowski, *Mussolini: Twilight and Fall* (New York: Roy Publishers, 1956), 122–23. According to

Duilio Susmel, *Vita sbagliata di Galeazzo Ciano* (Milan: Aldo Palazzi, 1962), 336, three booklets of the diaries, those for the years 1936, 1937, and 1938, were left at Como in the house of the Pessina family. Sources and the chronology in this complex matter, even from contemporary and firsthand sources, are not always consistent.

115 *Twilight came at 5:00 P.M.*: Kaltenbrünner to Ribbentrop, January 13, 1944, German Foreign Office Archives, Inland II geheim: "Geheime Reichssachen" 1944, vol. 15, box 3, fiche T-120, National Archives, Serial 712/262452-453.

116 *"As I said goodbye to her," Emilio remembered*: Niccoletti, "The Decline and Fall of Edda Ciano," n.p.

116 *"I don't know why, but at that point I didn't care"*: Mussolini Ciano, *My Truth*, 243.

117 *"[H]e was astonished and annoyed to hear me say that I was Edda Ciano"*: Mussolini Ciano, *My Truth*, 243.

117 *"[H]e conveyed, and I believe honestly," Dulles recorded*: Allen W. Dulles, *The Craft of Intelligence: America's Legendary Spy Master on the Fundamentals of Intelligence Gathering for a Free World* (Guilford, CT: Lyons Press, 2016), 169.

118 *Seeing her that day for the first time in months*: Moseley, *Mussolini's Shadow*, 218.

119 *Galeazzo, dressed in a sports coat*: Moseley, *Mussolini's Shadow*, 224.

119 *The trial was, as Galeazzo had written to the king*: Durgin, "Framed in Death," 83.

120 *There was one aspect of the trial, though, that attracted*: "Re. Trial

Against Minister Ciano and Others at Verona," translation, interview with Hildegard Beetz, Berlin, February 28, 1944, file MGKW-2371-ATT, Central Intelligence Agency Archives.

121 *"I went into a room where two girls were sleeping"*: Report, Emilio Pucci to Allen Dulles, May 24, 1945.

121 *To General Harster, Edda had written*: Smyth, "The Papers: Rose Garden."

124 *Sometime before dawn on the morning of January 10*: Niccoletti, "The Decline and Fall of Edda Ciano," n.p.

124 *"However, she has done well"*: Moseley, *Mussolini's Shadow*, 218.

125 *In the morning he rang for his personal secretary*: Durgin, "Framed in Death," 83.

126 *The fascist police chief covering the trial, Major Nicola Furlotti*: Durgin, "Framed in Death," 86.

127 *Zenone remembered how, after he had dried his eyes*: Mussolini Ciano, *My Truth*, 244.

127 *Galeazzo spoke of his love for Hilde*: Smyth, "The Papers: Rose Garden."

127 *"To her," Galeazzo confided to his friend, "I have entrusted"*: Smyth, "The Papers: Rose Garden."

128 *"I became aware: my heart was beating normally"*: Moseley, *Mussolini's Shadow*, 224.

128 *Thus began, Hilde said, the "most terrible night of my life"*: "Re. Trial Against Minister Ciano and Others at Verona," February 28, 1944.

128 *Later, when the Germans suspected that Zenone knew the location*:

"Copy of letter addressed to Countess Edda Ciano by Signor Zenone Benini," August 16, 1944, Personal Files of Allen W. Dulles, US, NA, RG 226, entry 190C, box 11, 1.

128 *"Forget about the plea for mercy"*: Durgin, "Framed in Death," 42.

128 *"When you return among men, and this cursed war will have finished"*: Durgin, "Framed in Death," 42.

129 *He did talk to Zenone of the diaries*: Durgin, "Framed in Death," 42.

129 *Sometime before six o'clock, the prison chief, Dr. Olas*: Moseley, *Mussolini's Shadow*, 224.

129 *"The German lady again was there"*: Smyth, "The Papers: Rose Garden."

130 *General Wolff advised him that Hitler's instructions*: Durgin, "Framed in Death," 42.

130 *"A failure to execute could harm me"*: Moseley, *Mussolini's Shadow*, 234.

130 *"Yes, very much so," the general advised him*: Moseley, *Mussolini's Shadow*, 234.

130 *What Mussolini did not know was that the clemency*: Mussolini Ciano, *My Truth*, 19.

131 *"I shall not give those who wanted my death"*: Mussolini Ciano, *My Truth*, 11.

131 *He slowly took off his overcoat and scarf*: Moseley, *Mussolini's Shadow*, 234.

133 *Only with the second shot did Galeazzo expire*: "Re. Trial Against Minister Ciano and Others at Verona," February 28, 1944; Mussolini Ciano, *My Truth*, 9.

134 *A German diplomat who witnessed the execution*: Moseley, *Mussolini's Shadow*, 236.

134 *Winston Churchill later said that it had been an act*: Durgin, "Framed in Death," 91.

134 *Only that afternoon would he come to understand*: Moseley, *Mussolini's Shadow*, 236.

134 *His son, Romano, remembered his father crying*: Romano Mussolini, *My Father Il Duce*, 103.

134 *An American nun who spent the war in Rome*: Jane Scrivener, *Inside Rome with the Germans* (New York: Macmillan, 1945), 87.

135 *"I was on my way to Sondrio, where I hoped I could make arrangements"*: Niccoletti, "The Decline and Fall of Edda Ciano," n.p.

135 *"Four machine guns were stuck against my throat"*: Report, Emilio Pucci to Allen Dulles, May 24, 1945.

136 *The Gestapo men threw him into the back of the car*: Walter Segna, Interrogation Report, May 13, 1945.

136 *"I stiffened to receive the blow, but it didn't come"*: Niccoletti, "The Decline and Fall of Edda Ciano," n.p.

136 *"few minutes after Count Ciano had been shot"*: Niccoletti, "The Decline and Fall of Edda Ciano," n.p.

137 *"[W]hat struck me," Emilio said later of the colonel*: "Pucci Story," Exhibit E, ECDAR, Personal Files of Allen W. Dulles, US, NA, RG 226, entry 190C, box 11.

137 *The colonel and his chief interrogator*: Major S. H. Shergold, "First Detailed Report on Five PW from SIPO und SD Aussenkommando Milan," CSDIC/CMF/SD 13, June 4, 1945, Central

Intelligence Agency, declassified 2001; "German Intelligence Officers: Walter Rauff," Security Services Archives, National Archives of the United Kingdom, KV 2/1970.

138 *"The worst thing," Emilio remembered later*: Report, Emilio Pucci to Allen Dulles, May 24, 1945.

138 *"Is it alright?" Emilio asked, giggling*: Report, Emilio Pucci to Allen Dulles, May 24, 1945.

138 *"I felt as if my bones were going to split and a cold sweat ran down my back"*: Report, Emilio Pucci to Allen Dulles, May 24, 1945.

138 *"I thought of the clear nights in Africa"*: Report, Emilio Pucci to Allen Dulles, May 24, 1945.

139 *By day's end, when Emilio was returned to his cell*: "The RSHA and Edda Ciano in Switzerland," interrogation of [Hilde] Burkhardt Beetz, June 16, 1945, SCI Detachment Weimar, Central Intelligence Agency.

139 *"I tried to slash the veins in my neck"*: Durgin, "Framed in Death," 35.

143 *She "said that she didn't care what I did"*: Report, Emilio Pucci to Allen Dulles, May 24, 1945.

143 *Finally, Emilio agreed that he would pass to Edda the message*: Durgin, "Framed in Death," 35.

143 *But on the morning of January 14 she was allowed*: Mussolini Ciano, *My Truth*, 248.

143 *The man—likely Franco Bellia*: Smyth, "The Papers: Rose Garden," 35.

144 *"Come, let's go for a walk," she told them*: Smyth, "The Papers: Rose Garden," 35.

144 *Despite the bitter cold, the children walked with her to the top of a hill*: Moseley, *Mussolini's Shadow*, 241.

144 *"Papa is dead," she said simply*: Mussolini Ciano, *My Truth*, 248.

144 *Her brother remembered later that "she shouted with an incredible force"*: Fabrizio Ciano, *Quando il nonno fece fucilare papa* (Milan: A. Mondadori, 1991), 97ff.; "La famiglia Pini è partita da Lugano, accompagnata dall'ispettore Camponovo, col treno ascendente delle 16.53," Rapporto, Bellinzona, 18 gennaio 1944, firmato Imperatori, in AFB, E 4320 (B) 1991/243 Bd. 97a, quoted in Renata Broggini, *La "famiglia Mussolini": I colloqui di Edda Ciano con lo psichiatra svizzero Repond, 1944–1945*, 338, n. 9.

144 *Fabrizio said of his grandfather's role in the execution*: Moseley, *Mussolini's Shadow*, 240.

144 *The next week, on January 18, Edda and the children*: Broggini, *La "famiglia Mussolini,"* 338. The family assumed various pseudonyms, including Santos and Pini.

145 *"The day came when Galeazzo was tried"*: Agnelli, *We Always Wore Sailor Suits*, 125.

145 *"As long as his tomb remained in Verona"*: Moseley, *Mussolini's Shadow*, 238.

145 *"I loved Galeazzo, Countess. And I still love him"*: "Fascismo: È morta Frau Beetz, la spia che doveva rubare i diari di Ciano," obituary, March 31, 2010.

146 *Two days later Emilio Pucci, alive but in bad shape*: "The RSHA and Edda Ciano in Switzerland," June 16, 1945.

146 *He landed ashore on January 19, at four o'clock in the morning*:

Rendleman, "Thinker. Tailor. Soldier. Spy." There is a discrepancy in dates, and I follow Hilde Beetz's interrogation notes as the more reliable source material.

146 *Hilde checked into the Hotel Alder, a lake-view villa*: "Vetting of Hilde Beetz," AB 16, Berlin to AB 17, Saint Amzon, May 24, 1946, LBX-317, Hildegard Beetz, vol. 1, 0136, Central Intelligence Agency Archives.

147 *"We have learned from a source"*: Neal H. Petersen, ed., *From Hitler's Doorstep: The Wartime Intelligence Reports of Allen Dulles, 1942–1945* (Philadelphia: Pennsylvania State Press, 2010), 202.

147 *"News of Edda's arrival has now been received"*: Petersen, *From Hitler's Doorstep*, 202.

148 *"steps [were] taken to intern Countess Ciano"*: *Journal de Geneve*, January 30, 1944; clipping is included in Central Intelligence Agency Archives, US, NA, RG 184, box 103, folder 800.2.

149 *"From her eyes ran a river of tears"*: Moseley, *Mussolini's Shadow*, 240.

149 *When an inspector came to interview the children*: Moseley, *Mussolini's Shadow*, 243.

149 *The police gave up and let the boy stay*: Moseley, *Mussolini's Shadow*, 243.

150 *Edda was desperately broke and, depressed*: Broggini, *La "famiglia Mussolini,"* 339.

150 *Edda's correspondence was very much under surveillance*: Broggini, *La "famiglia Mussolini,"* 339.

151 *"My dear lady," the letter reads*: Unidentified correspondence,

January 31, 1944, taken from Hilde Beetz and placed in her OSS intelligence file, item NWC-001899, Central Intelligence Agency Archives, declassified 2005.

152 *On January 27, Hilde made contact in Switzerland with a British intelligence agent*: Second Report, Emilio Pucci to Allen Dulles, June 20, 1945, 42; "The RSHA and Edda Ciano in Switzerland," June 16, 1945; Special Interrogation Report: Frau Hildegard Beetz, July 9, 1945, from SCI Detachment, United States Forces European Theater, to Chief CBI, United States Forces European Theater, AIC 166, declassified 2001.

152 *Officially, Garston was the vice consul in Lugano*: "Doctor Lancelot Cyril Brewster Garston," list identification G10, case reference Gb Eyh270, Hitler's "Black Book," Forces War Records.

152 *She forwarded to German intelligence all her communications*: Hildegard Beetz to Wilhelm Höttl, Como, Cernobbio, March 30, 1944, archive file 51, Central Intelligence Agency Archives.

152 *This message instructed the runner to "[i]nform Felicitas"*: "Hildegard Beetz," October 26, 1943.

153 *Mussolini, wanting to persuade Edda*: "The RSHA and Edda Ciano in Switzerland," June 16, 1945.

153 *He had balding hair and wore thick, round glasses*: Lieutenant Stewart French, "Hildegard Beetz, nee Burkhardt, SD Executive and Agent," interview, to CIB, G-2, 12th Army Group, June 18, 1945.

154 *I was friends with [Benito Mussolini's] children*: Renzo Allegri, "Nel racconto di un sacerdote, una pagina di storia sconosciuta

riguardante Edda Ciano e suo padre Benito Mussolini," March 11, 2011.

154 *General Harster assigned his second-in-command, Walter Segna*: Walter Segna, Interrogation Report, May 13, 1945.

156 *Höttl warned her to think of her reputation as an agent: "use this chance, you, who rule over all men"*: Wilhelm Höttl to Hildegard Beetz," Vienna, February 15, 1944, archive file 45, Central Intelligence Agency Archives.

156 *Susanna was living with her sister Clara*: "Subject: The Zimmer Notebooks," memorandum from AB to AB 52, JRX-3748, August 21, 1946, ref. LBX-495, Central Intelligence Agency Archives.

157 *"Would I try to get a permit to come and see him?"*: Agnelli, *We Always Wore Sailor Suits*, 124.

158 *"I saw a woman walking toward me"*: Agnelli, *We Always Wore Sailor Suits*, 93.

158 *"Are you Suni Agnelli?"*: Agnelli, *We Always Wore Sailor Suits*, 93.

158 *She said simply, "My name is Hilde B."*: Agnelli, *We Always Wore Sailor Suits*, 93.

158 *"I got him a vial of potassium cyanide"*: Agnelli, *We Always Wore Sailor Suits*, 93.

158 *"Galeazzo told me about you"*: Agnelli, *We Always Wore Sailor Suits*, 127.

158 *"You must help me"*: Agnelli, *We Always Wore Sailor Suits*, 127.

158 *After a moment of silence, Susanna said simply*: Agnelli, *We Always Wore Sailor Suits*, 127.

159 *"Get me a vial of real cyanide"*: Agnelli, *We Always Wore Sailor Suits*, 127.

159 *"But why don't you ask the Swiss for asylum?"*: Agnelli, *We Always Wore Sailor Suits*, 127.

159 *"My husband is a general on the Russian front"*: Moseley, *Mussolini's Shadow*, 236.

159 *Susanna here could not be as encouraging*: "Subject: RSHA and Edda Ciano in Switzerland," from L. E. de Neufville, SCI, to CO, SCI, Germany, July 19, 1945, Central Intelligence Agency Archives, declassified 2006.

160 *"Your husband died with calm"*: "Letter Written by Frau B, with Pucci, with Purpose of Sending [Similar] Information to Edda," n.d., Central Intelligence Agency Archives, declassified 2001.

161 *"My dear friend," Hilde wrote*: Letter from Hildegard Beetz, February 25, 1944, item 46, Central Intelligence Agency Archives.

162 *his "feeling of gratitude for his safety was rapidly changing"*: "The RSHA and Edda Ciano in Switzerland," June 16, 1945.

164 *Emilio mentioned this to the priest in passing*: "Subject: AMT VI Agents in Italy," diary of Frau Hildegard Beetz, August 12, 1945, XX8602, declassified 2001.

164 *"Edda was in Ingenbohl, in the Heiliger Kreuz convent"*: Allegri, "Nel racconto di un sacerdote."

165 *She would be given a brief extension, until March 20*: Hildegard Beetz, letter to [Mr.] Höttl, December 4, 1943, with handwritten note, item 30, Central Intelligence Agency Archives.

165 *Father Pancino had ongoing access to Edda*: Hildegard Beetz, letter to Wilhelm Höttl, Como, Cernobbio, March 30, 1944, item 51, Central Intelligence Agency Archives.

166 *On the other hand, her bosses considered*: Hildegard Beetz, letter to Wilhelm Höttl, German consulate, Lugano, March 3, 1944, item 48, Central Intelligence Agency Archives.

169 *In one of their communications in December 1943*: Hildegard Beetz, letter to Wilhelm Höttl, German consulate, Lugano, March 3, 1944.

169 *Her accuser had wanted the mission for himself*: Wilhelm Höttl to Hildegard Beetz, Vienna, February 15, 1944.

170 *Kaltenbrünner was confident the accusations were false*: Peniston-Bird and Vickers, *Gender and the Second World War*, 73.

170 *Her new assignment, though, took her right back*: "The RSHA and Edda Ciano in Switzerland," June 16, 1945.

170 *"[M]y mission," Father Pancino remembered*: Allegri, "Nel racconto di un sacerdote."

170 *"Edda Ciano was in possession of the famous diaries"*: Allegri, "Nel racconto di un sacerdote."

171 *"Once, Edda and I, to escape the German spies"*: Allegri, "Nel racconto di un sacerdote."

172 *Edda passed to the priest at least some of the original manuscripts*: French, "Hildegard Beetz, nee Burkhardt, SD Executive and Agent," June 18, 1945.

172 *"Only those who had pronounced a password"*: Moseley, *Mussolini's Shadow*, 244.

172 *"It was then Edda who picked up the Diaries"*: Allegri, "Nel racconto di un sacerdote."

173 *He hinted that maybe he should sit down with Edda and Hilde* *together*: [Hildegard Beetz], report to Dr. Hügel, Cernobio, June 7, 1944, item 53, Central Intelligence Agency Archives.

173 *Then, as good luck would have it*: Walter Segna, Interrogation Report, May 13, 1945.

174 *Hilde's intelligence briefings had assured Wilhelm Höttl*: Hildegard Beetz, letter to Wilhelm Höttl, German consulate, Lugano, March 3, 1944; Hildegard Beetz, letter to Wilhelm Höttl, Como, Cernobbio, March 30, 1944.

174 *He was transferred to an assignment in Budapest and replaced*: "Final Interrogation Report of SS Stubaf Klaus Hugel," June 12–13, 1945, XARZ-18937, Central Intelligence Agency Archives; Hildegard Beetz, letter to Dr. Hügel, Como, Cernobbio, June 7, 1944.

174 *Hilde confessed that she took pains to make it all "look difficult"*: "The RSHA and Edda Ciano in Switzerland," June 16, 1945.

175 *the feint was to send Radice in alone*: Walter Segna, Interrogation Report, May 13, 1945.

175 *The papers remained safely hidden in the electrical power plant*: [Hildegard Beetz], report to Dr. Hügel, Cernobio, June, 28, 1944.

176 *Dr. Elvezio Melocchi promptly turned over the manuscripts*: Walter Segna, Interrogation Report, May 13, 1945.

176 *"Why should I suffer torture to protect the papers"*: Niccoletti, "The Decline and Fall of Edda Ciano," n.p.

176 *"In trying to protect the papers," American intelligence reports*: Special Interrogation Report, Frau Hildegard Beetz, Chief CIB, United States Forces European Theater, to SCI Detachment, United States

Forces European Theater, July 9, 1945, X-106, Central Intelligence Agency Archives.

177 *Hilde was to hand-deliver the papers to Zossen*: Walter Segna, Interrogation Report, May 13, 1945.

177 *the Pessina family could be forgiven for having burned them*: Walter Segna, Interrogation Report, May 13, 1945.

178 *From late June or early July until August 24:* "The RSHA and Edda Ciano in Switzerland," June 16, 1945.

178 *Each afternoon, when her translation progress was completed*: "Subject: RSHA and Edda Ciano in Switzerland," July 19, 1945.

179 *"Interested parties are deliberately holding back the publication"*: Durgin, "Framed in Death," 41.

181 *"the Diaries…appear to be the most important single political document"*: Charlesworth and Salter, "Ensuring the After-Life of the Ciano Diaries," 568.

181 *The American ambassador, Alexander Kirk*: Durgin, "Framed in Death," 43.

181 *"Benini is convinced that, as a life-long friend of Ciano"*: Charlesworth and Salter, "Ensuring the After-Life of the Ciano Diaries," 578.

182 *"I was in the Verona prison from the 30th November"*: Durgin, "Framed in Death," 43.

182 *"I spent the last tragic night…with him"*: Durgin, "Framed in Death," 43.

183 *Sometime in July, just before the news story broke*: Moseley, *Mussolini's Shadow*, 244.

183 *The decision to move Edda to the Malévoz Psychiatric Hospital*: "Andre Repond, Psychiatrist, Headed World Health Unit," obituary, *New York Times*, March 15, 1973, 46.

184 *The next day, there would be intelligence concerns*: Letter from Hildegard Beetz, February 25, 1944, item 46.

184 *whose wife, it was said, spied for the Americans*: Interview, Jacqueline de Chollet, 2020.

185 *someone who "said atrocious things at which people trembled"*: Agnelli, *We Always Wore Sailor Suits*, 107.

189 *Frances and her daughters also spent long afternoons*: Interview, Jacqueline de Chollet, 2020.

190 *To Frances's considerable ire, Marie Thérèse, the Countess de Monléon*: Private manuscript, courtesy Jacqueline de Chollet, 2021.

190 *Accompanying the countess was her thirty-one-year-old daughter*: Interview, Jacqueline de Chollet, 2020; the de Chollet marriage ended in divorce in 1950, and Louis remarried in 1952, according to his daughter.

190 *Frances's daughter Jacqueline put it simply: "most of the visitors…were affiliated in some way"*: Private manuscript, courtesy Jacqueline de Chollet, 2021.

190 *The guest book at Le Guintzet recorded the comings and goings*: Le Guintzet, "Guest Book," courtesy Jacqueline de Chollet.

191 *Allen Dulles later said of Carl Jung*: Christopher Dickey, "The Shrink as Secret Agent: Jung, Hitler, and the OSS," *Daily Beast*, October 22, 2018; "Remembering Jung," Kairos Film Foundation, 2016; Deirdre Bair, *Jung: A Biography* (Boston: Back Bay Books, 2004), 493, quoted in Gord Barentsen, "Romantic Metasubjectivity: Rethinking the Romantic Subject Through Schelling and Jung," doctoral thesis (ref. 4784), Western University, 2017, x, n. 2.

191 *Her "great friend" Virginia Agnelli*: Interview, Jacqueline de Chollet, April 2020.

193 *Gerald Mayer, Allen Dulles's close associate*: Quibble, "Alias George Wood," Central Intelligence Agency Archives.

194 *Clara was the wife of the German-born Prince Tassillo von Furstenberg*: "Subject: The Zimmer Notebooks," June 28, 1946.

196 *move Edda to "a house or apartment somewhere in French Switzerland"*: "Edda Ciano: Una Agnelli l'aiuto a 'sopravvivere' in Svizzera," n.d., n.p.

196 *The clinic director, Dr. Repond, recognizing Edda's "deep depression"*: "Edda Ciano: Una Agnelli l'aiuto a 'sopravvivere' in Svizzera," n.d., n.p.

197 *"We should very much like to have this diary"*: Charlesworth and Salter, "Ensuring the After-Life of the Ciano Diaries."

198 *The Ciano Diaries seemed very likely to include smoking-gun war-crimes evidence*: Niccoletti, "The Decline and Fall of Edda Ciano," n.p.

199 *Cordelia was quickly recruited first by the military intelligence department*: "Intelligence Officer Did Fieldwork for OSS and CIA, Cordelia Dodson Hood '36, MA '41," obituary, *Reed Magazine*, December 2011.

199 *Cordelia contacted Emilio*: Second Report, Emilio Pucci to Allen Dulles, June 20, 1944, 45; Moseley, *Mussolini's Shadow*, 248.

199 *"Americans who had been living privately in Switzerland for various reasons'"*: Jennifer Hoover, "Secrets in Switzerland: Allen W. Dulles' Impact as OSS Station Chief in Bern on Developments of World War II & U.S. Dominance in Post-War Europe," thesis (ref. 240), William and Mary, 2009, 18.

201 *Gasoline, like nearly everything else, was strictly rationed*: "Switzerland's Economic Dependence During World War II," History of Switzerland (website), 2004.

201 *"On Thursday I went to see my new found friend Edda"*: Letters to Frances de Chollet from others, Frances de Chollet Collection, MC292, Public Policy Papers, Department of Special Collections, Princeton University Library; the author gratefully acknowledges the permission of Jacqueline de Chollet to quote from these materials.

202 *"Again Thursday and I have been to see my friend Edda"*: Letters to Frances de Chollet from others, Frances de Chollet Collection, Princeton University.

202 *"She is of the opinion that Hitler will kill himself"*: Letters to Frances de Chollet from others, Frances de Chollet Collection, Princeton University.

202 *"She is bored to tears…refus[es] to eat the food"*: Letters to Frances de Chollet from others, Frances de Chollet Collection, Princeton University.

203 *"I adore her because she never complains"*: Letters to Frances de Chollet from others, Frances de Chollet Collection, Princeton University.

204 *"I gave her some help and told her as her business manager"*: Letters to Frances de Chollet from others, Frances de Chollet Collection, Princeton University.

204 *St. Nicholas would alight from the donkey at the cathedral*: Dimitri Kas, "The unmissable St Nicholas' festival in Fribourg, Switzerland," House of Switzerland (website), Federal Department of Foreign Affairs, 2019.

205 *The diaries she had carried with her were bulky*: R. J. B. Bosworth, *Claretta: Mussolini's Last Lover* (New Haven, CT: Yale University Press, 2017), 18.

205 *Paul Ghali was in his late thirties*: James H. Walters, *Scoop: How the Ciano Diary Was Smuggled from Rome to Chicago Where It Made Worldwide News. An Historical Adventure* (privately printed, 2006), 103.

206 *Paul had been a foreign correspondent*: "Paul Ghali, Wrote for Chicago News," obituary, *New York Times*, June 4, 1970, 37.

206 *Most important, he was already working with Allen Dulles*: Walters, *Scoop*, 106.

206 *Paul Ghali recounted his version of the hunt for the Ciano Diaries*: Walters, *Scoop*, 109.

206 *"my blonde friend from Fribourg"*: Walters, *Scoop*, 108.

206 *"Mr. Dulles enlisted the services of a few people"*: Smyth, "The Papers: Rose Garden," citing interview with Allen Dulles, January 17, 1966; "Intelligence Officer Did Fieldwork for OSS and CIA: Cordelia Dodson Hood '36, MA '41," obituary, *Reed Magazine*.

207 *To this list, Allen Dulles later added two other names*: Charlesworth and Salter, "Ensuring the After-Life of the Ciano Diaries."

208 *She ferried multiple messages back and forth*: Walters, *Scoop*, 113.

209 *"Pucci wishes to see you. He will come this afternoon"*: Moseley, *Mussolini's Shadow*, 248.

209 *"The day before the papers had printed the news of my alleged marriage"*: Second Report, Emilio Pucci to Allen Dulles, June 20, 1944.

209 *"I was startled by Pucci's offer"*: Moseley, *Mussolini's Shadow*, 248.

210 *"I would intervene with Dulles only on the condition that Edda agreed to sell"*: Walters, *Scoop*, 135.

211 They *"told me that they were in touch with Edda"*: Charlesworth and Salter, "Ensuring the After-Life of the Ciano Diaries."

213 *He'd tapped a thirty-three-year-old spy for the OSS named Tracy Barnes*: Evan Thomas, *The Very Best Men. Four Who Dared: The Early Years of the CIA* (New York: Simon and Schuster, 1995), n.p. (e-book).

213 *One of his colleagues described him as "tall and blond"*: Thomas, *The Very Best Men*, n.p.

213 *"We all called him the Golden Boy"*: Thomas, *The Very Best Men*, n.p.

213 *He had already earned a Silver Star*: Thomas, *The Very Best Men*, n.p.

214 *Hitler's "ideas were not quite natural where women were concerned"*: Frances de Chollet, notes of meetings with Edda Ciano, 1945, Frances de Chollet Collection, MC292, Public Policy Papers, Department of Special Collections, Princeton University Library.

214 *"I had the impression that, despite her rupture with her father, she remained a Fascist"*: Moseley, *Mussolini's Shadow*, 248.

215 *"even if I... have to die, I want first to avenge Galeazzo"*: Smyth, "The Papers: Rose Garden."

215 *Allen Dulles wasn't sure whether it had ever made its way back*: Durgin, "Framed in Death," 43.

215 *"If she has not already received it"*: Durgin, "Framed in Death," 43.

216 *"Edda is a psychopathic case"*: Thomas, *The Very Best Men*, n.p.

216 *the strategy also created a new complication*: Smyth, "The Papers: Rose Garden."

216 *Ultimately, the State Department would agree—off the record—to backstop the payment*: Private manuscript, courtesy Jacqueline de Chollet, 2021.

217 *"when your 'important friend' comes I should like to talk with him"*: Edda Ciano letter to Frances de Chollet, Frances de Chollet Collection, MC292, Public Policy Papers, Department of Special Collections, Princeton University Library.

217 *Newspapers reported openly after the war*: "Drue Heinz, Philanthropist and *Paris Review* Editor, Dies at 103," obituary, *Seattle Times*, April 5, 2018.

218 *"Dear Frances," Edda wrote on December 30, "I was just wondering"*: Edda Ciano letter to Frances de Chollet, Frances de Chollet Collection.

218 *"Believe best line to take that Edda should desire"*: Petersen, *From Hitler's Doorstep*, 422.

220 *When lunch was over, Edda asked if she and Dulles could speak alone*: Durgin, "Framed in Death," 46.

220 *For an hour they talked, and Dulles wrote later*: Niccoletti, "The Decline and Fall of Edda Ciano," n.p.

220 *"I frankly admit she behaved with a good deal of dignity"*: Niccoletti, "The Decline and Fall of Edda Ciano," n.p.

222 *According to Father Guido Pancino, who claimed to already*: Allegri, "Nel racconto di un sacerdote."

226 *"I am no fool, or dumb, and I can help a lot"*: Niccoletti, "The Decline and Fall of Edda Ciano," n.p.; Smyth, "The Papers: Rose Garden."

227 *"Another thing, the rest. The complement of the diaries are still in Italy"*: Durgin, "Framed in Death," 48.

229 *"You mention the American lady, Mme. De Chollet"*: Walters, *Scoop*, 139.

230 *"For God's sake tell Paul to be very careful"*: Edda Ciano letter to Frances de Chollet, Frances de Chollet Collection.

232 *The Swiss press reported—accurately or not*: Wolfgang Achtner, "Edda Ciano," *The Independent*, obituary, October 23, 2011.

233 *When Allen Dulles was fully apprised of Emilio's role*: Durgin, "Framed in Death," 54.

234 *The charges would be crimes against the peace*: Robert D. Bush, "An Investigation into the Trial of a Nazi War Criminal: Joachim von Ribbentrop at Nuremberg, Germany, 1945–1946," thesis, University of Richmond, 1963, 18.

234 *"Dulles," he wrote, "has maintained an OSS post in Switzerland"*: Niccoletti, "The Decline and Fall of Edda Ciano," n.p.

235 *"I am not a criminal of war (how could I be?)"*: Niccoletti, "The Decline and Fall of Edda Ciano," n.p.

237 *"[A]n American girl married to a Swiss named Mrs. Frances Cholet"*: Allen Dulles letter to Charles G. Cheston, April 11, 1945, RG226, National Archives of the United States.

237 *"She is now applying through the Consulate for an amendment to her passport"*: Allen Dulles letter to Charles G. Cheston, April 11, 1945.

237 *"That," Jacqueline says, "was my mother"*: Interview, Jacqueline de Chollet, 2021.

239 *Harster, ultimately implicated in the murder of more than one hundred thousand Jews*: Richard Breitman, "Records of the Central Intelligence Agency (RG 263)," Interagency Working Group, National Archives of the United States, April 2001.

240 *she was inevitably asked about her role in obtaining for the Germans*: "Beetz, Hildegard, nee Burkhardt," interrogation notes, July 30, 1945, XX8382, Central Intelligence Agency Archives.

241 *"My youth, too, was buried in his grave"*: *Ciano Diaries*, 206, 257, 386, 524.

241 *She "preserved copies of diary entries"*: Smyth, "The Papers: Rose Garden."

241 *"Frau Beetz," Lieutenant French noted, "now discloses"*: Memorandum, on Hilde Beetz, from Spearhead, Amzon, to Hitor, Weimar, June 18, 1945, OSS 1366, Central Intelligence Agency Archives, declassified 2001.

243 *"[B]ecause of the extremely delicate...project she is undertaking"*: "Subject: Gambit's Lebenslauf and Analysis by AB 16," June 5, 1946, LBX-347, Central Intelligence Agency Archives.

244 *She was assigned, under cover as a secretary*: "Project Proposal for CIB: GAMBIT," July 13, 1946, LBX-435, Central Intelligence Agency Archives.

244 *"Our control over her is complete"*: "Project Proposal for CIB: GAM-BIT," July 13, 1946, LBX-435, Central Intelligence Agency Archives.

244 *"penetration agent," tasked with "aiding current and prospective"*: "CIA and Nazi War Crim. and Col.," working draft, chapter 3, "Persons from All Spheres of Influence (U)," Central Intelligence Agency Archives, 42; Moseley, *Mussolini's Shadow*, 264.

244 *"is probably better acquainted with the history of our organization"*: "CIA and Nazi War Crim.," 46.

245 *According to one of her biographers*: Judy Bachrach, "La Vita Agnelli," *Vanity Fair*, April 2001.

246 *"I miss our talks and mysterious rendez-vous"*: Edda Ciano letter to Frances de Chollet, Frances de Chollet Collection, MC292, Public Policy Papers, Department of Special Collections, Princeton University Library.

246 *"Frances dear, how is life? Did you succeed in getting away from Switzerland"*: Edda Ciano letter to Frances de Chollet, Frances de Chollet Collection.

247 *"she looked like a wounded small swallow"*: Livia Perricone, "Una rondine ferita dalle ali infrante: Edda Ciano e il comunista," *Lipari*, February 23, 2015; see also Marcello Sorgi, *Edda Ciano e il comunista: L'inconfessabile passione della figlia del duce* (Milano: Bur, 2011).

247 *"Come and live with me," she wrote in passionate letters*: Eliza Apperly, "Letters Show Mussolini Daughter's Love for Communist," Reuters (Rome), April 17, 2009.

248 *"I am sure that Allen Dulles's sudden death"*: Letters to Frances de Chollet from others, Frances de Chollet Collection, MC292, Public Policy Papers, Department of Special Collections, Princeton University Library.

249 *"There is in every true woman's heart a spark"*: Jacqueline de Chollet, personal correspondence, October 2021; the quote is from Washington Irving's *The Sketch Book* (1819).

250 *What did Frances think when she read in October*: The diaries were submitted as Document 2987-PS (Exhibit U.S.A.-166), Trial of the Major War Criminals before the International Military Tribunal, Nuremberg, November 14, 1945; see English edition, *Trial of the Major War Criminals Before the International Military Tribunal*, October 1, 1946, 31:434–38 and January 8, 1946, 4:567–68; Smyth, "The Papers: Rose Garden."

250 *"moments remain to make me thankful that we were so lucky"*: Letter from Frances de Chollet to Rosalie Harvie-Watt, Frances de Chollet Collection, Public Policy Papers, Department of Special Collections, Princeton University Library.

250 *"These diaries are unquestionably, incomparably"*: Smyth, "The Papers: Rose Garden."

252 *In the village of Erte*: Piergiorgio Grizzo, "Il segreto di Don Pancino era un diario perduto di Galeazzo Ciano?," *Vanilla Magazine*, n.d.

253 *He asked the boy to hide that box "in a small ravine"*: Grizzo, "Il segreto di Don Pancino era un diario perduto."

INDEX

ABOUT THE AUTHOR

Tilar J. Mazzeo is Professeure Associée at the University of Montreal, the former Clara C. Piper Associate Professor of English at Colby College, and the author of numerous works of narrative nonfiction. Her books have been *New York Times*, *San Francisco Chronicle*, and *Los Angeles Times* bestsellers.

The author acknowledges the support of the Canada Council of the Arts.

Canada Council Conseil des arts
for the Arts du Canada